Applied Social Network Analysis With R:

Emerging Research and Opportunities

Mehmet Gençer
Izmir University of Economics, Turkey

A volume in the Advances
in Computer and Electrical
Engineering (ACEE) Book Series

Published in the United States of America by
    IGI Global
    Engineering Science Reference (an imprint of IGI Global)
    701 E. Chocolate Avenue
    Hershey PA, USA 17033
    Tel: 717-533-8845
    Fax: 717-533-8661
    E-mail: cust@igi-global.com
    Web site: http://www.igi-global.com

Library of Congress Cataloging-in-Publication Data

Names: Gençer, Mehmet, 1969- author.
Title: Applied social network analysis with R : emerging research and
  opportunities / by Mehmet Gençer.
Description: Hershey, PA : Engineering Science Reference, [2020] | Includes
  bibliographical references and index. | Summary: "This book explores the
  structure of socio-economic relations, in particular, relations in
  business life"-- Provided by publisher.
Identifiers: LCCN 2019035515 (print) | LCCN 2019035516 (ebook) | ISBN
  9781799819127 (h/c) | ISBN 9781799819134 (s/c) | ISBN 9781799819141
  (eISBN)
Subjects: LCSH: Social networks--Statistical methods. | R (Computer program
  language)
Classification: LCC HM741 .G43 2020 (print) | LCC HM741 (ebook) | DDC
  302.3072/7--dc23
LC record available at https://lccn.loc.gov/2019035515
LC ebook record available at https://lccn.loc.gov/2019035516

This book is published in the IGI Global book series Advances in Computer and Electrical Engineering (ACEE) (ISSN: 2327-039X; eISSN: 2327-0403)

British Cataloguing in Publication Data
A Cataloguing in Publication record for this book is available from the British Library.

All work contributed to this book is new, previously-unpublished material.
The views expressed in this book are those of the authors, but not necessarily of the publisher.

For electronic access to this publication, please contact: eresources@igi-global.com.

Advances in Computer and Electrical Engineering (ACEE) Book Series

ISSN:2327-039X
EISSN:2327-0403

Editor-in-Chief: Srikanta Patnaik, SOA University, India

MISSION

The fields of computer engineering and electrical engineering encompass a broad range of interdisciplinary topics allowing for expansive research developments across multiple fields. Research in these areas continues to develop and become increasingly important as computer and electrical systems have become an integral part of everyday life.

The **Advances in Computer and Electrical Engineering (ACEE) Book Series** aims to publish research on diverse topics pertaining to computer engineering and electrical engineering. **ACEE** encourages scholarly discourse on the latest applications, tools, and methodologies being implemented in the field for the design and development of computer and electrical systems.

COVERAGE

- VLSI Design
- Computer Science
- Qualitative Methods
- Circuit Analysis
- Programming
- Optical Electronics
- Microprocessor Design
- Electrical Power Conversion
- Analog Electronics
- Algorithms

IGI Global is currently accepting manuscripts for publication within this series. To submit a proposal for a volume in this series, please contact our Acquisition Editors at Acquisitions@igi-global.com or visit: http://www.igi-global.com/publish/.

Titles in this Series

For a list of additional titles in this series, please visit:
https://www.igi-global.com/book-series/advances-computer-electrical-engineering/73675

Novel Approaches to Information Systms Design
Naveen Prakash (Indraprastha Institute of Information Technology, Delhi, India) and Deepika Prakash (NIIT University, India)
Engineering Science Reference • © 2020 • 299pp • H/C (ISBN: 9781799829751) • US $215.00

IoT Architectures, Models, and Platforms for Smart City Applications
Bhawani Shankar Chowdhry (Mehran University of Engineering and Technology, Pakistan) Faisal Karim Shaikh (Mehran University of Engineering and Technology, Pakistan) and Naeem Ahmed Mahoto (Mehran University of Engineering and Technology, Pakistan)
Engineering Science Reference • © 2020 • 291pp • H/C (ISBN: 9781799812531) • US $245.00

Nature-Inspired Computing Applications in Advanced Communication Networks
Govind P. Gupta (National Institute of Technology, Raipur, India)
Engineering Science Reference • © 2020 • 319pp • H/C (ISBN: 9781799816263) • US $225.00

Pattern Recognition Applications in Engineering
Diego Alexander Tibaduiza Burgos (Universidad Nacional de Colombia, Colombia) Maribel Anaya Vejar (Universidad Sergio Arboleda, Colombia) and Francesc Pozo (Universitat Politècnica de Catalunya, Spain)
Engineering Science Reference • © 2020 • 357pp • H/C (ISBN: 9781799818397) • US $215.00

Tools and Technologies for the Development of Cyber-Physical Systems
Sergey Balandin (FRUCT Oy, Finland) and Ekaterina Balandina (Tampere University, Finland)
Engineering Science Reference • © 2020 • 300pp • H/C (ISBN: 9781799819745) • US $235.00

For an entire list of titles in this series, please visit:
https://www.igi-global.com/book-series/advances-computer-electrical-engineering/73675

701 East Chocolate Avenue, Hershey, PA 17033, USA
Tel: 717-533-8845 x100 • Fax: 717-533-8661
E-Mail: cust@igi-global.com • www.igi-global.com

Table of Contents

Section 3
Contemporary Applications and Methods

Preface

Structural analysis of social relations promise insights into a variety of contemporary issues. These include business and economics areas such as digital marketing, human resources management, employee well-being management, and industry networks, and other areas such as crime investigation, disease epidemic simulations, etc. This network perspective is an emerging approach in several disciplines. Social network analysis methods supporting this perspective has their roots in social psychology and anthropology, ie traditionally applied to small social groups due to restrictions of these methods on data collection. However, recent explosion of data in business organizations and social media brings about a variety of research and application opportunities.

With its theoretical roots in social sciences, methodological roots in graph theory, and required software skills for its application, social network analysis can be quite demanding for both students, researchers, and practitioners alike, who want to pursue these research opportunities. Students, professionals, and researchers in social science and business fields have limited chance to develop analytics and coding skills that are necessary for cutting edge work in most fields. This book aims to provide an all-inclusive introduction for beginners and offers a bridge for those who aim to learn and apply network approach to their field, additionally making a range of further titles more accessible to them. Each chapter includes motivating examples, summarizes their theoretical conceptualization, explains methods and metrics that correspond to those concepts, and presents example applications of them using R statistics platform. With its unique approach, the book aims to provide an accessible entry for students, professionals, and researchers in several fields.

Our subject focus is the structure of socio-economic relations and, in particular, relations in business life. The primary purpose of analyzing social structure is to make it easier to explain the nature of human societies. During the 20th century, there were already remarkable advancements in the natural sciences and engineering. These advancements brought about "products" such as computers, cell phones and fast vehicles. But advancements in social sciences do not have results like those in natural sciences and engineering. However, particularly due to digital technology, a great and detailed pile of data about the functioning of individuals and societies has started to form. Our knowledge of the "social" increases significantly with the transformation of these data into information by processing and interpreting them. The methods and examples presented in this book deal with how to analyze these data about social functioning from a certain perspective, i.e. from a structural perspective, and with varying ways of interpreting the results. This book is created as an introductory practical guide for students and researchers of any level wanting to seize the research opportunities provided by the contemporary abundance of social data.

I grew up, like many from my generation, listening to trites concerning the state of our society. This discourse, in general, compares a society with another and imposes the fixed idea that the society compared has innate features, and thus it cannot change. At the same time, my generation also witnessed the glorification of science along with these commonplaces. These two patterns, the belief in scientific thought and the idea that a community has an "inexplicable" nature, are in contradiction. The impact of this contradiction on me was my interest in this "inexplicable" aspect. Even as an engineering student, I was always fascinated by the state of being "us" and its relation with "self". My focus on organizational theories at a certain point in my academic life stems mainly from this interest. What makes a human society different from or more/less successful than another? There are many factors to look at in order to explain the situation of a community, e.g. community culture or environmental conditions affecting the behavior of community members. Therefore, it is possible to handle this issue from various perspectives including those of political economy or social psychology. I, probably as a result of my professional background, lean more towards the structural perspective.

The structure of relations within a community is regarded as one of the essential elements of the *social* in many scientific disciplines. The presence, absence, strength or weakness, and amicable or hostile nature of relations has a profound impact on the state of a given community. Network analysis is a powerful approach to materialize and analyze the issue of structure in terms of its effects on human societies and the state of the individuals in these communities.

Even though the book is oriented towards business and work organizations, an approach underlining the ties of this field of study with broader social sciences is adopted throughout the book. Therefore, hopefully the methods presented here are useful for analyzing not only the organization of the business world but also for the organization of any given community. Many opportunities concerning the organization of business life will emerge if one accepts that whatever happens in the business world is, before anything else, "human" (and contemporary business education should develop accordingly). This assumption about business life has remarkable impacts on the studies on the ways of structuring of groups working together in an improved manner. With the right assumptions, the connection between "me" and "them" might be constructed in a better way and "smart" teams instead of flocks can be formed.

It is worth to take note of of some concerns regarding organizational theories and the field of sociology. At first glance, readers familiar with the field might think that the book adopts the approach of structuralist sociology. An alternative for this is the approach that can be labeled as cultural sociology. In its simplest sense, while the latter (cultural sociology) supposes that "similar people establish friendly relations", the former (structuralist sociology) assumes that "friends become gradually similar to one another". Personally, I do not think that trying to decide on this duality is constructive. For that reason, even though the notion of structure is primary in this text, I have also tried to emphasize frequently the role of non-structural elements (like culture) in cases where structural findings are interpreted.

Being an applied book, the content you will find here risks being outdated slowly and surely as the software it references keeps evolving. This is a risk, which I think is worth taking. I have seen many practitioners and researchers struggling to focus on a completely new set of concepts while at the same battling the hurdles of coding for them. The book specifically targets this difficulty. By taking this risk of being slightly outdated in time, it tries to make sure that it provides a smooth entry into social network analysis on time for the inter-disciplinary audience it appeals to.

Today, activities in every aspect of social life leave a digital trace about the relations among us. Structural analyses using these traces have become a valuable and avant-garde research area for many disciplines of social sciences. While writing this book, my aim was to position network analysis based on its contributions to social research. At the same time, I tried to cover the practical aspects that may prove tricky for learners of this new field of study. With the advancement of tools relevant to this subject, field and the related methods seem to be promising for an increasing number of researchers. Thus, this book aims to help this field to become more accessible for these individuals.

ABOUT THE BOOK

The foundations of this book started to be formed with the lecture notes I had written for an undergraduate course titled "Social Networks" which I have designed around 12 years ago, and have been teaching since then. However, considering the coverage it has reached, I hope the book can also be used on higher levels as well. As it is a textbook, there are repetitions, exercises, and questions for self-study included within the flow of the subject. I have tried to keep the number of repetitions and questions limited to an extent that would not disrupt the overall quality of the book but will support readability of chapters independently.

For instructors wishing to use this book as course material, each chapter accounts for approximately one week or three hours of class. There are exercises, questions and references to readings within the body of literature.

The data sets and necessary links to be used in some of the exercises and questions are available on the website I have created as a supplement to this book, http://appliedsna.mgencer.com. The data sets are also explained in the appendices.

In the appendices of the book, there is a chapter devoted to basic statistical definitions that might be necessary for students and readers coming from different disciplines. Furthermore, in another appendix, a mini guide on the use of R, a statistical software used for both basic statistics and network analysis, is given.

Many resources, all of them written in English, were used for the preparation of this book. John Scott's book titled "Social Networks: An introduction" (Scott, 2000) is probably the most suitable resource for beginners. "Social Network Analysis: Methods and applications" written by Stanley Wasserman and Katherine Faust (Wasserman & Faust, 1994) is still the most comprehensive reference on quantitative analysis techniques. These two are the most prominent references and would be my first recommendations for those seeking additional material to complement this text.

CONVENTIONS USED IN THE BOOK

The book intertwines theoretical explanations of social network analysis concepts with case studies and software applications in R statistical system. Throughout the book you will see code fragments that are given in grey boxes

Figure 1. A random graph produced in R code

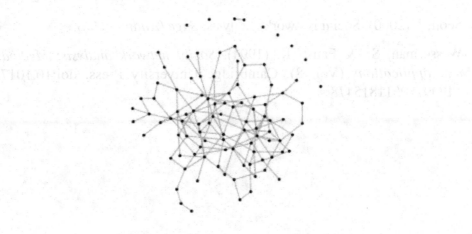

Plotting example: A random network

as follows. If the code outputs any information it is also shown in fixed fonts immediately following the code box. The output lines are marked with ##:

```
# This is an R code chunk
# with a simple code to sum a few numbers
sum(2, 2, 3)
## [1] 7
# all text following # is a comment in R
```

If any code fragment also produces a graphics, it is shown in the book as a figure box. In your own system, you will see the graphics in a separate screen or in a tab, depending on the R software components you prefer to use, such as plain R or RStudio.

```
require(igraph)
g <- sample_gnp(100, 3/100) #create a random graph
plot(g, vertex.label= NA, edge.arrow.size=0.025,
     vertex.size = 2, xlab = "Plotting example: A random
network")
```

REFERENCES

Scott, J. (2000). Social Network Analysis. *Sage (Atlanta, Ga.).*

Wasserman, S., & Faust, K. (1994). *Social network analysis: Methods and applications* (Vol. 8). Cambridge University Press. doi:10.1017/CBO9780511815478

Chapter 1
Introduction:
Social Systems and Relations

ABSTRACT

The traditional research approaches common in different disciplines of social sciences centered around one half of the social realm: the actors. The other half are the relations established by these actors and forming the basis of "social." The social structure shaped by these relations, the position of the actor within this structure, and the impact of this position on the actor are mostly excluded by the traditional research methods. In this chapter, the authors introduce social network analysis and how it complements the other methods.

WHY RELATIONAL APPROACH MATTERS?

The term "social sciences" encompasses a broad spectrum of disciplines ranging from economics and sociology to business management and industrial psychology. Throughout their histories, these disciplines have focused almost exclusively on individuals and their features (Marin and Wellman 2010). Virtually every research method, instrument and mathematical and statistical tool of these disciplines are shaped accordingly.

For instance, let us assume that we would like to find out the contributing factors to the success at university courses through traditional methods. In order to do so, we would start by collecting information about "personal" features of students such as age, sex, place of birth and family income level, and gather all the information in the form of a table. The data in the table are

DOI: 10.4018/978-1-7998-1912-7.ch001

then analyzed with descriptive statistical methods suitable for the study and theories and hypotheses are put forward. The hypotheses are then tested with regression models belonging to the same method category. The philosophical assumption behind this approach is as follows: The whole called "society" can be understood by analyzing all of its actors. Thus, in order to understand the functions of economic classes within the educational system, such an approach would first group students according to their income levels and then compare the average grades of each group (eg Turan and Aktan (2008); Silvester, Anderson, and Patterson (1999)). In this case, the "social" aspect of the phenomenon is reduced to an average. A more "social" study might be conducted with the same traditional methods; for example, a survey among students in order to study the effects of belonging to same or different income groups or those of gender groups on friendships. Once again, the "socialness" is analyzed through the average individual's point of view. In disciplines like economics, the unit of analysis is either companies or countries instead of individuals, but the basic assumption and methods are not essentially different.

Although this rather traditional approach common to different subdisciplines of social sciences reveal certain explanatory factors, it only looks at one side of the coin: social actors. On the other side of the coin, there are relations established by these actors and forming the "social". The social structure shaped by these relations, the position of the actor within this structure and the impact of this position on the actor are completely excluded by the traditional method.[1]

We are living in an increasingly interconnected society. Industrialization, urbanization, informatics and, most recently, developments in modern life under the title of globalization bring about new lifestyles entwined with more frequent and intense daily interactions between social actors. The issue of social networks research emerged in correspondence with these developments long before Facebook and will probably remain present even after it becomes obsolete. Within the framework of this term, many methods relying on computer sciences and mathematics are being developed. Media like Facebook and Twitter, the first items to come to one's mind upon the mention of social networks, are also included in this research activity. The abundance of data concerning social relations accumulating on such social platforms allows us to use suitable methods, and thus provides a unique opportunity to reveal the way contemporary social life functions. This fast developing field of network research has proven itself useful in a variety of fields: business relations (Artto et al., 2017;Dagnino et al, 2015), policy testing and development (Raberto et al, 2019), learning management (Saqr nad Alamro, 2019), etc. In fact the same base of network analysis tools and metrics are used beyond social sciences suchas biology (Shoshi et al, 2015) and informatics (Nyati et al., 2019). These developments highlights new research opportunies, and business applications, as well as presenting new methodological challenges (Crossley and Edwards, 2016), ethical issues related to use of data (Floridi and Taddeo, 2016), and challenges related to big data (Tinati et al., 2014).

A preliminary study conducted in the 1930s is worthy of particular interest as it makes visible the deficiencies of the traditional approach summarized above to which I refer as "individual oriented" or "actor oriented". Jacob Moreno, a social psychologist working at a girl's orphanage, and his researcher colleague Helen Jennings realized that traditional methods got them nowhere while trying to understand the behavior of girls escaping from the orphanage. The analysis of personal features of students escaping from the orphanage school such as age, sex, race and psychological history did not reveal any significant feature that separates the group from the rest of the orphanage. Approaching this phenomenon with a different assumption, Moreno and Jennings noticed that this behavior can be better understood by studying the social structure formed by the friendships among the students (Moreno and Jennings 1934). A group of students seemingly similar to others was excluded from the general structure and they developed a cultural pattern of escaping in their own exclusive "social zone". These "zones" put forward by this new approach are only visible in the social relation maps produced using data about the relations. Moreno's research has demonstrated the key promise of social network analysis that it can reveal the features of the social fabric that cannot be visible from the more traditional data, such as surveys applied to individuals. Several decades later, the social network analysis approach has this same substantial promise in key application areas such as business management (Brass et al, 2004; Borgatti et al, 2009) and marketing (Atefeh and Khreich, 2014), setting aside the variety of methods developed and scale of data that is available for use.

Although the network analysis approach I intend to introduce in this chapter dates back to Moreno and Jennings' study in the 1930s, it started to become widespread in the 1990s and has been popular to this day (Borgatti et al. 2009). In the chapters below, I will attempt to summarize the development of the network analysis approach, its potential contributions and the basics of the methods used within the scope of this approach. While doing so, rather than evaluating whether actor-oriented social sciences approach or network/relation-oriented approach is superior, I will attempt to underline that both approaches are different sides of a coin. The use of both approaches and methods they involve can only be possible if their differences are understood thoroughly and correctly.

Social Actors and Their Relations

The term "social network" and the studies for its analysis contribute significantly to the understanding of the social. This contribution derives from the rejection of the idea that the whole is a sum of the components. This rejection allows us to focus on the way the pieces come together (Emirbayer and Mische 1998; Granovetter 1985, 2005; Coleman 1988; Lazer et al. 2009). Therefore, the network or relation-oriented approach claims that the social can best be understood by studying features and patterns of relations rather than studying features of social actors, i.e. individuals. In disciplines like economics and business administration, the unit of analysis is not individuals but socioeconomic units, namely companies or economies of different countries.

Neither of these approaches is more correct or illuminating than the other. In fact, social network analysts often repeat the mistakes of the other camp. For example, when they say that the competitive power of a person or a company depends entirely on their relations with the market rather than on their individual features, social network approach leans towards social determinism (Burt 1992; Gulati 1995; Gulati and Gargiulo 1999). Preferring any one of the approaches would be as deceptive as opting for the other one.

Despite these deficiencies, in order to introduce this newly- developed approach, I will set individual-oriented methods (or, depending on the definition of the social, methods focusing on actors like companies or groups) aside here. Instead of these, I will focus on the functioning of the whole by studying the relations constituting the whole and the methods attempting to explain the impact of them on the individual. It is an important necessity that this approach is blended with the individual-oriented approach to explore a social phenomena extensively. However, such methodological blending develops rather slowly, and examples included in the pages ahead are relatively few. Thus, the focus of this book remains to clarify the differences in approaches and methods between the analysis of social actors (individuals) and that of networks, and introduce methods for the latter. While doing so, I will attempt to examine the difference between the data used for analysis of the whole networks and those used for analysis of individual actors and, finally, the way actor and network analyses complement each other. The analysis of actors and relations show orthogonal information on the social phenomenon. However, by combining these two, we can develop a multidimensional picture of the phenomenon. The repetition of the analysis at regular intervals has a potential of revealing movements/dynamics.

Let us go back to the example of student success in order to see the explanatory power of networks. Information about personal features can explain a part of the phenomenon (in this case, academic success). But in this example, course-related activities of these students continue outside the classroom setting. They probably discuss the subject covered after the class, share lecture notes and work together from time to time to do the assignments of the course. This socialization is certainly unequal, which means that the time spent with other students is not equal for every student. Due to different reasons, course-related interaction (or interaction for other matters) is limited to few people with whom the student gets along well. While some students interact with more colleagues, for others the case is the opposite. We might add other variables to the dataset consisting of information on ages of individuals, romantic relationships, etc. and thus attempt to broaden its explanatory power. But the real question for now is what kind of a data flow stems from a particular interaction.

The social structure of this imaginary classroom mentioned in our example is shown in Figure 1. The R code that reproduces the example and the figure is shown in the code box below (please inspect section 1.11, for the reasons behind choosing R for social network analysis). For those with little or no R experience, Appendic C provides a very quick introduction and pointers to learning resources. The code below demonstrates use of the R library igraph (Csardi and Nepusz, 2006), which is a generic library for visualizing, and analyzing graphs: a mathematical construct used for representing networks and other relational phenomena.

```
# In these code chunks throughout the book you will
# see the R codes to produce plots or analysis
# First load the igraph library
require(igraph)
# The graph.library() function produces a graph from
#   the given list of ties
g1 <- graph.formula("A"-"B",  "A"-"C",  "B"-"C",
        "C"-"D",     "A"-"D",     "D"-"E",     "E"-"F",
        "F"-"I",   "F"-"G",   "G"-"I")
# Finally plot the graph
plot(g1)
```

In this imaginary classroom, let us assume that student A is successful due to his/her various personal features. It is possible that students studying with A might be affected positively. However, if relatively less successful students B and C interact among themselves, it would not be of much benefit for either. Considering these factors, even if we added the number of ties of each actor to our classic data set, it would not explain the situation mentioned in this scenario because not all ties are equally useful. An approach dealing with actors individually as such inevitably excludes the effects due to social structure. But upon analyzing the structure of relations, we can see the reason behind the relative success of students having an interaction with student A or, more precisely, the aspects of this relative success that cannot be explained by the sum of the features like age and sex of individuals.

In the scenario given above, we based our argument on the differences between actors forming the social, e.g. some students being more successful. when compared with others. Let us now assume that all the actors are equal. In that case, we will encounter a case emphasizing even more the explanatory power of social network approach. The number of friends with whom the individual "D" is in contact is not so different from other students. However, upon looking at the position of this individual within the social structure, we see that he/she is in contact with two separate groups. It is possible that each of these two groups has better command of certain subjects of the course than the other. This is analogous to the case in which the chat topics within a group of friends are similar while being different from those discussed within

Figure 1. Study network among students (artificial)

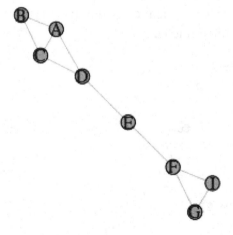

another group. Here, while the "amount" of knowledge of the two groups is not different, the content is. In that case, even though actor D has the same number of social relations with others, he/she also have the advantage of benefiting from different sources of information. What this second fictional scenario shows us is that even with a shallow assumption that every individual is the same, it is possible to discover the inequality of individuals in terms of their position within the social structure by looking at the features of the social structure. As far as a social process like information flow is concerned, the position of the individual within the social structure rather than the number of relations would make a difference. This is the fact completely overlooked by the research techniques of classical social sciences, i.e. collecting data on individuals as if they are completely independent.

A scientific discipline concerned with the way the individual is affected by the social environment is psychology. It would be accurate to say that the first studies on social networks emerged from this discipline. The aforementioned study of Jacob Moreno conducted at a girl's orphanage in the US in the 1930s is among these preliminary studies (Moreno, 1934). Historically speaking, Moreno's work coincides with an era during which the question how an individual's behavior is determined by the society was a topic of interest (Mcpherson, Smith-lovin, and Cook 2001; Brandes and Nick 2011). Moreno is of particular importance for us due to his methodological innovation in a period in which Gestalt psychology was the mainstream philosophy.

While he was researching on what was happening at Hudson Girl's Orphanage, Moreno relied on a principle right from the start. For him, in order to understand a society, it was necessary to look at the entirety of the society rather than individuals. The data he collected with this point of view and the way he interpreted them indeed resulted in novel explanations. For instance, in a certain period of several weeks, many girls ran away from the orphanage in focus of Moreno's research. The unusual character of such a phenomenon instantly catches the eye upon being registered among the statistical data. If the incidents of running away occur, let us say, once every two weeks on the average, then 14 girls running away in a single week becomes impossible to miss. But that is it. Even though an analysis based on individual-based data shows the "unusualness" of the phenomenon, it is not sufficient for explaining its reasons. Statistical data might have signified that, for instance, African-American girls or girls from a certain age group attempt to run away more frequently. But the data does not explain why all of them attempted to do so in that particular week or, more importantly, why those particular girls and not others tried to run away.

The analysis technique Moreno applied to this phenomenon was to map the social relations among the girls. When he did so, some other structural effects that could not be understood by other means started to come to the surface. For example, a group of girls were friends but they were also excluded from the other girls at the orphanage. Therefore, while deciding whether they would run away or not, they did not feel responsible to the rest of the students, and thus it was easier to make the decision.

While putting his theories into practice, Moreno developed certain techniques. Still used in the present day, **sociomatrix** is one of these techniques. At first, Moreno collected the traditional individual-based data while trying to gather information on the relations between the girls at the Hudson orphanage. We can arrange them as a table as seen in Table 1:

Each line of the table represents an individual in the data sample while each column shows the collected data about them.

However, social relation data must be collected in another way. That is where sociomatrices come into play. In this phenomenon, Moreno asked each girl to list her five best friends in order. A value of 5 represents the closest friend and the value 1 represents the least close one. If we continue to use the same little sample group as above, such data can be placed on the sociomatrix in Table 2.

In this sociomatrix, the number of rows is equal to columns and each corresponds to an individual. The diagonal cells of the matrix are blank as the girls cannot list themselves as their own best friend. The first row in the matrix shows Alice's relations. Alice listed Mary as her best friend because

Table 1. A sample dataset

Name	Age	Color	Residence
Alice	12	White	1
Jane	16	White	2
Mary	17	Black	1

Table 2. A sample sociomatrix

	Alice	Mary	Jane
Alice	x	5	1
Mary	4	x	0
Jane	3	1	x

the value 5, the highest scale, corresponds to her. In the second row, we can see that Mary sees Alice as a friend too but as the second best one (her best friend is not included in the sample because, in Mary's row, the value 5 is not shown in our sample matrix). She does not count Jane among her best friends. However, we can see that Jane considers Mary as a close friend (although as her fifth best friend).

In its current form, the sociomatrix is very useful to keep data on relations. Furthermore, in the phenomenon used by Moreno, the matrix shows the inequality in relations explicitly. Being a more isolated person, Jane considers Mary as her close friend, but Mary, a more popular student, probably does not reciprocate this intimacy. This information is invaluable for those working in the field of social psychology.

The original drawing by Moreno is shown in Figure 2. The blocks in the figure symbolize dormitory buildings. Thanks to this visualization, the relations among dormitories can also be seen clearly.

Such visualization of a social network seems to be quite interesting for most of us and creates the impression that we can understand a given social relation system at a single glance. Indeed, it might give us a clear idea about the social structure within the phenomenon. However, as useful as they may be, such drawings do not reflect the data in a sociomatrix in their entirety (Bender-Demoll and Mcfarland 2006). Even the asymmetry of relations in the girl's orphanage sample we have given corroborates this. Even if we would like to symbolize the closeness of a relation between two girls by placing them closer in a visual there are way too many constraints to do so, thus the visual proximity of points are different from these girls' own view of closeness. For such reasons, almost all social network visualizations are deceptive as much as they are informative; an issue taken up in Chapter 11.

Networks and Business Life

Every business having a certain size probably has a designated organizational chart. This chart shows who works for whom. We assume almost always that this chart shapes the reality for the business, meaning that a manager believes the person with whom the employees shown below him/her in the organizational chart interact the most is him/her. Similarly, when they need help from one of the other teams within the company, they might assume that the best thing to do is to reach the team manager. However, with social network research becoming more popular within the business administration

Figure 2. The student friendship network between orphanage dormitories presented by Moreno in his study

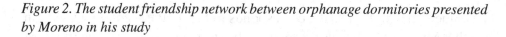

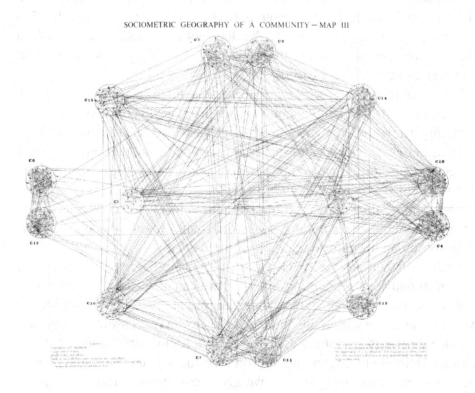

field, we know that the real interactions occurring within a business (informal networks) may be quite different from those shown in the organizational charts (formal networks) (Cross and Parker 2004; Kogut 2000).

Most of the time, it is not quite possible to see the real structure in its entirety. Before anything else, the possibility of such a difference between the formal and the informal business organization is troublesome and the very thought of it is often suppressed. In addition, each individual within the business is aware of only their own relations; it is not easy for anyone to see the general view regarding the social structure of the business. As it is the case in social research, individuals are generally evaluated separately from the factors concerning social structure. This is also applicable to the evaluation of employee performance. Two people with similar educational backgrounds and skills might perform very differently. This, of course, may stem from personal qualities. On the other hand, the communication networks of individuals within the business are different. For this exact reason, their problem-solving skills and paces might differ. In fact, significant disparities that are observed while evaluating employee performance may stem from social structure.

Apart from increasing or decreasing the performance of individuals, the informal social structure within the business might produce various and unexpected effects. For instance, as seen in studies about different professional or working groups within the same business, teams working in the field may develop their own isolated cultures and sets of habits when compared with those working in the headquarters of a company (Wellman, 1997; Orr 2006; Wenger 1998). It will not be possible to take precautions against or manage such structural effects sourcing from the disconnection (or the excessive connectedness) in the social structure unless we approach them systematically.

Such effects are more visible in businesses claiming to be highly productive and innovative. For example, in a classical approach, in order to solve a technical problem, teams are set up from employees working exclusively on the subject matter. This might work well for routine affairs. However, research shows that teams of individuals with varying experiences representing different stakeholders and different zones within the social structure work more efficiently within a shorter time frame in cases requiring creative solutions. The issue here is the features of the information flow. This information flow takes place through the channels, i.e. relations, within the social structure. Therefore, forming teams of individuals with varying characteristics and experience may create an abundance of knowledge. In summary, information flow processes made visible only by the social network approach are constantly at work within a company. Managing the information processes accurately in the business becomes possible only if steps toward network analysis are taken. Following the realization of these effects, many businesses now adopt this novel point of view and use related techniques in order to foster a more creative and innovative working environment (Cross and Parker 2004).

The Changing World and the Impact of the Internet

Moreno's research in the 1930s coincided with a period during which urbanization has accelerated in the Western world, the population density in cities increased, and thus social relations became more intense. A lot more changes has taken place to this day. A considerable majority of human population now lives in mega-cities with populations exceeding 10 million inhabitants. The companies at which we work, the schools we attend and other social settings are more crowded and more connected than they were in the past. Even people in rural areas maintain relations with more people regardless of distances thanks to means of communication such as smartphones.

This current situation highlights the importance of understanding the relation networks present in our lives and their impact. Scientists have started to use these techniques with unexpected creativity. For instance, making predictions on the spread rate of HIV based on sexual relation patterns or developing methods to counter terrorism by studying the relations among terrorist groups are among these unusual scientific applications (Neblett et al., 2011; Knoke 2015).

While the phenomenon "social network" becomes increasingly popular it might also be presented with terms unrelated with the essence of the subject and concepts distorting or blurring the phenomenon. As far as a field of study developing at the intersection of different disciplines (psychology, sociology, business administration etc.) such as social networks is concerned, these complicating terms and concepts prevent and mislead learners. Since we deal with a subject integrated with many disciplines and theoretical backgrounds, the way it is presented here inevitably includes certain simplifications. In this chapter, I attempt to give a general overview of this new field of study, to summarize what these new theories and methods can or cannot offer and to foreground the unique value of this field (and its theoretical background) with practical examples.

Representation and Analysis of Social Networks

To analyze social networks, we need to begin with defining a given social network based on the relation shaping it. Such an effort includes the collection of data depending on the definition of the social relation. The representation methods of various kinds of relations forming a social network differ from one another. Making sense of these data and answering the research questions by using them require certain analysis techniques unique to these data structures.

Imagining groups of individuals with social relations among them is not a difficult task. However, when we use the term "a social network" we mean a sum of relations regarding "a certain social relation". For instance, relations such as kinship or business partnership might be present and intermingled within a group. We define a social network by picking only one of these relations. Only then can we talk about the effect of, let us say, the social network of marriage relations on that of business relations or their assimilation (or vice verse). Besides, information on the presence/absence of a social relation or, in some cases, on its strength, will be necessary. But analyzing multiple relations as if they were a single pattern of relations would harm the objectivity and straing methodology. It would make the operationalization problematic and unreliable.

Once we make the definition of subjects and relations constituting the social network in question, we can answer certain fundamental questions regarding the social network data, e.g. the question whether this relation is a directional one. In the friendship relation of Moreno, we see a unilateral relation. The values usually differ even when the friendship is more or less reciprocated. However, for instance, marriage relations are non-directional. A marrying B is not a unilateral relation where B is in a different position from A within the relation. But in an extreme case, e.g. in a case within a context where women's rights are not established and women are "given away as wives" outside their will, a different relation definition might be made. In this extreme example, the objects are women and men; the relation may be considered as a unilateral marriage relation. In this particular case, the male and female actors form two sets of actors who are completely separated from one another and the relation is always from an actor in one set to an actor from the other set (i.e. a bipartite or bimodal network). These concepts will be explained further in the section below and in Chapter 2.

Different relations mentioned above require the collection of data as different datasets. But if we construct an identity among the actor sets of these different networks, it might be possible to analyze the facts together within a relation of causality. For instance, Padgett's study (Padgett 2010) investigates the marital and commercial bonds among Florentine families between the 13th and 15th centuries and examines the similarity between the two social networks.

Due to this wide range of social relations, social networks emerging from these relations and, consequently, datasets of these networks are diverse. Reference sources on the issue include lengthy and usually complex chapters on the classification of social network data. It would be beneficial to start with concrete social facts and analyzing basic examples rather than trying to classify the relations forming a social network in a systematic manner. After doing so, a systematic classification would be much easier to understand.

Types of Social Relation Data

The variety of datasets mentioned above can be classified entirely based on the nature of the social relation being analyzed. Basic types are as follows:

- **Directed/Undirected Relations, also Known as Asymmetrical/ Symmetrical Relations:** Relations of "liking" are unilateral; they are evaluated on the basis of a single individual or actor within the relation. Similarly, "borrowing" relations are also directional. This type of relations ihave a directional flow, i.e. an asymmetry. However, in marital or business joint venture networks, for example, such asymmetry does not exist.
- **Weighted/Unweighted (Binary) Relations:** A marital relation is either present or absent between two individuals, i.e. the relation either exists or not. Therefore, such relations are called binary or, more commonly, unweighted relations. But relations of "liking" or "borrowing" can be qualified as we can measure, for instance, "how much two people like each other" or "how much money a party borrowed from the other". Such relations are weighted. For weighted relations, the value of the weight depends on our evaluation technique. For example, if we ask someone to "evaluate how much do you like your friend on a scale from 1 to 10", due to our instruction, we determine a maximal value. But in a "borrowing" relation, there is no maximal value in the question. The existence of a maximal value might make it easier to make certain evaluations that are problematic for weighted relations.

Apart from these basic classifications, some others that might not seem familiar may also exist:

- **Bipartite Network:** The parties of a social relation might be from two different groups of actors. For instance, in the relation of "students taking classes", one party is the cluster of students and the other is that of classes. This is, once again, embedded within our definition of the relation. It is possible to transform such a dataset into a relation of "taking common classes" among students (a monopartite network); such transformation is a common practice for analysis purposes. A similar relationship is in the business world between individuals in the executive boards of companies. The relation of "membership of the executive board" is formed with individuals on one side and companies on the other, i.e. from one side of a bipartite network to the other. By transforming such networks to monopartite ones (e.g. co-membership to boards), the social structure formed by executive boards can be analyzed (Kogut, 2012).

- **Multiple Relation Networks:** In some cases, the relation we define might be established between the same two individuals more than once. The relation of "meeting" is an example of such relations. In the majority of such relations, transforming the definition into a weighted relation by calculating the number of interactions between actors is feasible. For instance, let us consider the network of executive board membership. If individuals A and B are together in not one but two executive boards of two different companies, there is a case of multiple relations. Multiple networks, or multinets, are similar to weighted networks and usually can be transformed to the latter.

- **Temporal Dataset:** In some cases, we can deal with the time frame in which the relation exists rather than the presence and volume of the relation. If we gather the times of getting together and departing in a "meeting" relation, such a data is visible. In that case, transformation into weighted relation is still possible by using the duration of meetings in which people come together, but some data will be lost. Temporal datasets are still quite an advanced and under studied subject within social network analysis.

An Example: Personal Friendship Network

Nowadays, many of us use online platforms called "social networks" such as Facebook. As most of our friends are also present in these platforms, our social environment is in fact represented digitally on them. For instance, when checking out a Facebook profile, mutual friends are also listed. In this section, we will discuss such personal friendship networks, with a small fictional example. Such a friendship network, lets assume yours, (1) includes your bonds of friendship with your friends and (2) encompasses related bonds if your friends are also friends. Let us assume that we gathered the relevant information or were able to extract the information as data and look at the features of your social network. I will name this network "personal friendship network" for reference. A fictional example is provided in Figure 3.

The initial observations regarding the "personal friendship network" will concern the relation forming this network, i.e. your "perception of friendship" among your group of friends. While collecting data about this network or thinking what to analyze regarding this network and what questions to ask based on these data, our starting point will be *exclusively* focused on this perception. But the results will concern the entirety of the network.

"The friendship network of the individual" includes a single type of relation compatible with our description: Friendship. Other types of relations like "taking the same course together", "being from the same family" or "being lovers" might be present between you and the people in this network or between these people. However, we have focused on a single type of relations. If we have focused on a different type of relation, we would reveal an entirely different social network. For instance, we can opt for "taking the same course together" and collect the data about with whom we take the same course at the university as a second social network dataset. This "taking the same course network" still will be a social network about me, but it is different from the first one. At best, we can ask the question whether there is a correlation between taking the same course and being friends and compare these two social networks. In this respect, these two social networks are related as they consist of the same actors (my close friends and me) and as such provides many research opportunities. But they are different social networks and the relational data cannot be added as apples and pears.

After determining the scope of the "personal friendship network", let us look at its features. A significant feature of this social network is its individual nature. We did not try to collect the relations among all the individuals constituting a social group, we only collected data regarding a single individual. We will name such a network as an ego-network: the network around a particular actor (the ego). The purpose of analyzing such a network is to understand the social structure around a single individual and not the whole group of individuals. In a typical social network research, the researcher may want to collect ego-network data for a sample of individuals, and use structural metrics alongside other, actor related variables.

The social relation underlying the "personal friendship network" is "the perception of friendship". This is both easy and hard to evaluate and measure. It is easy because I can think of my friends and my intimacy with them quickly without actually collecting data. But it is also hard as the objectivity of my evaluation is debatable. What we need to do is to define the social network we deal with. We evaluate the way "I" see the friendships within the group consisting of me and my close friends. We could have chosen a different relationship and collected a different dataset. For example, I could have kept a track of how many times I was together with each friend or how many times

I called each friend on the phone; then, I could have used those numbers. The social network would be "the network phone communication". This is another network as the underlying relation is different. If I can manage to gather this information, I will have two ego- network datasets. By comparing them, I can attempt to understand the difference (or similarity) between my perception of friendship and the demonstration of this friendship by getting together data. Such social network data based on "the perception of friendship might not be interesting for some individuals (e.g. business managers). On the other hand, such a comparison might be quite exciting for those interested in psychology. As for businesses, studies may be conducted by creating networks from e-mail correspondences or other similar interaction data (Gençer 2007).

This example shows us a noteworthy aspect of studying social networks: It might not always be easy to evaluate social relations and the precision of our measurements might be limited. What is to be taken into consideration here is to define the relation we want to evaluate accurately. Only then can we interpret and use the data correctly. In our example, comparing the perceptions of friendship of different individuals within the same group makes sense for a social psychologist as it is a measurement of social perception. On the other hand "the frequency of getting together" is a different relation that needs to be interpreted differently, althoug it too gives a social ego-network for the same individual.

Another feature of the "personal friendship network" is that it is based on an undirected or symmetric relation. When we speak of friendship, we mean something conceptually reciprocal. However, if we have asked each person to state how much they "liked" one another and to evaluate their perceptions on a scale from 1 to 10, the results could be different at two sides of a friendship and may not be reciprocal.

Another aspect of the social relation we deal with in this example is that the relations are "weighted". We have collected data about not only the presence or absence of the relation but also its strength (or weight). The strength of relations in our dataset is different from one another. This will be important for the numerical methods we will choose while analyzing the social network, which will be explained in the coming chapters. In some cases, the relation may be unweighted or, more accurately, dichotomous. Marital relations can be considered as an example. This relation may or may not present between two individuals; we cannot say that a couple is "more married" than another.

Here, we have dealt with an example of a seemingly-simple social network and we can ask many questions regarding social effects or outcomes of the relational structure. We can answer these questions in a systematic manner.

Our principle is to take the nature of the relation underlying the social network into consideration. When we determine the features of the relation accurately, the meaning of our quantitative evaluations becomes clear and thus helps us to raise the right questions concerning the phenomenon systematically.

Each researcher would work with social network data compatible with their discipline. A "subjective" evaluation like the one mentioned in this example may seem hardly useful for some, but for someone else (e.g. a psychologist) this is the exact feature that makes it interesting. On the other hand, a researcher coming from the field of business administration may prefer to base their arguments on an objective definition of a relation.

Representation of Social Network Data

Now, let us see how we will analyze this social network. While working with personal (non-relational) datasets, we first tabulate the data we have and then apply the standard empirical methods suitable for the question we want to answer to the data. After that, we evaluate the accuracy of our hypotheses regarding the phenomenon or we try to come up with new ones by interpreting the results. This is similar to the steps we are going to follow for relational analysis. However, before doing that, we need to deal with the problem of how to represent such kind of a dataset.

The first data format to be used to represent social networks is the format known as **sociomatrix** or **adjacency matrix**. In this matrix structure, both rows and columns represent the actors of the social network we analyze (i.e. individuals). The "personal friendship network" data mentioned in our example can be represented with this method as given in Table 3.

The relations in the matrix are visualized in Figure 3. The following code chunk reproduces this example.

Table 3. An example of a network sociomatrix.

	Me	**Adam**	**Jane**	**Joe**	**Mary**
Me	0	8	4	6	10
Adam	8	0	9	0	5
Jane	4	9	0	3	0
Joe	6	0	3	0	6
Mary	10	5	0	6	0

```
require(igraph)
d<- data.frame(Me  = c(0, 8, 4, 6,10),
               Adam= c(8, 0, 9, 0, 5),
               Jane= c(4, 9, 0, 3, 0),
               Joe = c(6, 0, 3, 0, 6),
               Mary= c(10, 5, 0, 6, 0),
               row.names = c("Me","Adam","Jane","Joe","Mary"))
m=as.matrix(d) # Convert data frame to a matrix
net=graph.adjacency(m, # Create graph from adjacency matrix
               mode="undirected", # Set the graph type
since it is not
                                  # apparent from the
matrix
               weighted=TRUE,  # Use weights as $weight
attribute of edges
               diag=FALSE)
# The difference above from the previous plot:
# we designate weighted=TRUE
plot.igraph(net,
           vertex.label=V(net)$name, #igraph functions are
versatile
           # but cumbersome! This parameter is necessary to
produce
           # vertex labels on the plot
           layout=layout.fruchterman.reingold, # graph layouts
           # are discussed much later in the book. This one
           # is a good default for small networks
           edge.color="black",
           edge.width=E(net)$weight, # The E() function
extracts
                                  #  the set of network
edges
           vertex.size=40)
```

The structure of the matrix reflects all the aspects of the mentioned social relation. Let us look at those features:

- The value in the diagonal cells of the matrix (Me-Me, Adam-Adam etc.) is always 0 as this relation in question is a *social* one. Therefore, I do not have a relationship with myself or Joe does not have a relationship with himself. But if the subject matter were an economic relation, e.g. "money transfer", it would be normal to have a value other than zero if I sent money from one of my own accounts to another. Similarly, certain social relations like "e-mail correspondences" might result in

Figure 3. Personal friendship network

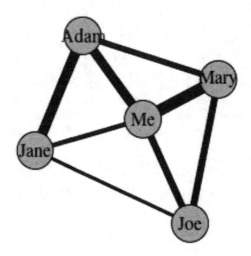

values different from zero. But the diagonal cells are not used in most cases.

- There is symmetry around the diagonal of this matrix, meaning that the value in the cell "Adam-Jane" is equal to the value in "Jane-Adam". The reason is that the relation in question is an *undirected(symmetric)* one.

- There are values other than 0 and 1 in the cells because this relation is weighted. The strength/weight of a tie may differ from another. If it was a binary/unweighted relation, our data matrix would exclusively include the values 0 (no relation) or 1 (relation exists) only.

CASE STUDY: BASIC STRUCTURAL FEATURES OF THE PERSONAL FRIENDSHIP NETWORK

Features of the structure surrounding an individual are determined based on the data representation mentioned above. The number of cells within the rows and columns of a matrix with values other than zero shows a wide range of information on the individual. The sum of a row is the amount of relations that the individual establishes (or presupposes in this case); the sum of a column signifies the amount of relations established towards the individual. In an undirected (symmetric) relation such as the one given in the example, these values are equal.

In social relations, there are cognitive tensions in triads. Two of my close friends meeting each other is almost an obligation, as is the case in the example. There is an expectation for them to meet sooner or later and to become friends. If they do not meet or do not like each other, tension occurs. This dynamic within triads are called transitivity (Krackhardt 1987).

The "density" of social networks is a common topic. The density of the network indicates its comprehensiveness. In its simplest sense, it shows how many of all the possible relations exist in reality. Apart from a general density value regarding the overall network, it is also possible to talk about individual (ie. ego) network density. This signifies the density of relations among the social structure around an individual.

Social ego-networks are usually dense. The cognitive tension in triads causes ego-networks to close: a topic of social dynamics that is covered in Chapter 5. However, ego-networks within certain contexts, e.g. in business life, might scatter differently. Another example would be the significant differences of quality and density between the ego-networks of a person living in a more closed environment (e.g. a housewife) and another person engaging in a wider range of daily activities (e.g. a salesperson).

When there is a unilateral relation such as "liking" instead of "friendship" as it is the case in Moreno's data, some other features come into play. Reciprocity is among the most significant of these features. Such a relation is usually reciprocal. This feature is present in many social and economic relations and its absence is interesting in itself.

Upon looking at the visualized network in Moreno's dataset, we can see that it is, unlike the personal friendship network, divided into social groups. The density of such networks is low. Density generally decreases as the network grows (as the number of actors increases). For instance, it is quite possible for everyone within a group of 10 people to know each other, but same is highly unlikely for a group of 1000 individuals as only a small portion of possible relations would actually exist. For that reason, we cannot compare the densities of networks of different sizes.

Besides these, the most important metric regarding the actors of a network is "centrality". Originally a topographical term, centrality is a difficult aspect to define in social networks. Therefore, there are as many types of centrality measurement as there are disciplines using this approach (Freeman, 1978; Das et al., 2018). One of the simplest of these types, **degree centrality** is defined as the number of ties of a social actor. However, this metric concerns exclusively the local social structure surrounding the actor only. Let us think of an individual who is outgoing within its own group but does not have any relations with other groups. This individual's degree centrality is high. **Betweenness centrality**, the exact opposite of degree centrality, is about the position of the actor as a bridge within the wider social structure. Individuals serving as a bridge connect different social groups, therefore they are able to access certain opportunities in the social or economic system. We will discuss the definition both types of centrality in the chapters 3 and 5. A good discussion on centrality can be found in the works of Scott (Scott 2000) or Borgatti (Borgatti and Foster 2003; Borgatti and Everett 2006; Borgatti et al. 2009).

Some Sources and Software on Social Networks

I made use of many resources, all of them in the English language, while compiling this book. Even though these resources are discussed within the body of the book, some readers might require a short list of recommendations. The best option for beginners, in my opinion, would be "Social Networks: An Introduction" by John Scott (Scott 2000). Besides this, a comprehensive resource on quantitative analysis techniques would be "Social Network Analysis: Methods and applications" by Stanley Wasserman and Katherine Faust (Wasserman and Faust 1994). These books would be my first recommendations for those seeking additional resources on the subject matter.

Many researchers and research groups coming from different disciplines and institutions have created their own software solutions for network analysis. You can find certain guidelines regarding some of these software tools within the main text but a more comprehensive list and evaluation is provided in appendix E. This section provides a very brief overview of the relative merits of these software tools. For those who would like a quick introduction to the subject, I would recommend the software called Gephi (Bastian, Heymann, and Jacomy, 2009; Aggrawal and Arora, 2016). Based on my experience with students, I would recommend Gephi for beginners. With is graphic interface, it is very well designed and therefore it is easy for a beginner to navigate. Gephi is only one of the many contemporary software solutions for social network visualization and analysis. As Java programming language is used in its coding, it can be used on many platforms (Windows, Linux, Mac). Furthermore, it is relatively easier to start using. The software and basic user guides are available on http://gephi.org/ free of charge. You can use this software for the initial steps of social network research. However, for serious analyses, R statistics package and related libraries provide more control over the processes.

Another software solution for network analysis is Pajek (Nooy, Mrvar, and Batagelj 2005). This is one of the earliest and commonly-used network visualization and analysis software. Having benefited from the disciplines of mathematics (random networks) and physics, the interface of the software reflects these fields of study. It is an efficient system for the analysis of larger networks. You can download the software from http://pajek.imfm.si/doku.php free of charge and access additional material like user guides. However, my initial recommendation for those working in social sciences would be Gephi. I would like to remind you that you can find the datasets for the examples given in the remainder of the book on http://appliedsna.mgencer.com.

A few more tools, in different categories, worth mentioning here. First is NodeXL, which is an extension to Microsoft's popular spreadsheet tool Excel. It allows very basic visualization of network data stored as an Excel spreadsheet. Therefore, offers an easy exploration for users who feel comfortable with Excel. Another tool, in the opposite end of the spectrum, is NetworkX, which is a software package in the popular Python programming language. NetworkX is interesting for those who feel more comfortable to start off in Python, rather than R. It should be preferred for research or applications in which one needs to develop new metrics or algorithms.

R as a Platform for Social Network Analysis

R is a software environment for statistical computing and graphics. Over its long history R has attracted researchers from almost all disciplines to use it as the platform for statistical analysis in scientific research. Social network analysis is just one of these disciplines. Therefore, R is neither not a tool specifically designed for network analysis, nor it outstands other social network analysis tools in terms of features. But it does have several key advantages that are the basis of our choosing it for the platform of application in this text.

One key reason is that R is open source and multi platform. You can obtain files to install R from its website (http://r-project.org). It is available for all major platforms (Linux/Unix, Windows, MacOS). This was an important reason for our choice as it makes R a tool which most of our readers can get their hands on. As with many open source tools R has a rich variety of documentation and materials for novice users as well as more experienced ones. These resources come from a large and global community of R users and developers, who support one another in Internet forums by answering each other's questions and exchanging experiences.

As with most open source software R has a lot of community contributed packages, with varying quality and maturity levels. This includes the packages on social network analysis (SNA), that seem to come from different disciplines. Despite the variance in quality, these packages provide an excellent coverage of SNA methods and metrics.

Another key advantage of using R for social network analysis is that, being a general statistical computing platform, R allows you to integrate SNA as part of a bigger pipeline of data processing or quantitative research. You can take data resulting from a social network related analysis and use it for more conventional operations, or vice versa; such as visualizing distributions or linear modeling with non-network data.

Last but not the least; R is an increasingly popular platform for data analysis. On the one hand developing R skills promises better prospects to us as analysts. In addition, one can expect to see a growing ecosystem of tools and materials in R when compared to other alternatives for social network analysis.

REVIEW EXERCISES

1. Create a sociomatrix for your own personal friendship network, using pen and paper.
2. Produce the R data object for your personal friendship network, using graph.formula() function. Then visualize the network.
3. Consider the "work relations network" of (a) an individual with a relatively introvert job, such as accounting, and (b) an individual with a relatively extrovert job such as merketing. How would you expect the densities of these two networks to compare to each other?

REFERENCES

Aggrawal, N., & Arora, A. (2016). *Visualization, analysis and structural pattern infusion of DBLP co-authorship network using Gephi. In 2016 2nd International Conference on Next Generation Computing Technologies (NGCT)* (pp. 494–500). IEEE; doi:10.1109/NGCT.2016.7877466.

Artto, K., Ahola, T., Kyrö, R., & Peltokorpi, A. (2017). Managing business networks or value creation in facilities and their external environments: A study on co-location. Facilities, 35(1/2), 99–115. doi:10.1108/F-07-2015-0049

Atefeh, F., & Khreich, W. (2015). A survey of techniques for event detection in twitter. *Computational Intelligence*, *31*(1), 132–164. doi:10.1111/coin.12017

Bastian, M., Heymann, S., & Jacomy, M. (2009). Gephi: An Open Source Software for Exploring and Manipulating Networks. International Aaai Conference on Weblogs and Social Media. http://www.aaai.org/ocs/index.php/ICWSM/09/paper/view/154

Bender-Demoll, S., & Mcfarland, D. A. (2006). The art and science of dynamic network visualization. *Journal of Social Structure : JOSS*, *7*(2), 1–38.

Borgatti, S. P., & Everett, M. G. (2006). A Graph-theoretic perspective on centrality. *Social Networks*, *28*(4), 466–484. doi:10.1016/j.socnet.2005.11.005

Borgatti, S. P., & Foster, P. C. (2003). The network paradigm in Organizational research: A review and typology. *Journal of Management*, *29*(6), 991–1013. doi:10.1016/S0149-2063(03)00087-4

Borgatti, S. P., Mehra, A., Brass, D. J., & Labianca, G. (2009). Network Analysis in the Social Sciences. *Science*, *323*(5916), 892–895. doi:10.1126/science.1165821 PubMed

Brandes, U., & Nick, B. (2011). Asymmetric relations in longitudinal social networks. *IEEE Transactions on Visualization and Computer Graphics*, *17*(12), 2283–2290. doi:10.1109/TVCG.2011.169 PubMed

Brass, D. J., Galaskiewicz, J., Greve, H. R., & Tsai, W. (2004). Taking stock of networks and organizations: A multilevel perspective. *Academy of Management Journal*, *47*, 795–817.

Burt, R. S. (1992). *Structural holes: The social structure of competition.* Cambridge, MA: Harvard University Press.

Coleman, J. S. (1988). Social Capital in the Creation of Human Capital. *American Journal of Sociology*, *94*, S95–S120. http://www.jstor.org/stable/2780243 doi:10.1086/228943

Cross, R., & Parker, A. (2004). The Hidden Power of Social Networks: Understanding How Work Really Gets Done in Organizations. Harvard Business School Press. Retrieved from http://www.amazon.com/exec/obidos/redirect?tag=citeulike07-20{\&}path=ASIN/1591392705

Crossley, N., & Edwards, G. (2016). Cases, mechanisms and the real: The theory and methodology of mixed-method social network analysis. *Sociological Research Online*, *21*(2), 1–15. doi:10.5153/sro.3920

Csardi, G., & Nepusz, T. (2006). The igraph software package for complex network research. InterJournal. *Complex Systems*, *1695*(5), 1–9.

Dagnino, G. B., Levanti, G., Mina, A., & Picone, P. M. (2015). Interorganizational network and innovation: A bibliometric study and proposed research agenda. *Journal of Business and Industrial Marketing*, *30*(3/4), 354–377. doi:10.1108/JBIM-02-2013-0032

Das, K., Samanta, S., & Pal, M. (2018). Study on centrality measures in social networks: A survey. *Social Network Analysis and Mining*, *8*(1), 13. doi:10.1007/s13278-018-0493-2

De Nooy, W., Mrvar, A., & Batagelj, V. (2018). *Exploratory social network analysis with Pajek: Revised and expanded edition for updated software* (Vol. 46). Cambridge University Press; doi:10.1017/9781108565691.

Emirbayer, M., & Mische, A. (1998). What Is Agency? *American Journal of Sociology*, *103*(4), 962–1023. doi:10.1086/231294

Floridi, L., & Taddeo, M. (2016). What is data ethics? Philosophical Transactions of the Royal Society A: Mathematical, Physical and Engineering Sciences, 374. PubMed

Freeman, L. C. (1978). Centrality in social networks conceptual clarification. *Social Networks*, *1*(3), 215–239. doi:10.1016/0378-8733(78)90021-7

Gencer, M. (2007). Increasing Modularity of Production in Computer Markets: Common Business Strategies and the Case of IBM Eclipse Project. Proceedings of the International Coloquium on Business and Management. Retrieved from http://mgencer.com/files/ICBM2007.pdf

Granovetter, M. S. (1985). Economic Action and Social Structure: The Problem of Embeddedness. *American Journal of Sociology*, *91*(3), 481–510. doi:10.1086/228311

Granovetter, M. S. (2005). The Impact of Social Structure on Economic Outcomes. *The Journal of Economic Perspectives, 19*(1), 33–50. doi:10.1257/0895330053147958

Gulati, R. (1995). Social Structure and Alliance Formation Patterns: A Longitudinal Analysis. *Administrative Science Quarterly, 40*(4), 619–657. doi:10.2307/2393756

Gulati, R., & Gargiulo, M. (1999). Where do Inter-organizational Networks Come From? *American Journal of Sociology, 104*(5), 1439–1493. doi:10.1086/210179

Knoke, D. (2015). Emerging trends in social network analysis of terrorism and counterterrorism. Emerging Trends in the Social and Behavioral Sciences: An Interdisciplinary, Searchable, and Linkable Resource, 1-15.

Kogut, B. (2000). The network as knowledge: Generative rules and the emergence of structure. *Strategic Management Journal, 21*(3), 405–425. doi:10.1002/(SICI)1097-0266(200003)21:3<405::AID-SMJ103>3.0.CO;2-5

Kogut, M. (2012). The Small world of corporate governance. The Small Worlds of Corporate Governance, 1–52. doi:10.7551/mitpress/9780262017275.001.0001

Krackhardt, D. (1987). Cognitive social structures. *Social Networks, 9*(2), 109–134. doi:10.1016/0378-8733(87)90009-8

Lazer, D., Pentland, A., Adamic, L., Aral, S., Barabási, A. L., Brewer, D., ... Jebara, T. (2009). Computational social science. *Science, 323*(5915), 721–723. doi:10.1126/science.1167742 PubMed

Marin, A., & Wellman, B. (2011). Social network analysis: An introduction. The SAGE handbook of social network analysis, 11. doi:10.1017/CBO9781107415324.004

McPherson, M., Smith-Lovin, L., & Cook, J. M. (2001). Birds of a feather: Homophily in social networks. *Annual Review of Sociology, 27*(1), 415–444. doi:10.1146/annurev.soc.27.1.415

Moreno, J. L., & Jennings, H. H. (1938). Statistics of social configurations. *Sociometry, 1*(3/4), 342–374. doi:10.2307/2785588

Neblett, R. C., Davey-Rothwell, M., Chander, G., & Latkin, C. A. (2011). Social network characteristics and HIV sexual risk behavior among urban African American women. *Journal of Urban Health*, *88*(1), 54–65. doi:10.1007/s11524-010-9513-x PubMed

Nyati, U., Rawat, S., Gupta, D., Aggrawal, N., & Arora, A. (2019). Characterize ingredient network for recipe suggestion. International Journal of Information Technology, 1-8.

Orr, J. E. (2006). Ten years of talking about machines. *Organization Studies*, *27*(12), 1805–1820. doi:10.1177/0170840606071933

Padgett, J. F. (2010). Open Elite? Social Mobility, Marriage, and Family in Florence, 1282–1494. *Renaissance Quarterly*, *63*(2), 357–411. doi:10.1086/655230 PubMed

Raberto, M., Ozel, B., Ponta, L., Teglio, A., & Cincotti, S. (2019). From financial instability to green finance: The role of banking and credit market regulation in the eurace model. *Journal of Evolutionary Economics*, *29*(1), 429–465. doi:10.1007/s00191-018-0568-2

Saqr, M., & Alamro, A. (2019). The role of social network analysis as a learning analytics tool in online problem based learning. *BMC Medical Education*, *19*(1), 160. doi:10.1186/s12909-019-1599-6 PubMed

Scott, J. (2000). *Social Network Analysis*. Atlanta, Ga.: Sage.

Shoshi, A., Hoppe, T., Kormeier, B., Ogultarhan, V., & Hofestädt, R. (2015). GraphSAW: A web-based system for graphical analysis of drug interactions and side effects using pharmaceutical and molecular data. *BMC Medical Informatics and Decision Making*, *15*(1), 15. doi:10.1186/s12911-015-0139-5 PubMed

Silvester, J., Anderson, N. R., & Patterson, F. (1999). Organizational culture change: An inter-group attributional analysis. *Journal of Occupational and Organizational Psychology*, *72*(1), 1–23. doi:10.1348/096317999166464

Tinati, R., Halford, S., Carr, L., & Pope, C. (2014). Big data: Methodological challenges and approaches for sociological analysis. *Sociology*, *48*(4), 663–681. doi:10.1177/0038038513511561

Turan, S., & Aktan, D. (2008). Okul Hayatında Var Olan Ve Olması Düşünülen Sosyal Değerler. *Türk Eğitim Bilimleri Dergisi*, *6*(2), 227–259.

Wasserman, S., & Faust, K. (1994). Social network analysis: Methods and applications (Vol. 8). Cambridge university press. doi:10.1017/CBO9780511815478

Wellman, D., & Orr, J. E. (1997). Talking about machines: An ethnography of a modern job. *Contemporary Sociology*, *26*(5), 626. doi:10.2307/2655659

Wenger, E. (1998, June). Communities of practice: Learning as a social system. *The Systems Thinker*.

ENDNOTE

[1] Even though certain disciplines such as political science analyze the social structure, they do not have a fully-developed structural analysis method.

Section 1
Structure and Structural Measurements

Chapter 2
Structural Analysis
With Graphs

ABSTRACT

Graphs are mathematical formalisms that represent social networks very well. Analysis methods using graph theory have started to develop substantially along with the advancement of mathematics and computer sciences in recent years, with contributions from several disciplines including social network analysis. Learning how to use graphs to represent social networks is important not only for employing theoretical insights of this advanced field in social research, but also for the practical purposes of utilizing its mature and abundant tools. This chapter explores structural analysis with graphs.

GRAPHS

Graph is a mathematical term, which provides us a representation method that is completely equivalent to sociomatrices and adjacency matrices mentioned in the previous chapter. In its most basic and theoretical sense, using one or other of these methods does not contribute to how easily we gather information on or how well we represent a social network phenomenon. Matrix algebra has been a stronghold of mathematics and was the choice of early social network researchers. However, analysis methods using the graph theory have started to develop substantially along with the advancement of mathematics and computer science in recent decades. Therefore, learning how to use graphs to represent social networks is important not for theoretical aspects but for

DOI: 10.4018/978-1-7998-1912-7.ch002

practical purposes, i.e. using these methods in practice. While dealing with the question of how structural features are found from the data set, we will also see how they are reflected in graph and matrix features simultaneously. As a result, your early exposure to different social network representation methods with their corresponding analysis tools would make it easier for you to develop an oversight and benefit from books and articles written within the scope of different disciplines and in different time periods.

The mathematical concept of a graph is a structure which consists of "vertices" which are connected by "edges". As the mathematical term is defined regardless of what it is meant to represent, mathematicians named the components in the graph as geometric terms. They further differentiate between edges and "arcs", a term used for the ties in a directed or asymmetrical relation (Valiente 2002). Software people prefer the word "node" instead of vertex, and "tie" instead of edge or arc. Social researchers would feel home with the term "actors" instead of a mathematical or computational term like "vertices" or "nodes", and "relation" or "tie" instead of edge or arc. Figure 1 shows a visual of a fictional personal friendship network. As far as our example is concerned people are vertices and the friendships among them are edges of the graph in this visualization.

Here, I will opt for the terms "actor" and "tie" to maintain a style in accordance with the social sciences perspective, but I will also use the more neutral term "component" instead of "actor" from time to time while handling theories on graphs. The reason for this is that not every socio-economic component is "active" or is an "actor" and that some of them might be passive as well, e.g. the "country" in the case of trade network between countries. Even though the varying terminology does not affect the underlying mathematical processes, it allows us to talk about phenomena in various and appropriate ways. It takes some terminological versatility to use the same mathematical apparatus when talking about, for example, electrical networks of a city versus a network of political relations.

The mathematical framework used for the representation of graphs is also quite suitable for social networks. Furthermore, it is more clear and more compact in representing social networks, when compared with sociomatrices. Let us see this method at work in an example. The example below is a social network data file written in the particular graph format of the Pajek software, which is commonly used as input format in many other software packages as well:

```
*Vertices 4
1 "Albert"
2 "Richard"
3 "Betty"
4 "Louis"
*Edges
1 3 7
1 4 11
2 1 12
2 3 21
```

Even without a detailed explanation of the data format used, the data above can be read easily by looking at the English terms regarding graphs, if you are familiar with graph terminology. The data format shown here is used in the Pajek software (Nooy, Mrvar, and Batagelj 2005) and is compatible with many social network analysis software developed later on. You can save the graph representation above as a file named "example.net" and then open the file with Gephi for visualization and analysis purposes. Similarly, you can also export one of the sample social networks included in Gephi (and visible on the opening screen) in this format and then use it. Relatively newer software such as Gephi recognize the formats of Pajek and other preceding programs, define their own usually-richer data formats and allow the conversion between two formats.

The social network in this example consists of four actors (the part starting with the term "Vertices"). The first rows include the numbers given to these actors and the names or labels of these actors. Labels are not necessary for the computer but allows us to interpret the produced visualizations easily. In each row starting with "Edges", there are three numerical values. The first two are the actor numbers and signify that a tie is present between these two actors. The weight of the tie is given as the third value in each row. There would not be a third number if the relation in question was an unweighted one. In the case of directed relations, the term "Edges" would be replaced by "Arcs". The R code to produce this example is given below. The code example does not read any input file yet. We will come to social network data input from files later in this chapter. For now, the code below produces a network data object manually, as in the previous examples:

```
require (igraph) #load the igraph library if it is not already
loaded
# the following line forms the graph data object
g1 <- graph.formula(Albert--Betty,
                    Albert--Louis,
```

```
                        Richard--Albert,
                        Richard--Betty)
V(g1)$size <- 50 # Set the vertex sizes to the same fixed value
E(g1)$weight <- c(7, 11, 12, 21)
E(g1)$label <- E(g1)$weight
plot(g1, # Visualize the graph
     edge.curved=0.0, # make the edges curved, for aestetic
purposes
     edge.width=E(g1)$weight)
```

Comparing the use of Graphs and Sociomatrices

If we represented the example social network data given in Pajek graph format above with a sociomatrix instead, it would look like as follows:

There are many cells with the value "0" in our sociomatrix. The majority of the cells will include the value "0" as the number of actors (nodes) in the social network increases; this would seriously undermine the usefulness of

Figure 1. A sample personal friendship network

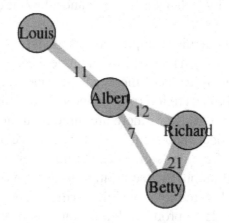

Table 1.

.	Albert	Richard	Betty	Louis
Albert	0	12	7	11
Richard	12	0	21	0
Betty	7	21	0	0
Louis	11	0	0	0

matrices as a representation method. For instance, imagine a social network of friendship in which 1000 individuals are present and each individual has a friendhip tie with approximately 10 others. We would need a square matrix with a size of 1000x1000 to hold the social network data. But the number of all relations is actually only around 1000x10, thus 99% of the matrix is full of zeros. Besides, the graph would obviate the necessity of repeating relations twice in such an undirected network. Instead the matrix is symmetrical diagonally, meaning that the same values are repeated twice (e.g. the value for Albert-Richard is equal to Richard-Albert). Therefore, graph representation is much more economical when compared with matrices. Considering that the datasets with which social scientists deal nowadays become increasingly larger, the use of the graph format instead of matrix format facilitates both the preparation of datasets and the processing of these datasets with computer software.

For these reasons, although matrices are more eligible for smaller networks, the graph method is generally preferred for networks of every size. Another justification would be, in addition to being more economical for the representation of larger networks when compared with matrices, the rapid development of graph analysis methods and tools. Nevertheless, matrix algebra has a long history and encompasses a wide range of advanced methods. Therefore, new matrix-based analysis methods are still among the most active areas of study (e.g. Newman (2006)).

Graph Data

A graph is a combination of nodes and ties. In mathematical terms, we denote a graph as follows: $G=(N,T)$. The set of nodes can be shown as $N=n_1,n_2,...,n_n$, and the set of ties as $T=t_1,t_2,...,t_m$. The number of nodes, $n = N \vee$, and that of relations, $m = T \vee$, are the sizes of these sets.

Here, each tie is shown with the two nodes it connects: $t_k=(n_{k1},n_{k2})$. If the relation is weighted, the strength of the tie is also added to the notation: $t_k=(n_{k1},n_{k2},s_k)$. We can see the set of nodes and then that of ties in the graph data shown above in Pajek format. In our example given in Pajek format, the list of nodes ("vertices") correspond to the set N while the set of ties ("edges") to the set T.

Different software tools use different formats for the representation of actors and relations in a graph representing a social network. There is no standard format in this respect. For instance, how do we show directed or undirected relations? You can indicate an undirected relation as two directed ones, but this means a doubling in the size of the data file, just like the redundancy in a sociomatrix which is symmetrical around its diagonal. Therefore, in some data formats, features of the graph such as being directed/undirected are also given at the beginning of the data format. For example, the content of GEXF files of Gephi using an XML-based format is similar to the example given below (taken from Gephi website), which uses the software terminology of "node" and "edge" for graph content:

```
<gexf version="1.2">
    <meta>
        <creator>Gexf.net</creator>
        <description>A hello world! file</description>
    </meta>
    <graph mode="static" defaultedgetype="directed">
        <nodes>
            <node id="0" label="John" />
            <node id="1" label="Jane" />
        </nodes>
        <edges>
            <edge id="0" source="0" target="1" />
        </edges>
    </graph>
</gexf>
```

In this example, the type of the relation, a feature at the graph level, is stated as "directed" by the defaultedgetype attribute of the file format. Thus, information on the direction of the ties ("edges") are not given; only the two nodes a tie connects (source and target) are indicated. Furthermore, it is also indicated in this format that the social network is "static" with the "mode" attribute, i.e. a social network dataset without temporal dimension. Apart from that, some "meta" information is alson given at the graph level that are not a part of any node or tie but concerning the dataset level, such as the "creator" of the dataset along with a brief "description".

Social network data, in reality, may include more than basic graph data. For instance, demographic information on the actors, such as age and gender, can be collected. Such "non-graph" data can also include features of relations as well, like the time of establishing the tie within a social network with a temporal aspect. "Label" information about the actors (nodes) in the Gephi/GEXF format given above is such an example that does not give a measurement about the ties forming a graph. The "label" data in this example is used for saving the real name of the actor in addition to the actor number.

Therefore, we can easily see the identity of an individual whom we find to have interesting structural features and make use of these labels in order to make it more comprehensible while visualizing and interpreting the network structure.

While Pajek format is more suitable for manual aditing, formats like GEXF are not. Instead of manual efforts, software tools like Gephi offer easy-to-use data entry screens similar to those given in tabular software and they use their own formats to save rich data although they are less readable.

A handy format you may find useful is *edgelist* format. This is a simple file format which you can manipulate in a plain text editor or a spreadsheet program. A simple edgelist will be a two column csv (comma separated values) spreadsheet as the following that reproduces our example. Note that the first row gives column names of our choosing; in this case I have chose V1 and V2 to denote vertex 1 and vertex 2:

```
V1,     V2
Albert, Louis
Albert, Betty
Albert, Richard
Betty,  Richard
```

Let's assume that you have stored this content in a file in dataexampleEdgelist1.csv`. You can read this data file and convert it into graph format as in the following example. You will find all such examples at http://appliedsna.mgencer.com:

```
require(igraph)
d <- read.csv("data/exampleEdgelist1.csv",header=TRUE)
edgelist <- as.matrix(d) # coerce the data into
                         #  a matrix format for igraph's liking
g <- graph.edgelist(edgelist,directed=FALSE)
plot(g) # plot if you like
```

Note that the file does not provide certain meta info such as whether the graph is directed or not. This is unlike more feature rich formats such as GraphML. But the advantage is that the format is simple and versatile to manipulate with a wide range of software choices.

You may need to use the format for weighted graphs as well, which was our original example in the previous section. This can be accomplished in two steps: first by reading the graph structure then by assigning the edge weights. To do this we need a csv file which provides edge weights in a third colum as follows:

```
V1, V2, weight
Albert, Louis, 11
Albert, Betty, 7
Albert, Richard, 12
Betty, Richard, 21
```

Let's assume that the above representation is stored in file data/exampleEdgelist2.csv. We can read the data and create a weighted graph object as follows:

```
library(igraph)
d <- read.csv("data/exampleEdgelist2.csv",header=TRUE)
edgelist <- as.matrix(d[,1:2]) # Use only the structure data
g <- graph.edgelist(edgelist,directed=FALSE)
E(g)$weight <- d[,3] # Now assign the weights to edges
E(g)$label <- E(g)$weight
plot(g, edge.width=E(g)$weight)
```

Graph Topology (Structure) and Density

Since graph is an abstract mathematical concept it is used in a variety of scientific disciplines. One of the earliest uses was the problem in which Euler questioned the paths around the rivers, bridges, and islets in Königsberg, his native city, where he used a precursor of the modern graph concept. Apart from such use in a geographical context, phenomena in many fields like biology or computer networks can be represented with graphs. As a result, definitions, concepts, and criteria used to evaluate the structure of networks are shared among these disciplines. For that reason, some concepts to be defined here may not seem "social" at first glance.

We can talk about, for example, a **walk** along the graph. A walk is a series of uninterrupted ties traversed starting from one node and continuing along neighbouring ties. If the walk does not stop by the same nodes and ties, this walk is called a "**path**". These were important concepts in Euler's original problem: Can we draw a path without going at a place twice but still using all the bridges. Today, this is a question of practical importance for the areas of marketing and logistics (e.g the "traveling salesman problem").

There may be more than one path between two nodes These paths are vital for analyzing, for instance, the information flow between nodes in graphs. The number of ties (the length) in the shortest path connecting two nodes gives us the **distance** of nodes. Finding and using such paths is an important task, for example, in routing the Internet data traffic.

At first, it might seem odd to use such concepts reminding of geography or physics for social phenomena. However, these quantifications prove to be useful for understanding the topology and the positions of individuals or other social actors within a social structure. For example, the farthest distance among those starting from one individual to all others is called the individual's **eccentricity** and the comparison of these measurements among individuals shows us how central or peripheral (eccentric) an individual is within the network in comparison with others. Similarly, the largest value of eccentricity, i.e. the distance between the individuals positioned the farthest from one another, gives us the **diameter** of the network. To make things clearer, you can think of the social network as a circle. Two points at opposite sides of the circle would be the most distant and the distance shows the diameter. Points closer to the sides of the circle are the ones with larger eccentricity values. In contrast, points closer to the center of the circle have smaller eccentricity.

We will use such measurements both to determine how well the social network is connected and to understand and compare the positions of each individual within the network. Such measurements regarding the position of the individual and their uses will be handled in detail in Chapter 3 dedicated to centrality.

Here, we will deal with the calculation of density, one of the basic measurements regarding the general structure of the network. This concept is not borrowed from geometry like most other terms but it is borrowed from physics; it is one of the most common metrics used while quantifying a network structure. We can find the density of the entire social network by calculating the ratio of "number of existing relations / number of all possible relations". In the example above, the density is $\frac{4}{6}$. There are 4 relations present in the network. The number of all possible relations is calculated as follows: If each of the 4 people had a relationship with every 3 remaining individuals, there would be 6 ties, i.e. combinations of 4 by 2: $\frac{4\cdot2}{2!}$. Therefore, the density value for the network is $\frac{4}{6}$. As an illustration, we can think of a physical object. The gaps in this object would decrease its density. As far as a social network is concerned, non-existing relations among individuals decrease its density. If all the gaps are filled, the density value becomes 1.0.

The definition of mathematical density depends on whether the relation is directed or not. Let us assume that there are n nodes and m ties. Density of a directed/asymmtric graph is defined as

$$d = \frac{m}{n \cdot (n-1)}$$

since there may be relations between each of the n actors and each of the remaining n-1. As for an undirected/symmetric graph, density is defined as

$$d = \frac{m}{n \cdot (n-1)/2}$$

because the two directions of a symmetric tie between two nodes are the same, meaning that we need to divide the denominator of the formula by 2 in order not to count a symmetric tie twice.

Density calculation for the entire network is informative within certain assumptions. If we calculate the density of the same social group at two different times, the change in density signifies that the fabric of social relations have become tighter or looser, and thus gives us information on the evolution of the social network. But if we want to compare two different social systems instead of understanding the dynamics of the same network over time, density calculation anc comparison must be done with care. Density comparison may not be useful as it highly depends on the number of nodes in a network. Therefore it is not possible to make comparisons between social groups of different sizes. In other words, density calculation is not **scale-free**. Comparing the density of relations within a small neighborhood and that of relations in a metropolis does not make any sense since the scales in each case are significantly different.

Analyzing **"ego-network" densities**, on the other hand, might prove to be quite interesting. Such an evaluation shows how tightly knit the ties around an individual's immediate social environment are. A network of tightly knit relations brings about a strictness of social rules. Such networks may be supportive and restrictive for the individual at the same time. While calculating "ego network density", we take an individual considered as the center (the "ego") of the network and find the density of the network formed among the people with whom this central individual has ties to. But while doing so, we first need to take this individual out of the network surrounding him/her. In other words the ego-network consists of the ties between an individual's/ ego's friends, except the ego.

Consider the small network given in our example in Figure 1. The ego network of Betty consists of two nodes: Albert and Richard (ie. $n=2$). If we cut out the part of network containing only Albert and Richard we see that there is only on possible tie and it exists ($m=1$), thus the density of Betty's ego network is

$$d = \frac{m}{n \cdot (n-1)/2} = \frac{1}{2 \cdot (2-1)/2} = 1.$$

Same is true for Richard. For Louis, her ego-network only contains Albert. With an ego network of a single node, density is undefined. For Albert on the other hand ego network contains the other three individuals ($n=3$). Thus three ties are possible but only one between Betty and Richard exists ($m=1$). So the density is

$$d = \frac{m}{n \cdot (n-1)/2} = \frac{1}{3 \cdot (3-1)/2} = \frac{1}{3}.$$

The measurement of ego network density should be interpreted in accordance with the social phenomenon in question. The high density of friendship and family networks is supportive for the individual, but there is also a restrictive aspect stemming from strict rules arising from being in an environment that is integrated in its own right. High density in commercial relation networks is a sign of blockage, but it also provides stability. Low density in such a network may signify that the actor maintains simultaneous relations with separate commercial societies and is in a position open for opportunities as it serves as a commercial bridge. However, this kind of structure may be unsafe and lacks the stability of a closely-bound environment.

Wellman's research on the relations among families living in suburban areas is a good example of the use of ego network density (Wellman 1979). Conducted with 845 adults, the study showed that individuals with denser ego networks formed these networks mostly with their relatives. The average ego network density was calculated as 0.33, lower than expected, and Wellman concluded that the relations in this neighborhood were not as "local" as it was thought and that they reached unrelated groups. Naturally, the more interesting part of the study was to research why those with and without dense ego networks differentiated, like the differences between working women and housewives or the fact that dense networks included many relatives. Therefore, comparing ego network densities makes more sense when combined with actor data. Similarly, comparing the averages and distributions of ego network densities of different social groups may give us some hints regarding the overall pattern of the network.

CASE STUDY: FLORENTINE FAMILIES

Collected by Padgett (Padgett 2010), the dataset on the marital and business relations among Florentine families is only one of the sample datasets used in this book. Explanations on and links to this and other datasets are available in the appendices.

In Padgett's dataset, marital and business relations among prominent families of medieval Florence are given and, as actor information, wealth level of each family is stated. The Pajek version of these data on 16 families is given below partially. You can also find a digital copy of this dataset on the book's website http://appliedsna.mgencer.com as "PadgettMarital.net". Starting with the line "Edges", relation data is given with actor numbers: For instance, the line "1 9 1" states that there is a single marital relation between the first and ninth families, and its strength is 1. While looking at these relations, we can see which families are represented by the two nodes by looking at the list of "vertices" at the beginning. For example, the first family is "Acciaiuoli" and the ninth is "Medici":

```
*Vertices      16
  1 "Acciaiuoli"
  2 "Albizzi"
  3 "Barbadori"
  4 "Bischeri"
  5 "Castellani"
  6 "Ginori"
  7 "Guadagni"
  8 "Lamberteschi"
  9 "Medici"
 10 "Pazzi"
 11 "Peruzzi"
 12 "Pucci"
```

```
 13 "Ridolfi"
 14 "Salviati"
 15 "Strozzi"
 16 "Tornabuoni"
*Edges
   1   9 1
   2   6 1
   2   7 1
   ...
*Vector Wealth
*Vertices 16
 10
 36
 55
 ...
```

A different file which we will explain later, provides an extra data vector indicating the wealth levels of families in the order of definition. For instance, while the wealth level of the Acciaiuoli family is given as 10, and the wealth level of the Medicis as 103.

Simple Drawing of Social Networks

At times, you may want to make an initial visualization of a small network with a hand drawing. The simplest way of drawing a social network like the one in Padgett's example is to create a circular representation. Place the nodes around a circle and make sure that the distances are as equal as possible. Then draw a line between nodes for each tie on your list. In a directed relation, we need to put an arrow to the end of a tie according to the tie direction. A sample drawing is given in Figure 2.

The following R code fragment first reads the data file. Make sure that you create a file named PadgettMarital.net containing the data above, or simply donwload it from the book's website. Make sure that the graph() function has the correct path where you put your file in your own computer. If you are not sure about the path you can instead use the commented version of the command using file.choose() function which opens a dialog box to choose the data file. You can consult the help pages for plot.igraph for alternative graph layouts:

```
require(igraph)
g <- read.graph("data/PadgettMarital.net", format="pajek")
```

```
#g <- read.graph(file.choose(), format="pajek") # to choose a
file with dialog
gu<-simplify(as.undirected(g))
V(gu)$size <- 40
plot(gu, layout=layout_in_circle)
```

This circular drawing is not the most optimal way of visualization but it is easy to do by hand and helps us to see the actors in which relations become denser and to calculate their centrality easily. A more "legible" drawing like the one in Figure 2 is generated by using advanced actor placement algorithms, more commonly called as **layout algorithms**, with the "mode" parameter. The R commands used for it is given in the box below. Please note that this example uses the R package network instead of igraph. You may want to experiment with the "mode" parameter by consulting the manual page for plot.network function.

```
require(network)
n<-read.paj("data/PadgettMarital.net")
plot(n, displaylabels=T,
     mode="fruchtermanreingold",
     vertex.cex=3, usearrows=FALSE)
```

These code fragments also welcome you to the inter-disciplinary world of social network analysis. The network library has its origins in the social network research, unlike the igraph library. It provides different implementations of

Figure 2. Network of Florentine families' marriage relations, visualization with circular placement

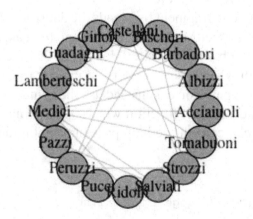

Figure 3. Florentine families' visualization with advanced layout by network package

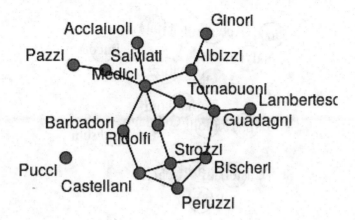

data importing and drawing which we may like in some applications of social network analysis. But the social network data object that is returned from data importing function read.paj() is of a data type we cannot use with other packages like igraph, as you can see by consulting its object class:

```
require(network)
n<-read.paj("data/PadgettMarital.net")
class(n)
## [1] "network"
```

Therefore it is handy to have the capacity to convert between such formats while doing social network analysis. A package called intergraph provides exactly this functionality as shown below. Since the network package uses a matrix based data storage it is problematic to deduce graph features such as being directed or undirected. Parts of the code fixes such missing information after translation. Nevertheless the igraph objects are compatible with a wider variety of graph libraries, hence the conversion is well worhted:

```
require(network)
require(igraph)
require(intergraph)
n<-read.paj("data/PadgettMarital.net")
g<-asIgraph(n) # translate network object into igraph object
class(g) # See how classes are different
## [1] "igraph"
gu<-simplify(as.undirected(g)) # fix the missing info in
translation
V(gu)$size <- 30
```

Figure 4. Florentine families visualization after igraph conversion

```
V(gu)$label <- network.vertex.names(n)  #add vertex names
plot(gu)
```

If you want to play with the plotting function, please note that this time you must consult the manual page for plot.igraph(), not plot.network().

EXERCISES

1. Calculate the density of the Florentine network.
2. Find the ego networks and ego network densities for two families of your choosing.

REFERENCES

De Nooy, W., Mrvar, A., & Batagelj, V. (2018). *Exploratory social network analysis with Pajek: Revised and expanded edition for updated software* (Vol. 46). Cambridge University Press. doi:10.1017/9781108565691

Newman, M. E. (2006). Modularity and community structure in networks. *Proceedings of the National Academy of Sciences of the United States of America*, 103(23), 8577–8582. doi:10.1073/pnas.0601602103 PMID:16723398

Padgett, J. F. (2010). Open Elite? Social Mobility, Marriage, and Family in Florence, 1282–1494. *Renaissance Quarterly*, *63*(2), 357–411. doi:10.1086/655230 PMID:20552737

Valiente, G. (2002). *Algorithms on trees and graphs*. Springer. Retrieved from http://books.google.com.tr/books?id=NSfIWxqPlbcC

Wellman, B. (1979). The community question: The intimate networks of East Yorkers. *American Journal of Sociology*, *84*(5), 1201–1231. doi:10.1086/226906

Chapter 3
Neighborhood and Position:
Local Centrality

ABSTRACT

An important contribution of studying social structure is that it allows us to analyze the inequalities and differences in a complex web of social relations with concrete metrics. The 'centrality' of individuals is an important metric used in this respect. The concept of 'center' is borrowed from geometry, and there are several centrality metrics of social structure. This chapter looks into a particular centrality that gives information about the position of individual within his/her local structural neighbourhood. The concepts in this chapter also lay the foundation for understanding further variants of centrality in the following chapters.

One of the most interesting aspects of social networks and relational inquiry is that they allow us to analyze the inequalities and differences in the complex nature of a social structure. In other words, this approach focuses on the heterogeneity of the social network in a concrete manner. When talking about social or economic systems we use qualifications such as an actor being peripheral or disadvantageous, or another having a 'strong position'. Social network analysis aims to measure such qualities, and numerous methods has been proposed for a variety of research contexts.

The centrality of actors/individuals has been one of the first measures used in this respect for measuring positional differences of actors in a social system. In time, alternative centrality measurement methods were developed.

DOI: 10.4018/978-1-7998-1912-7.ch003

While some of them are suitable for general purposes, some of them are better for certain types of social phenomena.

The concept of "center" has geometric connotations. In geometry, the center of a circle is a point equidistant to all points on the circumference. It also has the lowest eccentricity value, meaning that the distance between the center and a circumferential point to which it is the farthest is shorter than the same distance for all other points. As far as social networks are concerned, however, things are more complicated, leading to many definitions for centrality in order to measure different social factors. We will start our analysis from the simplest and earliest type.

CENTRALITY - LOCAL

One of the first definitions to be used for centrality measurement defines centrality as the number of ties of an actor with the reest of the actors. In the statement above, we actually define the social notion of "popularity" in a measurable manner. In graph terms then number of relations of a vertex is called its *degree*. Thus this particular centrality measure is called **degree centrality**

Let us take the network shown in Figure 1 into consideration (you can find information on how to generate the visual with R commands in the box below, using igraph library by Csardi and Nepusz, 2006). Upon looking at the graph visualization, we can see that d and b are the actors with the highest degree centrality values (3 for each).

```
# The small network in the example is generated with R commands
# In a real data analysis we would upload the network from the
data file
library(igraph) #load the library
# the function below forms the network
g1 <- graph.formula(a--b, b--c, c--g, b--d, d--e, d--f)
V(g1)$size <- 25 # arrange the size of "Vertex" or nodes
V(g1)$color <- "white"
plot(g1) # Network visualization function
```

It is easy to count the centralities in this network manually, but let us see how do we do it with a computer. The degree() function in the igraph library provides the degree centrality metric. This function computes the metric for

Figure 1. A sample personal friendship network

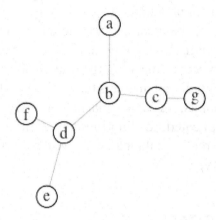

each of the nodes in the graph and reports the node names and centrality measurements as a numeric vector whose rows are named with vertex/node names:

```
degree(g1)
## a b c g d e f
## 1 3 2 1 3 1 1
```

I would like to emphasize that our definition here is quite *local*. If we think of the social network as a wide geographical area encompassing many individuals, this definition takes into consideration only the relations in the individual's closest neighborhood. Therefore, it does not provide information on the position of the individual within the broader structure of the network. For instance, the social network visualization above, in a way, suggests that b is "slightly more central" than d. But the centrality measurement does not indicate such a difference: The centrality values are the same for both individuals. It would not be possible to notice this difference only by looking at the centrality values without visualization if we were dealing with a large social network. Despite this fact, local centrality was widely used for social network research and is still a good criterion for certain features of a social phenomenon. We will see other centrality measurements taking the general structure of the network into consideration in the next chapter.

Local centrality may be used for comparing different actors within the same social network. However, it is not suitable for making comparisons between social networks of different qualities or sizes. For example, the density of business partnership relations among a group of people might be different from that of friendship network between them. The sizes of these two networks are the same as they concern the same group, but it is not possible to make a centrality comparison. This is the main problem in this respect even though more comparable criteria were also tested (e.g. Freeman relative centrality measurement, Scott (2000)).

Variations in Calculating Centrality

Centrality, like other social network metric, should be measured considering the type of the relation that underlies the network definition (e.g. directed/undirected, weighted/unweighted). If you are using sociomatrices, the sum of rows indicates the **"out-degree"** of the actor because each matrix cell in the row contains a number indicating presence/absence (ie. 0 or 1 for an uweighted graph) or strength of a relation (for a weighted graph) that goes "out" from the actor to whom the row corresponds to, to each of the actors the columns of the cells correspond to. Likewise, the sum of columns indicates its **"in-degree"** of the actor to whom the column corresponds to. These two values would be equal in a symmetrical (undirected) relation and this value would be simply called **"degree"**. For directed relations the out-degree centrality and in-degree centrality values of an actor may be different.

In unweighted relations the cells include only 1s and 0s, indicating a tie being present or not present. Thus sum of a row or a cell amounts to the number of relations. For unweighted but directed relations the number of incoming and outgoing relations are different. For weighted relations on the other hand the matrix cells may include values other than simply 1 and 0. The degree centralities defined above can be calculated in the same way for the weighted case as the total of weights instead of the number of relations (but there are also alternative approaches, see Opsahl, Agneessens, and Skvoretz, 2010).

When one uses graph based representaitons instead of matrix based representations, such calculations are more computationally feasible, especially for large networks. Because for large networks the matrix would include mostly zeroes, but they will enter the summation (or whatever operation a metric involves). But for the moment we let these problems to algorithm designers and implementors, and let us focus on the use of social network metrics.

Heterogeneity of Centrality

Closely related to degree centrality is degree distribution. This distribution can be obtained as a histogram of degree values for all nodes. Being a common measure, it is provided by the igraph package with the following function call on the graph we have created in the previous code chunk:

```
degree.distribution(g1)
## [1] 0.0000000 0.5714286 0.1428571 0.2857143
```

The degree_distribution is a numeric vector of the same length as the maximum degree, and plus one more for the zero value. The first element shown above is the relative frequency of vertices with zero degree centrality, the second value is the relative frequency of vertices with a degree of one, etc.

Similar to some other cases in social or natural phenomena, degree centrality also shows a power (or exponential) distribution and not a normal distribution as seen in many other phenomena. An example is given in Figure 2. Power distribution is formulated as follows:

$$f(x) = ax^k$$

For instance, think of x as centrality and take the value of k as -1, then $f(x)$ will give us the number of individuals with a centrality value of x. Therefore, this mathematical formula provides us with a template regarding real social networks with many individuals with low centrality and few individuals with high centrality. The constant a depends on the number of individuals within a network. Naturally, the power (-1) varies according to the social phenomenon. Some networks are more unequal, meaning that the value of k might be smaller than others (in other words, the curve descends faster). Figure 2 shows a large-scale social network. The figure is created with the following R code fragment that employs a function to construct a random network with a power law degree distribution. You may consult the igraph documentation or function help for additional information and other random network generators:

```
library(igraph)
g <- static.power.law.game(500, 1000, #numbers of actors and
ties in the random network
      exponent.out= 2.2, #power distribution parameter
      exponent.in = -1) #undirected network
```

```
plot(g, vertex.label= NA, edge.arrow.size=0.02, vertex.size =
0.5)
```

The distribution given in Figure 3 is the distribution of degree centralities of the nodes in this network. Such a distribution plot can be produced as follows. The code also adds (in red) the theoretical power law distribution line of $f(x)=1.x^{-22}$ for the given example to facilitate comparison:

```
plot(degree_distribution(g),type="l",
xlab="Degree",ylab="Relative frequency")
x<-0:20
fx<-x^(-2.2)
points(x, fx, type="l", col="red")
```

As seen in the distribution, a majority of the individuals have one of the few low degree centrality values; in this example most have a degree of less than 5. The remainder is distributed to ascending values more scarcely. In other words there are a handful of very popular actors. Of course, real networks do not manifest an exact mathematical certainty but almost all of them show a similar distribution. Please note that the power law is a continuous function, and some of the differences is due to the fact that the degrees here are integers by definition of unweighted graphs.

The parameter k determining the form of centrality distribution in a network also shows a hint regarding the scale of heterogeneity and centralization of the network. A high negative value for k, signifying a rapidly-descending

Figure 2. A large, randomly-generated network

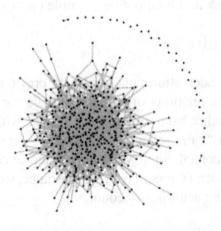

Figure 3. Degree centrality distribution within the random network

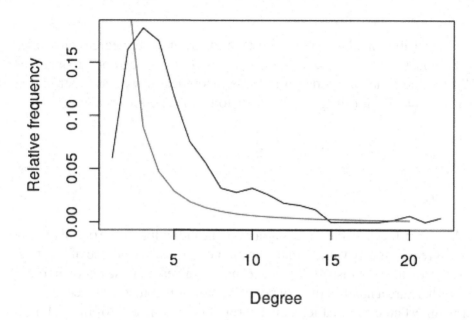

distribution graphic, means a large mass with low centrality and few individuals with high centrality.

An interesting aspect of the power/exponent distribution is that it is **"scale-free"**. This means that as far as the social relational phenomenon is concerned, the distribution of centralities for a crowded social network and that of a smaller network are similar in terms of the form of the distribution curve; at most, the constant a is different in each case. In other words you would have a similar plot shape but with different values if you have created a much larger network in the following example (see exercises).

Variations of Centrality

The degree centrality calculation mentioned in the previous section exclusively takes the first-degree relations of the individual/actor into consideration. We can say, on the other hand, that making friends with influential people makes an individual "more related", compared to someone whose friends are generally less infuential. Some variations of degree centrality calculation attempt to consider such factors as well. For instance, we can take neighbors of the neighbors of the actor into account.

In the normal degree centrality calculation we count the number of individuals to whom our focal actor is directly tied to, ie. tied with paths with the length value of 1. In order to count "firends of firends" this time we need to take the number of individuals to whom our focal individual is tied with paths with a length value up to 2. Let us call this count as "second-degree centrality". If we apply this to the previous example above in Figure 1, the "second-degree centrality" of node d is equal to 5 and it is 6 for node b. Thus, we make it possible to calculate centrality by looking further in the graph/network. Similarly, we can also mention third or fourth-degree centralities but they are hard to interpret in a social sense. Plese note that these variations of degree centrality are essentially "local", but they have an extended range of locality.

Application Case: Florentine Families

We can argue that in the Florentine families example there is a correlation between wealth of a family and its centrality within the network. This social network was visualized in Chapter 2, Figure 3. We can find degree centrality values easily by looking at the visual or use the degree() function we have learned. The family wealth information was also provided by Padgett with the original network data (Padgett, 2010). You can find this in a separate file PadgettWealth.csv in the book's website. Following code can be used to combine both information. Furthermore the wealth values are used as the vertex size in drawing Figure 4, by a factor for visual adjustment:

```
require(igraph)
g <- read.graph("data/PadgettMarital.net", format="pajek")
wealthData <- read.csv("data/PadgettWealth.csv",header=TRUE)
V(g)$size <- wealthData$wealth/5
plot(g)
```

Let us put the wealth values given in the original dataset side by saide the degree values and have a look at the result. We will use knitr::kable function to produce Table 1 from these vectors:

```
require(igraph)
g <- read.graph("data/PadgettMarital.net", format="pajek")
wealthData <- read.csv("data/PadgettWealth.csv",header=TRUE)
d<-data.frame(degree=degree(g), wealth=wealthData$wealth)
require(knitr)
```

Figure 4. Florentine families marriage network: node size indicates family wealth

```
kable(d,caption="Relation of degree and wealth for Florentine
families")
```

Although our findings suggest a correspondence between degree and wealth at first glance, we need to calculate this with numerical methods even for such a small dataset.

An easy way for measuring the correspondence between two measures regarding the set of actors is to look at the correlation between the two variables (there are also more complex and advanced methods like linear modeling). The correlation estimates the correspondence (or contrast) between two variables of the actors. Details on how to calculate correlation with the Pearson correlation method are given in the appendices.

The correlation we find takes a value between 1 and -1. A high positive value shows correspondence between two variables while the opposite indicates contrast. In this case, even though centrality is about relations, once calculated, it becomes a feature of the actor. Therefore, it can be used for a comparison with other variable regarding the actor. Correlation is computed using the cor standard function in R. For our example the correlation is found as follows:

```
require(igraph)
g <- read.graph("data/PadgettMarital.net", format="pajek")
wealthData <- read.csv("data/PadgettWealth.csv",header=TRUE)
cor(degree(g), wealthData$wealth)
## [1] 0.5589956
```

The correlation value between centrality and wealth for the Florentine families dataset is 0.56. This is a positive value and considerably close to 1

Table 1. Relation of degree and wealth for Florentine families

	degree	wealth
Acciaiuoli	2	10
Albizzi	6	36
Barbadori	4	55
Bischeri	6	44
Castellani	6	20
Ginori	2	32
Guadagni	8	8
Lamberteschi	2	42
Medici	12	103
Pazzi	2	48
Peruzzi	6	49
Pucci	0	3
Ridolfi	6	27
Salviati	4	10
Strozzi	8	146
Tornabuoni	6	48

than it is to 0, meaning that there is a significant correspondence between the wealth and centrality in the marriage network, for Florentine families.

CASE STUDY: RELATIONS AMONG MANAGERS

In this example, we will use Krackhardt's dataset on a high- technology company. This dataset (Krackhardt 1987) was collected from a company that was going through a merger and includes the relations of giving advice, friendship or being superior/subordinate between managers. These advices were influential on the eventual success of the merger, thus the social network under study has an important business outcome. In addition to relational information, information on the age and seniority (years worked in the company) of managers was also available. Additional explanations on and Internet sources providing access to this dataset and others are given in the appendices.

The best way of uploading this dataset for application is to use an existing R library (NetData library, Nowak et al., 2012) as seen in the code below.

The NetData library provides Krackhardt's dataset and some others which you can use for exercising social network analysis. The data, an extract of which is shown below the code, is not directly suitable to import into igraph so we do some manipulation to obtain an edgelist from it. Please consult the help page for advice_data_frame. The edges in this graph indicate "to whom one goes to take advice". The code also plots the network:

```
require(NetData) #https://cran.r-project.org/web/packages/
NetData/NetData.pdf
data(kracknets)
head(advice_data_frame,3) # show an extract of data
##    ego alter advice_tie
## 1   1     1           0
## 2   1     2           1
## 3   1     3           0
edgelist <- as.matrix(  # turn data into edgelist suitable for
igraph
    advice_data_frame[advice_data_frame[3]==1,1:2])
    #a 1 in the third column of data indicates a tie
require(igraph)
g<-graph_from_edgelist(edgelist)
plot.igraph(g, layout=layout_with_kk)
```

The visual generated with this code is shown in Figure 5. Alternatively, you can use the file available for download on the website of the book as in the following code chunk. Note that the file format is different this time. The DL format is used by the software UCINET, which was popular at the

Figure 5. Krackhardt's network of company managers

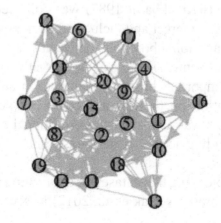

time of Krackhardt's research (Borgatti et al, 2014). In this version of the visualization we use the in-degree centrality as the size of the nodes:

```
require(igraph)
g <- read.graph("data/HigTech-advice.dl",format="dl")
V(g)$size <- degree(g, mode="in")*1
plot(g)
```

The out-degree values in the advice-giving network of the actors are used as the indicators of their impact on the social system in the code given below and, as seen in Figure 6, are visualized as the size of graph nodes. Note that such sizing creates a visual narrative that effects the observer.

In our exercise, we will focus on a single network data type within our dataset: The relation of giving advice. This is a noteworthy phenomenon for businesses as we talk about an informal network not visible in the organizational charts of companies. Such an informal network may have a significant impact upon the business, information flow and decision- making processes. In fact, the focus of Krackhardt's study was the question who is affected the common decision during unionization following the merger. Today, such issues are a principle domain of study in high-performance businesses (Cross and Parker 2004).

First, we will find the individuals in a central position in the advice-giving relations within this dataset. Then, we can find the parallels between this structural feature and the ages and seniorities of these individuals. We

Figure 6. Krackhardt's network of relations among company managers, a visualization where node size indicates out-degree centrality

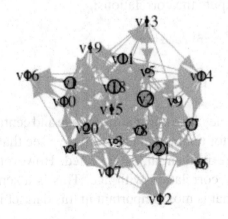

can reveal this with a simple correlation. We will attempt to interpret this correlation taking the social phenomenon into consideration.

For a small or medium-sized dataset as the one in our example we can try to make a manual circular drawing and make centrality estimates. Similarly, we can make the same estimate by counting the rows concerning a actor in the data file. However, if you prefer doing these estimates with the help of a software, you need to overcome a problem that might arise quite frequently in similar cases. The dataset in the Pajek format consists of multiple social networks. But we only want to use a single network. The .DL file, the file format of UCINET, is more compatible with some software tools we use but not others. You need to be alert in case of such circumstances as social network analysis is a young discipline and the software in this field are not always compatible.

Out-degree estimates from the data file are given below along with information on age and seniority. These additional data is provided in NetData library and displayed in Table 2 with the following code:

```
require(NetData)
data(kracknets)
g<-graph_from_edgelist(
  as.matrix(
    advice_data_frame[advice_data_frame[3]==1,1:2]))
d<-data.frame(individual=as.numeric(V(g)),
              Age=attributes$AGE,
              Tenure=attributes$TENURE,
              DegreeCentrality=degree(g,mode="in"))
require(knitr)
kable(d,caption="Relation of degree centrality and individual's
features in Krackhardt dataset")
```

We can now compute the correlations:

```
cor(d$Age,d$DegreeCentrality)
## [1] -0.0407932
cor(d$Tenure,d$DegreeCentrality)
## [1] 0.5419909
```

We find a slightly negative correlation for age and centrality and a strongly positive correlation for tenure and centrality. We see that tenured managers are likely to be more influential, as expected. However the influence has a slightly negatively correlation with age. This is a sensible and intuitive result. Of course, what is more important in this dataset is that it reveals the

Table 2. Relation of degree centrality and individual's features in Krackhardt dataset

individual	Age	Tenure	DegreeCentrality
1	33	9.333	13
2	42	19.583	18
3	40	12.750	5
4	33	7.500	8
5	32	3.333	5
6	59	28.000	10
7	55	30.000	13
8	34	11.333	10
9	62	5.417	4
10	37	9.250	9
11	46	27.000	11
12	34	8.917	7
13	48	0.250	4
14	43	10.417	10
15	40	8.417	4
16	27	4.667	8
17	30	12.417	9
18	33	9.083	15
19	32	4.833	4
20	38	11.667	8
21	36	12.500	15

influencers. If the company management was to use this data for practical purposes they would knew exactly which handful of individuals they need to convince, so that the rest will follow suit.

Centralization

Hierarchical social structures, e.g. relations in an army, are quite concentrated around a central as it is the case in the star-shaped network shown in Figure 7.

By contrast, relations within the circular network in Figure 8 are not centralized.

Network researchers needed a network level measurement of how centralized its structure is. In other words a metric that evaluates the centralization of a network, that goes beyond local degree centralities of its nodes. This is not a

Figure 7. Star-shaped network structure

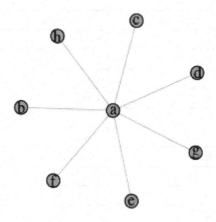

starightforward task because a good metric should allow the analyst to make comparisons between different networks (or same network at different times) even if the network sizes are different. However in larger networks the degree distributions would be different.

Generally speaking, centralization estimate is made by looking at the difference between the most central actor(s) and the least central one(s). While the degree centrality value of an actor in the star-shaped network structure is 7, that of every other actor is 1. In the circular network structure, however, all actors share the same value of 2, the lowest and highest possible centrality

Figure 8. Circular network structure

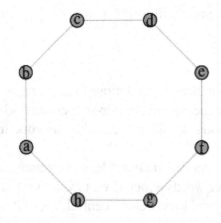

value. Based on this conceptual definition, centralization in a network x can be calculated as follows (Newman 2006):

$$C_x = \frac{\sum_{j=1}^{N} C_x(p) - C_x(p_i)}{max \sum_{j=1}^{N} C_x(p) - C_x(p_i)}$$

In this equation, $C_x(p)$ is the maximum centrality estimate among actors within a network while $C_x(p_i)$ values indicate the centrality of each p_i actor. Therefore this metric evaluates how degree centrality of nodes in a network compares to the most central node. The denominator denotes the theoretical maximum of the sum and provides a normalization so that the value can be compared across networks of different sizes.

The igraph library provides this metric without the normalization as follows. The code also calculates numerator and denominator of the centralization metric formula separately, for your exploration:

```
library(igraph)
stargraph <- graph.formula(a--b,a--c,a--d,a--e,a--f,a--g,a--h)
centr_degree(stargraph, normalized=FALSE,
loops=FALSE)$centralization
## [1] 42
centr_degree_tmax(g)
## [1] 42
centr_degree(stargraph, normalized=TRUE,loops=FALSE)$centraliz
ation
## [1] 1
circulargraph <- graph.formula(a--b,b--c,c--d,d--e,e--f,f--g,
g--h,h--a)
centr_degree(circulargraph, normalized=TRUE,loops=FALSE)$centra
lization
## [1] 0
```

As you can see from the result the centralization measure for circular graph is zero, as there is no hint of centralization in this structure. The star graph on the other hand has the maximum possible centralization value of 1.

Distance, Centrality and Diameter

To what extent a network is heterogeneous and central, and who is positioned in the center? Different methods put forward in order to estimate these features are interesting as far as social phenomena are considered.

The **distance** between two actors is the length of the shortest path connecting them. For example, the only path connecting the actors b and e in our star-shaped network is the one going through a and its length is 2. In the circular network, on the other hand, there are two possible paths between b and e, namely b-c-d-e or d-e-f-g-h-a-b. The length of the shortest one is 3. Since both of these networks are unweighted networks each tie simply denotes a distance of 1, thus the length of a path can be found intuitively as the number of ties on it.

The geometrical analogy of distance is also valid while defining the diameter and periphery of a network. The highest value among the distance values between one actor and all the other ones is the **eccentricity** of that single actor. We can say that we find eccentricity by thinking of the network as a circle and take the longest distance between the actor and the periphery. Therefore, the actor with the lowest eccentricity value is the **center** of the network. In the star-shaped network, while the eccentricity of node a is 1, and eccentricity of any other actor is 2, making node a the center of the network. As for the circular network, all eccentricity values are equal to 4, indicating that there is no center. We can already see this in simple visualizations. However, we can't use such simple methods in crowded networks, so such calculations are the only ways of understanding the center and centralization.

Within the scope of the same analogy, the highest eccentricity value in a network gives us the **diameter** of the network (2 for the star-shaped network and 4 for the circular network). If we take it further, we can also talk about the "**volume**" of the network, but there is no consensus regarding the validity and usefulness of this concept. On the other hand, the term "density", mentioned in the previous chapter and calculated using the number of relations within the network, is frequently used. While the physical definition of density requires both mass and volume, the network density computation does not require a volume, but instead uses the maximum number of ties.

Accessibility, Connected Networks and Isolates

The definition of distance given above implicitly assumes that there is at least one path from each actor in the network to all others. However, this is not the case for all networks. Let us look at the example shown in Figure 9.

The code produces this example is shown below.

```
library(igraph)
g <- graph.formula(a--b,b--c,a--c,c--d,a--d,  #one actor
                   f--e,f--i,f--g, g--i)       # and another
V(g)$color<-"white"
plot(g)
```

There two groups that are not connected. This is an example of a disconnected network. In such a network, there is no path between, for instance, individual D and individuals E, F, I and G. Therefore, the distance of D from all these individuals would be infinite. We cannot speak of the diameter of a disconnected network; in other words, depending on our definition, we need to assume the diameter as infinite, which is not informative. Please note that the eccentricity calculations are still possible as in the following example:

```
library(igraph)
g <- graph.formula(a--b,b--c,a--c,c--d,a--d,  #one actor
                   f--e,f--i,f--g, g--i)       # and another
eccentricity(g)
## a b c d f e i g
## 1 2 1 2 1 2 2 2
```

Figure 9.

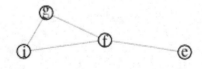

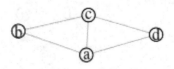

When we analyze a network using software capable of making standard distance calculations, infinite distances might indicate one of two cases: (1) an individual separate from the network or (2) a closed group. The first one is quite common. In the Florentine families example, the Pucci family with no marital relations with any of the other families may be an example. As a result, our sample network can be as shown in Figure 10. The R code below produces this graph. As different from our previous examples, this code adds a vertex separately but does not add any edges for it, thus creating an isolate.

```
library(igraph)
g <- graph.formula(a--b,b--c,a--c,c--d,a--d,f--i,f--g, g--i,f-
-d)
g<-add_vertices(g,1,name="e")
V(g)$color<-"white"
plot.igraph(g)
```

The state of Individual E in our example is a frequently seen situation. A disconnected network can be rendered compatible with certain analyses (e.g. finding distance, diameter or the center) by excluding such isolates. Indeed the standard function for finding diameter does exactly that:

```
library(igraph)
g <- graph.formula(a--b,b--c,a--c,c--d,a--d,f--i,f--g, g--i,f-
-d)
g<-add_vertices(g,1,name="e")
diameter(g)
## [1] 4
```

Figure 10. A network structure with isolates

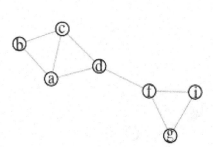

However, apart from isolates, a network consisting of two or more disconnected groups must be examined by analyzing each of them. If we do not do so, estimations (like calculating density) may be extremely misleading. Let us say that we have a network of 200 people, but this network is composed of a group of 20 and another group of 180. The density estimate for the group of 20 must be made separately and evaluated along with the group dimension. Otherwise, other estimations made using the disconnected network of 200 like density would be completely meaningless and unsuitable for comparison.

REVIEW EXERCISES

1. Consider the network and its degree distribution in figures 2 and 3. Create a network which has ten times more number of nodes, and produce the degree distribution plot. Are the results different? How can you explain whatever differences are there?
2. Find the centralization measure for the random networks in the previous question.
3. Find the centralization measure for the random networks you have created in the previous questions. How does the measures compare for two networks?
4. Find the diameter and eccentricities for the random networks you have created in the previous questions.

REFERENCES

Borgatti, S. P., Everett, M. G., & Freeman, L. C. (2014). Ucinet. Encyclopedia of social network analysis and mining, 2261-2267.

Cross, R., & Parker, A. (2004). *The Hidden Power of Social Networks: Understanding How Work Really Gets Done in Organizations*. Harvard Business School Press. Retrieved from http://www.amazon.com/exec/obidos/redirect?tag=citeulike07-20{\&}path=ASIN/1591392705.

Csardi, G., & Nepusz, T. (2006). The igraph software package for complex network research. *InterJournal. Complex Systems, 1695*(5), 1–9.

Krackhardt, D. (1987). Cognitive social structures. *Social Networks*, *9*(2), 109–134. doi:10.1016/0378-8733(87)90009-8

Newman, M. E. (2006). Modularity and community structure in networks. *Proceedings of the National Academy of Sciences of the United States of America*, *103*(23), 8577–8582. doi:10.1073/pnas.0601602103 PMID:16723398

Nowak, M., Westwood, S. J., & Messing, S. (2012). *NetData: Network Data for McFarland's SNA R labs.* R Package Version 0.3.

Opsahl, T., Agneessens, F., & Skvoretz, J. (2010). Node centrality in weighted networks: Generalizing degree and shortest paths. *Social Networks*, *32*(3), 245–251. doi:10.1016/j.socnet.2010.03.006

Padgett, J. F. (2010). Open Elite? Social Mobility, Marriage, and Family in Florence, 1282–1494. *Renaissance Quarterly*, *63*(2), 357–411. doi:10.1086/655230 PMID:20552737

Scott, J. (2000). Social Network Analysis. *Sage (Atlanta, Ga.).*

Chapter 4
Non-Local Centrality

ABSTRACT

The previous chapter focused more on assessment of the local and immediate structure surrounding a social actor. In this chapter, the authors look at the actor's relative importance by considering his/her position in the whole network. Some actors fill critical gaps in the broader social structure (e.g., by brokering between two otherwise detached social groups). Hence, their importance emerges from their structural qualities at the whole network level rather than local level. In this chapter, the authors develop the concepts and metrics to assess the broader structural features of individuals.

In the previous chapter, we focused more on local features of the social network structure, e.g. ego-network density and local centrality. Furthermore, we also mentioned a measure of density regarding an entire network. Among these measures, general density indicates "to what extent a network is connected" while individual density shows us to what extent the social environment of the individual/actor analyzed is connected within its local environment. Local centrality, on the other hand, measures around which actor the ties are clustered.

In this chapter, we will look at different roles within a given social network, in terms of structural qualities, by primarily analyzing the distribution of local measures over network components. Then, we will cover some non-local measures and how they are interpreted.

DOI: 10.4018/978-1-7998-1912-7.ch004

EVALUATING AN ACTOR'S NETWORK POSITION FEATURES WITH RESPECT TO GENERAL STRUCTURE OF NETWORK

Each actor within a social network has different structural features in terms of their social environment. Some individuals/actors have more friends or other types of connections, immediate circles of some actors form a closely-tied group and others have relationships with individuals from other "circles".

We have analyzed Krackhardt's network of advice-giving relations among company managers before (Krackhardt, 1987). Let us look at the distribution of local centralities in this network. We can generate the degree distribution histogram in Figure 1 by using the following commands:

```
require(NetData)
data(kracknets)
require(igraph)
g<-graph_from_edgelist(
  as.matrix(
    advice_data_frame[advice_data_frame[3]==1,1:2]))
hist(degree(g,mode="out"),xlab="Out-degree centrality",ylab="Fr
equency",main="Histogram")
```

The degree values can also be plotted, which in this example forms some groups nicely, as seen in Figure 2, with the following code:

```
require(NetData)
data(kracknets)
require(igraph)
g<-graph_from_edgelist(
  as.matrix(
    advice_data_frame[advice_data_frame[3]==1,1:2]))
plot(degree(g,mode="out"),type="l")
```

The out-degree centrality values used in this directed example indicate the popularity of the actor in terms of "advice-giving". This distribution roughly shows us that the individuals within the social group form four different clusters as far as degree centrality goes. Each cluster corresponds to certain roles in our social phenomenon (community leader, popular person, marginal person etc.). For instance, a few individuals with a high centrality value between 15-20 are community leaders whose advice is sought by many. Those with a centrality value between 10-15 have a relatively "normal" popularity. As for those with a value between 5-10, they are in the periphery in terms of

Figure 1. Distribution of local centrality within Krackhardt's network of company managers.

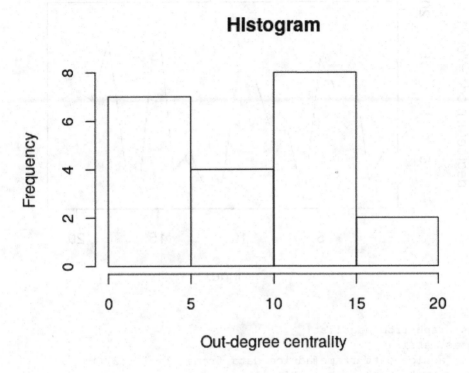

"advice-giving". There is a group with even lower centrality values, meaning that nobody asks their opinion. These individuals are socially isolated.

It is usually beneficial to analyze measures regarding individuals as a whole. Let us place the ego network density and local centrality together. The **ego network density** is calculated as the density of an ego's (an actor or a node) network without the ego. The **ego network** is a first step to evaluating the structure that surrounds an actor. It is defined as the ties between the actors to whom the selected ego actor has connections. In other words it is the friendships between your friends, if you think of yourself as the 'ego' in this definition. The igraph library provides some routines to produce ego networks. The make_ego_graph() functions produces ego graphs for all nodes in the graph. Let us visualize one such ego network, for node 6, the plot from the code below is shown in Figure 3:

```
require(NetData)
data(kracknets)
require(igraph)
```

71

Figure 2. Plot of local centrality within Krackhardt's network of company managers

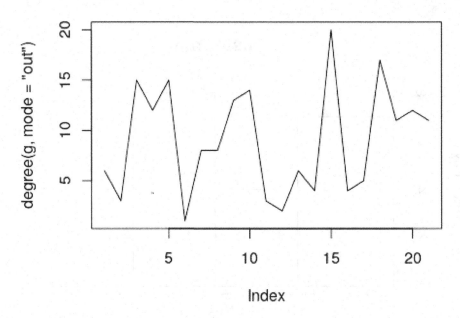

```
g<-graph_from_edgelist(
  as.matrix(
    advice_data_frame[advice_data_frame[3]==1,1:2]))
g1 <- make_ego_graph(g,1)[[6]]
plot(g1)
```

Now we can proceed to calculate density of ego networks. What we will do here is to examine ego network densities together with degree centralities. These data are visualized in Figure 4. We use the sapply() function in R to compute ego network densities for all nodes, as follows:

```
require(NetData)
data(kracknets)
require(igraph)
g<-graph_from_edgelist(
  as.matrix(
    advice_data_frame[advice_data_frame[3]==1,1:2]))
V(g)$yogunluk <- sapply(make_ego_graph(g,1), graph.density)
plot(degree(g,mode="out"), V(g)$yogunluk, xlab="Out-degree
centrality",ylab="Ego netwrok density")
```

Here, we can see that ego-network density and centrality values may be quite different. For example, there is a group with a very high centrality value

Figure 3. Extraction of ego network for node 6

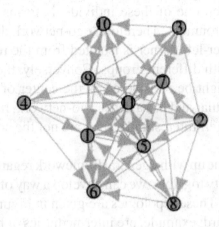

but a very low ego-network density value (lower-right). These individuals are clearly intermediaries connecting different groups. Ego-network density is low as individuals with whom each of these is in a relationship are in different groups. But local centrality is high since they have many relations. On the other corner of the graphic, there is a group of individuals with

Figure 4. Distribution of ego network density u versus degree centrality in Krackhardt's network

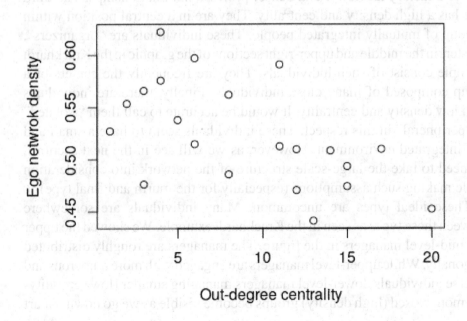

low centrality and high ego-network density, the exact opposite of the case mentioned above. Each one of these individuals forms relations within a small and closed environment. Therefore, ego-network density is high. The individual on the lower-left corner is isolated from the rest of the network, has fewer relations with different groups. Conversely, the individual on the upper-right corner might be considered as the center of the network. This individual is both popular and has a dense ego-network, meaning that he/she is probably the manager. Interestingly, they are not the actors whose advice is sought the most!

If we attempt to come up with a general framework regarding the evaluation of centrality and density together, we can develop a way of interpreting based on certain typologies. These typologies are given in Figure 5. The first type, as seen in the Krackhardt example, are intermediaries or brokers in the local environment, having relatively low ego-network densities but high centrality, signifying their central position within an otherwise poorly connected set of actors. The second type, the exact opposite of the first one, has high ego-network density by low centrality, live and introvert life in a small and closed environment. Housewives in Wellman's study (Wellman 1979) may be considered as an example because they leave their neighborhoods less often and form relations in a circle consisting of relatives and neighbors all of whom know one another; therefore, they live in a "closed" or "introvert" manner within the social network. Similarly, a worker working in a certain part of a factory has fewer and denser professional relationships. The third type has a high density and centrality. They are in a central position within a group of mutually integrated people. These individuals are "organizers". Clusters in the middle and upper-right sections of the graphic in the Krackhardt example consist of such individuals. They are frequently the centers of a group composed of many close individuals. Finally, there are individuals with low density and centrality. It would be accurate to call them "isolated" or "peripheral" in this respect. These individuals seem to have a small and non-integrated environment. However, as we will see in the next sections, we need to take the large-scale structure of the network into consideration while making such assumptions (especially for the fourth and final type).

These ideal types are uncommon. Many individuals are somewhere between these types as seen in the Krackhardt example. We showed the upper and mid-level managers in the figure. The managers are roughly distributed diagonally. While upper-level managers are engaged with more numerous and diverse individuals, lower-level managers managing smaller (low centrality) and more closed (high density) groups become visible as we go down. Apart

Figure 5. Social roles occuring in different combinations of ego-network density and local centrality

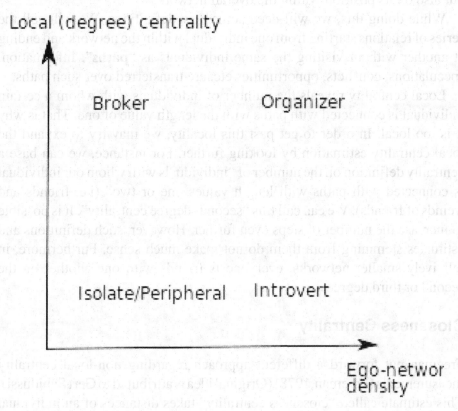

from those, there are also low-level managers/employees in the lower parts of the figure (low centrality). Some of them work within a more closed team (lower-right, high-density) and some of them conduct affairs between teams (lower-left, low-density). A more focused discussion regarding the impact of these roles on professional organizations is available in Cross and Prusak's article (Cross and Prusak 2002).

Non-Local Centrality Measures

Local centrality and density measures examine only the closer circle of an actor. However, we need to look at its location within the general structure of the network in order to understand its position in the social network. In this section,we will discuss completely different, non-local centrality measures.

These measures reveal information not only on an individual's close circle but also on its position within the overall network.

While doing this, we will need some new definitions. We will call the series of relations starting from one individual within the network and ending at another without visiting the same individuals as "**paths**". Information, speculations, conflicts, opportunities etc. are transferred over such paths.

Local centrality reveals the number of individuals with whom a certain individual is connected with paths with the length value of one. That is why it is too local. In order to get past this locality, we may try to expand the local centrality estimation by looking further. For instance, we can base a centrality definition on the number of "individuals with whom our individual is connected with paths with length values one or two" (i.e. friends and freinds of friends). We can call this "second- degree centrality". It is possible to increase the number of steps even further. However, such definitions and estimates stemming from them do not make much sense. Furthermore, in relatively smaller networks, everyone is friends with one another on the second or third degree.

Closeness Centrality

Freeman put forward a different approach regarding non-local centrality measurements (Freeman,1978) (Original idea is attributed to Gert Sabidussi). This estimate called "closeness centrality" takes distances of an individual from all others within a social network into account. Before defining this estimate developing some terminology is necessary. We will name the shortest path between two individuals as "**geodesy**" (a term borrowed from the field of geography meaning air distance). Furthermore, we will define the length of this shortest path as "the **distance** between two individuals". Indeed, if there is a flow of information between these two individuals, information is probably transferred primarily from this shortest path. Therefore, geodesies should be taken into consideration.

To find the closeness centrality of an individual, b_i, we start by calculating the sum of distances between our individual and all others: $U_{b_i} = \sum_{\forall b_j \neq b_i} u_{ij}$. Here

u_{if} is the geodesic distance between two individuals b_i and b_j. "Closeness centrality" must be higher for an individual that is closer to others within the network compared to another, i.e. when an individual is more central within the overall network. Thus, the closeness centrality of the individual, denoted as $C(b_i)$, must increase when the geodesisc of the individual with all others decreases. It may be found as the inverse of the sum we have written above:

$$C'(b_i) = \frac{1}{U_{b_i}} = \frac{1}{\sum_{\forall b_j \neq b_i} u_{ij}}$$

However, this measure is not scale-free. It depends on the number of actors in the social network. For example, if there are n people in the network and one individual is directly connected with all others (i.e. he/she is as close as possible to eveneryone else), the sum of distances is n-1 and closeness centrality is $\frac{1}{n-1}$. Thus it changes as n changes in this example, so depends on network size. For that reason, this estimate is not suitable for comparison between social networks of different sizes. Thus, we make an adjustment, or normalization by using the size of the network. The final version of closeness centrality is therefore defined as follows:

$$C(b_i) = \frac{n-1}{U_{b_i}} = \frac{n-1}{\sum_{\forall b_j \neq b_i} u_{ij}}$$

The significance of closeness centrality estimate can be seen in Figure 6, produced with the code below. There are 9 individuals in this network. Individual "a" is the one with the highest local centrality (4 connections). The local centrality value of individuals "e" and "f" are each 3. But we can see that "e" is positioned in the middle of the network, connecting different groups. Thus it is more central despite its relatively lower degree centrality. The sum of distances between "a" and other eight individuals is 14 (1 from b, c, d, and e; 2 from i and f; 3 from g and h). Thus, the closeness centrality of "a" is 8/14. The same measure is 8/13 for "e".

```
require(igraph)
g <- graph.formula(a--b, a--c, a--d, a--e, e--i, e--f,f--h,f-
-g)
V(g)$size <- 25
V(g)$color <- "white"
plot(g)
```

Therefore, individual "e" seeming to be less important in terms of local centrality measure becomes the most central individual as far as a global centrality estimate such as closeness centrality is concerned.

Surely, as the outlook of the network would be quite complex in large networks and it would not be possible to make arguments just by looking at it, the existence of such an measure becomes vital. You can use the function "closeness()" in the igraph library to make closeness centrality measurements on R:

```
require(igraph)
g <- graph.formula(a--b, a--c, a--d, a--e, e--i, e--f,f--h,f-
-g)
closeness(g)
##           a         b         c         d         e
i
## 0.07142857 0.04761905 0.04761905 0.04761905 0.07692308
0.05000000
##           f         h         g
## 0.06250000 0.04347826 0.04347826
```

We must also remember that closeness centrality cannot be calculated for a "disconnected" network. If there are non-connected groups, the distance between individuals from these two groups is undefined. Therefore, it is not possible to calculate their closeness centrality. In undirected networks, the direction of the relationship changes the measure. We can say that the example below given regarding Krackhardt's dataset measures the impact of advice-giving as it uses the "outward" relation. The example uses closeness()

Figure 6. An example small network and closeness centrality

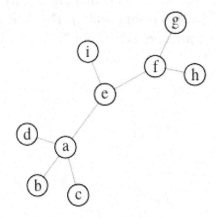

function but wraps its results to show them in a nice tabular form, showing only first ten values.

```
require(NetData)
data(kracknets)
edgelist <- as.matrix(# turn data into edgelist suitable for
igraph
    advice_data_frame[advice_data_frame[3]==1,1:2])
    #a 1 in the third column of data indicates a tie
require(igraph)
g<-graph_from_edgelist(edgelist)
head(
  data.frame(
    node=as.vector(V(g)),
    closeness=closeness(g,mode="out")),
  n=10)
##      node   closeness
## 1       1 0.02941176
## 2       2 0.02222222
## 3       3 0.04000000
## 4       4 0.03571429
## 5       5 0.04000000
## 6       6 0.02083333
## 7       7 0.03125000
## 8       8 0.03125000
## 9       9 0.03703704
## 10     10 0.03846154
```

Betweenness Centrality

Another global centrality measure aims to define the level of an individual being an intermediary between others. This measure is called "betweenness centrality" (Freeman, 1978) and is used especially regarding competitive power in economics (Burt, 1992). Roughly, for an individual it measures the proportion of shortest paths on which he/she sits in between any other pair of individuals.

This measure is quite difficult to calculate because there might be more than one geodesics, i.e. multiple shortest paths, connecting two actors in the network. Let the number of geodesics connecting two individuals, b_k and b_l, be denoted as j_{kl}. The number of geodesics on which the individual we are concerned with, b_i, is located is denoted as j_{kl}^i. An example network demonstrating betweenness centrality is shown in Figure 7. This artificial network is loaded from a data file as shown in the code chunk below:

```
require(igraph)
g<- read_graph("data/globcentralityexample2.
net",format="pajek")
plot(g)
```

One of the shortest paths in the network between "a" and "b" passes by "c" and the other one passes by "d". Therefore, we find j_{ab}=2 and $j_{ab}^{c}=1$. On the other hand, there is only one geodesic between "a" and "i", and it passes by "e".

By using these definitions, we find the betweenness of "c" for "a" and "b" as $j_{ab}^{c}/j_{ab}=1/2$, i.e. "c" sits on half the geodesics between "a" and "b". This measure is the basic element of betweenness centrality. Firstly, we will need the *betweenness sum* below in order to calculate the betweenness centrality of the actor, namely b_i:

$$a(i)=\sum_{k\neq l}j_{kl}^{i}/j_{kl}$$

In measuring betweenness, this sum, as it was the case in "closeness" centrality, produces a value depending on the size of the social network and does not allow us to compare networks of different sizes. Normalization by dividing the betweenness sum by the number of pairs excluding the actor is

Figure 7. An example of global centrality: Betweenness centrality

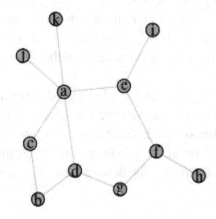

necessary. In a social network with n actors, the number of all possible pairs excluding the focal actor is $(n-1)(n-2)/2$. Therefore, betweenness centrality can be calculated as:

$$A(i) = \frac{a(i)}{(n-1)(n-2)/2} = \frac{\sum_{k \neq l} j_{kl}^i / j_{kl}}{(n-1)(n-2)/2}$$

The manual calculation of betweenness centrality is quite complex. We will make use of R for this example, but note that the betweenness centrality function in R gives us the betweenness sum:

```
require(igraph)
g<- read_graph("data/globcentralityexample2.
net",format="pajek")
betweenness(g)
##    a    b    c    d    e    f    g    h    i    j    k
## 26.0  1.0  2.5  9.5 17.0 11.0  4.0  0.0  0.0  0.0  0.0
```

If you rather want a normalized betweenness value, you can use the parameter for the `betweenness()` function as below

```
betweenness(g, normalized = T)
##          a          b          c          d          e
f
## 0.57777778 0.02222222 0.05555556 0.21111111 0.37777778
0.24444444
##          g          h          i          j          k
## 0.08888889 0.00000000 0.00000000 0.00000000 0.00000000
```

There are some differences here that are quite striking, for example between "f" and "g"." Here, "f" is in a more advantageous position arising from the fact that for node "h", it is the only connection with rest of the network, ie. it has high betweenness for that particular node. If this is a commercial network, "f" can make use of this position and gain considerable profit over "h". Compare this to "g". "g" is not the only connection for neither "f" or "d", the neighbours to which it is connected. Thus it does not have such an influence over them. This is the exact reason why betweenness centrality is used in economic networks and competition. Like closeness centrality, betweenness centrality cannot be calculated in a "disconnected" network. There is no geodesic between disconnected groups; the numerator and denominator in the formula above would, therefore, be zero. For that reason, it is not possible to calculate closeness centrality nor betweenness centrality for disconnected graphs.

Information Centrality

There have been some objections regarding betweenness centrality. One of the most significant counter arguments was put forward by Stephenson and Zelen (Stephenson and Zelen 1989). These two researchers underline that geodesics between two actors have varying importance in terms of information flow but betweenness centrality, nevertheless, assumes that all geodesies are equivalent. Stemming from this counter argument, "information centrality" is calculated by attaching importance commensurate with the local centrality of actors to geodesies. This new type of centrality is thought to make more sense when it comes to information flow and the related centrality. We will not make a detailed definition here since it is a quite complicated calculation. A comprehensive discussion and formulation are available in Wasserman and Faust's reference book (Wasserman and Faust 1994). We can calculate the information centrality for the first example above by using a different library, "statnet", in R. Please note some details in the following code for this. By using sna package we create a mix of graph related functions from multiple packages, some with same names. To avoid confusion we will detach the package after we are done:

```
require(statnet)
##                    Installed   ReposVer  Built
## ergm               "3.9.4"     "3.10.4"  "3.5.1"
## ergm.count         "3.3.0"     "3.4.0"   "3.5.1"
## network            "1.13.0.1"  "1.15"    "3.5.1"
## networkDynamic     "0.9.0"     "0.10.0"  "3.5.1"
## statnet            "2018.10"   "2019.6"  "3.5.1"
## statnet.common     "4.1.4"     "4.3.0"   "3.5.1"
## tergm              "3.5.2"     "3.6.1"   "3.5.1"
## tsna               "0.2.0"     "0.3.0"   "3.5.1"
g<- read.paj("data/globcentralityexample2.net")
infocent(g)
##  [1] 0.9720930 0.6807818 0.7037037 0.8530612 0.8360000
0.7655678 0.7359155
##  [8] 0.4707207 0.4964371 0.5414508 0.5414508
detach("package:statnet")
```

Note that the difference between f and g is more minor according to this measure.

Eigenvector Centrality

Unlike other centrality measure, the eigenvector centrality does not regard the neighbors of an individual as equals. Instead, it reflects the impact of powerful/more central neighbors on the centrality of the individual/actor. This approach is also the basis for the PageRank method used by Google to list web pages in order of importance. The aim here is to achieve a ranking based on importance and popularity rather than distance only.

Let us denote the graph representing a network as $\varsigma = (B, 0)$ and the sociomatrix as A. In an undirected social relation, each element of this matrix, $a_{i,j}$, takes the value 1 if there is a tie from node i to node j, and if not, it takes the value 0. Let us name the set consisting of neighbors of i as K_i. The eigen value centrality of this individual, denoted x_i, is calculated as follows:

$$x_i = \frac{1}{\lambda} \sum_{t \in K_i} x_t = \frac{1}{\lambda} \sum_{t \in B} a_{i,t} x_t$$

Here, λ is a positive constant. What is noteworthy in this centrality formula is that the centrality of the individual depends on that of all its neighbors (and, therefore, viceversa) with a positive constant. This is because x values appear on both the left and right hand side of the equation, so it relies on eigenvalue computation. From a social perspective, an individual having high-centrality neighbors would also have high centrality.

This requires eigenvector mathematics as these centrality values are mutually dependent to one another. We limit the vector x giving the eigenvector centrality of all individuals/actors by writing this equation as an eigenvector equation as follows:

$$Ax = \lambda x$$

There are fast algorithms for finding eigenvectors. As eigenvector centrality values must be positive, the highest one among many eigenvalue/eigenvector couples to be found is taken for centrality calculation. We can make this calculation for our example by using the "eigen_centrality()" function in the "igraph" library:

```
library(igraph)
g<- read_graph("data/globcentralityexample2.
net",format="pajek")
```

```
V(g)$name=c("a","b","c","d","e","f","g","h","i","j","k")
eigen_centrality(g)$vector
##          a          b          c          d          e          f
g
## 1.0000000 0.4780869 0.5538392 0.7220798 0.6434824 0.4762140
0.4490007
##          h          i          j          k
## 0.1784374 0.2411129 0.3747000 0.3747000
```

Google's PageRank method adopts an essentially similar approach while defining a centrality corresponding to a much easier algorithm, calculated with large networks rapidly. This way, Google lists at top of its results list not the websites with most links but ones having links from more popular websites. The aim of both PageRank and eigenvalue centrality calculations is to make it possible to evaluate web pages linked by popular websites as more popular than those linked by non-popular sites.

Kleinberg's Authority and Hub Centrality

This meaasure, developed for hyperlink relations among websites, is similar to the eigenvector centrality measure: The purpose is to make a ranking based on popularity (Kleinberg 1999b, 1999a). But this measure, developed by Kleinberg, takes into account the fact that hyperlinks compose a directed network and, based on this, makes a distinction between pages of "authority" linking important pages and hub pages linked many times, especially by these authorities.

This centrality measure is frequently referred to as HITS, an abbreviation for "Hyperlink-induced Topic Search". In this approach, definitions of authorities and hubs mutually depend on each other. We define an authority as a page including links to important web pages, i.e. hubs. Symmetrically, a hub is a web page linked by authority pages (and not by unimportant ones!). We can formulate this as follows:

$$x^{(p)} \leftarrow \sum_{q:(q,p)\in E} y^{(q)}$$

$$y^{(q)} \leftarrow \sum_{p:(p,q)\in E} x^{(p)}$$

Here, (q,p) denotes a directed and unweighted tie within the set of relations, E.

If vectors x^* and y^* start with a reasonable value (e.g. all of them are one) and get mutually updated, it will converge to their real values at some point. But this problem has a better, algebraic solution: If the set A given in the formula is the adjacency matrix of this social network, the solution for x^* is the eigenvector of $A^T A$, and the solution for y^* is the eigenvector of AA^T.

Although similar to the eigenvector and Kleinberg centralities, Google PageRank does not have such an algebraic solution. However, it converges to its real value so rapidly that it allows the use in large-scale cases. If you are interested in the details, you can check the original article written by Larry Page and Sergei Brin, founders of Google (Page et al. 1998). These two algorithms are developed within the same time period . Kleinberg's HITS algorithm was later used for the search engine www.Ask.com.

One of the analyses the HITS algorithm used for commercial networks. Commercial networks are directed, but there are fewer algorithms available for analysis of directed networks, whereas many are available for undirected ones. HITS is suitable for directed networks. A version of HITS suitable for weighted networks can also be used for this analysis (Deguchi et al. 2014). These analyses, unlike methods exclusive to undirected networks, may reveal interesting trends. For instance, the primary authority feature of the United States declines in global trade networks while that of China rises. On the other hand, while China transforms from a production center into a consumer market, it turns into a consumption authority from a production hub. As for Japan, while it has transformed into a balanced economy from a production hub, its authority centrality has decreased and its hub centrality has increased (Deguchi et al. 2014).

Distribution of General Centrality Values

As we did previously with local centrality, analyzing the distribution of centrality measures over actors may prove to be illuminating. For example, let us how information centrality is distributed within Krackhardt's network of advice-giving among managers (Figure 8). There seem to be two clusters in this distribution. But there were four of them in local centrality distribution. Thus, it means that local centrality reflects the company hierarchy more directly. Yet as far as information centrality goes, there are only two "roles" in this social network. The code chunk below uses 'statnet` library which provides information centrality:

```
require(statnet)
##                    Installed    ReposVer  Built
##  ergm              "3.9.4"      "3.10.4"  "3.5.1"
##  ergm.count        "3.3.0"      "3.4.0"   "3.5.1"
##  network           "1.13.0.1"   "1.15"    "3.5.1"
##  networkDynamic    "0.9.0"      "0.10.0"  "3.5.1"
##  statnet           "2018.10"    "2019.6"  "3.5.1"
##  statnet.common    "4.1.4"      "4.3.0"   "3.5.1"
##  tergm             "3.5.2"      "3.6.1"   "3.5.1"
##  tsna              "0.2.0"      "0.3.0"   "3.5.1"
g<- read.paj("data/HighTech-advice.net")
hist(infocent(g),
     main="Distribution of information centrality",
     xlab="Information centrality",
     ylab="Frequency")
```

Interesting details concerning the social system in question are revealed in Figure 9 with two measures combined. Some individuals with very low local centrality, like others with very high values, have high information centrality. Even though they are low-level managers, they are strategically positioned in information flow processes.

```
require(statnet)
g<- read.paj("data/HighTech-advice.net")
plot(sna::degree(g,cmode="outdegree"),infocent(g))


detach("package:statnet")
detach("package:sna")
```

Such analysis of different centrality estimates would contribute to the better understanding of the roles within the network and to the planning of the further steps in the analysis.

CENTRALIZATION AND CONDENSATION

Estimates about individuals, their distributions etc. give us only limited information on the overall state of the network. Particularly, the question who/ where is the center of a network has attracted considerable interest. Because

Figure 8. Information centrality distribution within Krackhardt's network of company managers

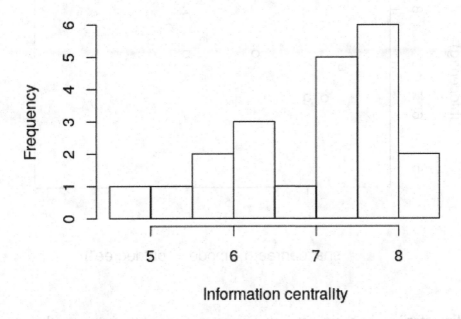

Distribution of Information centrality

Information centrality

the answer to this question may produce results strikingly different than, for instance, the official organizational chart in a network of professional relations (Cross and Parker 2004). In the definition regarding the whereabouts of the center of the network, certain explanations were made by drawing analogies between social network structure and geography/geometry. Some definitions like "distance, center, and diameter" mentioned in the previous chapter can be related to non-local estimation techniques discussed here.

One of these analogies was **"eccentricity"**. There are many geodesics connecting one actor of the network with all other actors. The length of the longest among these geodesics is called eccentricity. What underlies this definition is an analogy drawn from geometry: If we think of a social network as a circle, the eccentricity of an object is the distance between it and the farthest point in the circle. We say that actors with relatively low eccentricity values are in the center, if we continue with this analogy.

On the other hand, the actors with the highest eccentricity values are on the periphery. Furthermore, the highest value among eccentricities is the

Figure 9. Information centrality and degree distribution within Krackhardt's network of company managers

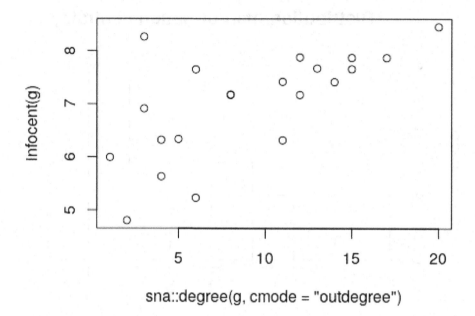

sna::degree(g, cmode = "outdegree")

"**diameter**" of the social network. Diameter is one of the measures that can be used to compare the size and the centralization level of networks. If the diameter of one of two networks of similar sizes is smaller than the other, this indicates that it has a more centralized structure.

In the example given in Figure 6 while we were discussing closeness centrality, the eccentricity of the actor "e" is 2 and, as far as this definition is concerned, is the center of the network. We have already concluded that it was the center of the network based on our closeness centrality calculations; this new measure confirms the former. However, a few actors like "b" and "c" are on the periphery and their eccentricity value is 4, hence the diameter of the network. In the example given for betweenness centrality in Figure 7, the eccentricity of individuals "e" and "a" is 3. Therefore, considering this definition, both of them are centers. Considering closeness centrality, on the other hand, we found that "a" is more central. Making a preference between these centralization measures seems to be problematic; it must be interpreted in accordance with the relational phenomenon. The diameter of the network is 4, which is the same as the network in Figure 7. But one of these social networks with the same diameters has 9 actors while the other has 11.Thus, we can intuitively infer that the latter network is "more centralized".

In addition to centralization, the average of local (degree) centralities of actors would give us the condensation level of the network. We can find this for the two examples above as follows:

```
g1 <- graph.formula(a--b, a--c, a--d, a--e, e--i, e--f,f--h,f-
-g)
mean(igraph::degree(g1))
## [1] 1.777778
g2<- read_graph("data/globcentralityexample2.
net",format="pajek")
mean(igraph::degree(g2))
## [1] 2.181818
```

The second network, in addition to being more centralized, is also denser. Because each actor has 2.18 ties on average, higher than the first network. Our calculation of condensation level, unlike network density, does not depend on the number of actors within the network, therefore it can be used to compare networks of varying sizes. For that reason, we can say that the second network is more condensed than the first one.

To underline the difference between centralization and condensation, let us look at the example given in Figure 10 in which actors in the second example are connected differently. The diameter of the network is only 2 in this example, therefore it is much more centralized than the others. Condensation level (the average local centrality of actors), on the other hand, is 1.81, less dense than the second example. This shows that condensation and centralization are two different things that need to be interpreted together.

```
library(igraph)
g3<- read_graph("data/globcentralityexample3.
net",format="pajek")
V(g3)$name=c("a","b","c","d","e","f","g","h","i","j","k")
plot(g3)
```

```
mean(igraph::degree(g3))
## [1] 1.818182
```

Figure 10. Difference between centralization and condensation

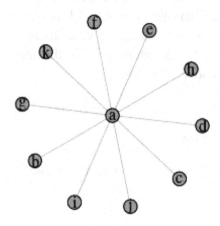

Other Centrality Measures

There have been other measures proposed to measure centrality of actors in a network (Das, Samanta, and Pal, 2018). These measures have originated in a variety of disciplines and used for a variety of purposes. In this chapter we have covered only a few that are used most frequently in social research. For the curious readers the R library CINNA (Ashtiani et al., 2018) provides a rich collection of centrality measures by combining functions from various other R libraries. An example is shown below. Here the example is adapted to exclude some centralities which are not computable for this example. The names of centralities are printed only. You may examine the content of data frame d to explore the centralities. Note that we need to detach several libraries which CINNA automatically loads, to clean up the R namespace:

```
library(igraph)
g<- read_graph("data/globcentralityexample2.
net",format="pajek")
V(g)$name=c("a","b","c","d","e","f","g","h","i","j","k")
library(CINNA)
centralities <- calculate_centralities(g,
            except=c("Communicability Betweenness
Centrality",
                "Community Centrality",
                "Hubbell Index",
                "Closeness Vitality"))
d<-as.data.frame(centralities)
names(d)
```

```
##    [1] "subgraph.centrality.scores"
##    [2] "Topological.Coefficient"
##    [3] "Average.Distance"
##    [4] "Barycenter.Centrality"
##    [5] "BottleNeck.Centrality"
##    [6] "Centroid.value"
##    [7] "Closeness.Centrality..Freeman."
##    [8] "ClusterRank"
##    [9] "Decay.Centrality"
##   [10] "Degree.Centrality"
##   [11] "Diffusion.Degree"
##   [12] "DMNC...Density.of.Maximum.Neighborhood.Component"
##   [13] "Eccentricity.Centrality"
##   [14] "eigenvector.centralities"
##   [15] "K.core.Decomposition"
##   [16] "Geodesic.K.Path.Centrality"
##   [17] "Katz.Centrality..Katz.Status.Index."
##   [18] "Kleinberg.s.authority.centrality.scores"
##   [19] "Kleinberg.s.hub.centrality.scores"
##   [20] "clustering.coefficient"
##   [21] "Lin.Centrality"
##   [22] "Lobby.Index..Centrality."
##   [23] "Markov.Centrality"
##   [24] "Radiality.Centrality"
##   [25] "Shortest.Paths.Betweenness.Centrality"
##   [26] "Current.Flow.Closeness.Centrality"
##   [27] "Closeness.centrality..Latora."
##   [28] "Cross.Clique.Connectivity"
##   [29] "Entropy.Centrality"
##   [30] "EPC...Edge.Percolated.Component"
##   [31] "Laplacian.Centrality"
##   [32] "Leverage.Centrality"
##   [33] "MNC...Maximum.Neighborhood.Component"
##   [34] "Semi.Local.Centrality"
##   [35] "Residual.Closeness.Centrality"
##   [36] "Stress.Centrality"
##   [37] "Load.Centrality"
##   [38] "Flow.Betweenness.Centrality"
##   [39] "Information.Centrality"
##   [40] "Weighted.Vertex.Degree"
##   [41] "Harary.Centrality"
##   [42] "Dangalchev.Closeness.Centrality"
##   [43] "Group.Centrality"
##   [44] "Harmonic.Centrality"
##   [45] "Local.Bridging.Centrality"
##   [46] "Wiener.Index.Centrality"
detach("package:CINNA")
detach("package:erqm.count")
detach("package:tsna")
```

```
detach("package:tergm")
detach("package:networkDynamic")
detach("package:ergm")
detach("package:network")
```

CASE STUDY: FLORENTINE FAMILIES WEALTH AND CENTRALITY

We can examine which of the centrality measurements better explain wealth in our Florentine families example we have studied before (Padgett, 2010). We have already done this for degree centrality:

```
require(igraph)
g <- read.graph("data/PadgettMarital.net", format="pajek")
wealthData <- read.csv("data/PadgettWealth.csv",header=TRUE)
cor(degree(g), wealthData$wealth)
## [1] 0.5589956
```

One problem with this example is that it is a disconnected network as seen in Chapter 3, Figure 2. For this reason an attempt to compute closeness centralities, for example, would fail with an error message:

```
require(igraph)
g <- read.graph("data/PadgettMarital.net", format="pajek")
wealthData <- read.csv("data/PadgettWealth.csv",header=TRUE)
V(g)$wealth <- wealthData$wealth
cor(closeness(g), V(g)$wealth)
At centrality.c:2617:closeness centrality is not well-defined
for disconnected graphs[1]
```

For this reason we need to modify out graph to remove isolated nodes and continue our examination with the connected main component of the graph. The delete.vertices() function can be used with a selector to remove nodes with degree zero:

```
require(igraph)
g <- read.graph("data/PadgettMarital.net", format="pajek")
wealthData <- read.csv("data/PadgettWealth.csv",header=TRUE)
V(g)$wealth <- wealthData$wealth
gconnected <- delete.vertices(g, which(degree(g)==0))
```

```
cor(closeness(gconnected), V(gconnected)$wealth)
## [1] 0.2877389
```

Let us note the positive correlation between closeness and wealth for the moment; although it is smaller than that for the degree centrality and wealth.

We can repeat the correlation calculation for betweenness centrality and wealth:

```
require(igraph)
g <- read.graph("data/PadgettMarital.net", format="pajek")
wealthData <- read.csv("data/PadgettWealth.csv",header=TRUE)
V(g)$wealth <- wealthData$wealth
gconnected <- delete.vertices(g, which(degree(g)==0))
cor(betweenness(gconnected), V(gconnected)$wealth)
## [1] 0.3103916
```

Considering all these results together we conclude that a local measure of centrality is more closely related with wealth in this particular case.

EXERCISES

1. Remember that a random network can be created with a command as follows:

```
require(igraph)
g <- static.power.law.game(500, 1000, #numbers of actors and
ties in the random network
        exponent.out= 2.2, #power distribution parameter
        exponent.in = -1) #undirected network
Find and plot the ego network densities of the nodes in this
network.
```

2. Make a degree vs ego network density plot for your random network in the previous question. Do you see the described role types in Figure 5 in the random network? Why or why not?

3. Find the closeness centralities in the random network you have created and plot a histogram of them. Remember to remove isolates, if any, before this computation. What kind of distribution the centralities show?

4. Find the betweenness centralities in the random network you have created and plot a histogram of them. What kind of distribution the centralities show?

REFERENCES

Ashtiani, M., Mirzaie, M., & Jafari, M. (2018). CINNA: An R/CRAN package to decipher Central Informative Nodes in Network Analysis. *Bioinformatics (Oxford, England)*, *35*(8), 1436–1437. doi:10.1093/bioinformatics/bty819 PMID:30239607

Burt, R. S. (1992). *Structural holes: The social structure of competition.* Cambridge, MA: Harvard University Press.

Cross, R., & Parker, A. (2004). *The Hidden Power of Social Networks: Understanding How Work Really Gets Done in Organizations.* Harvard Business School Press. Retrieved from http://www.amazon.com/exec/obidos/redirect?tag=citeulike07-20{\&}path=ASIN/1591392705.

Cross, R., & Prusak, L. (2002). The people who make organizations go–or stop. *Networks in the Knowledge Economy*, 248-260.

Das, K., Samanta, S., & Pal, M. (2018). Study on centrality measures in social networks: A survey. *Social Network Analysis and Mining*, *8*(1), 13. doi:10.100713278-018-0493-2

Deguchi, T., Takahashi, K., Takayasu, H., & Takayasu, M. (2014). Hubs and authorities in the world trade network using a weighted HITS algorithm. *PLoS One*, *9*(7), e100338. doi:10.1371/journal.pone.0100338 PMID:25050940

Freeman, L. C. (1978). Centrality in social networks conceptual clarification. *Social Networks*, *1*(3), 215–239. doi:10.1016/0378-8733(78)90021-7

Kleinberg, J. M. (1999a). Authoritative sources in a hyperlinked environment. *Journal of the Association for Computing Machinery*, *46*(5), 604–632. doi:10.1145/324133.324140

Kleinberg, J. M. (1999b). Hubs, authorities, and communities. *ACM Computing Surveys*, *31*(4es), 5, es. doi:10.1145/345966.345982

Krackhardt, D. (1987). Cognitive social structures. *Social Networks*, *9*(2), 109–134. doi:10.1016/0378-8733(87)90009-8

Padgett, J. F. (2010). Open Elite? Social Mobility, Marriage, and Family in Florence, 1282–1494. *Renaissance Quarterly*, *63*(2), 357–411. doi:10.1086/655230 PMID:20552737

Page, L., Brin, S., Motwani, R., & Winograd, T. (1999). *The PageRank citation ranking: Bringing order to the web*. Stanford InfoLab.

Stephenson, K., & Zelen, M. (1989). Rethinking centrality: Methods and examples. *Social Networks*, *11*(1), 1–37. doi:10.1016/0378-8733(89)90016-6

Wasserman, S., & Faust, K. (1994). *Social network analysis: Methods and applications* (Vol. 8). Cambridge University Press. doi:10.1017/CBO9780511815478

Wellman, B. (1979). The community question: The intimate networks of East Yorkers. *American Journal of Sociology*, *84*(5), 1201–1231. doi:10.1086/226906

Section 2
Network Dynamics and Models

Chapter 5
Microdynamics in Networks:
Homogenization, Structural Balance and Transitivity

ABSTRACT

This chapter focuses on relations between two individuals and their interactions with third parties. The dynamics at this level have common effects in terms of network structure. Certain common behaviors observed at dyad and triad level (i.e., at a micro level) help social networks acquire similar structural features. These features constitute a significant part of the development dynamics of the network structure. Feedback from such common behavioral patterns balances the micro-level structure of the network. These structural balances play a determining role in the similarity or difference between behaviors, languages, current issues, or opinions regarding basic concepts and so on.

Expressions such as "Any friend of a friend is a friend of mine" or "The enemy of my enemy is my friend" summarize certain behavioral patterns related to the formation of social relations affecting all of us. In this chapter, we will handle, in particular, relations between two individuals (dyads) and their interactions with third parties (triads) in terms of network structure. Certain common behaviors observed at dyad and triad level, i.e. at a micro level, help social networks acquire similar structural features. These features constitute a significant part of the development dynamics of the network structure.

DOI: 10.4018/978-1-7998-1912-7.ch005

There are common behaviors such as this "friend of a friend" effect that is at work and continuously shaping social structures. The behaviros at work in a social system and their relative importances may change from case to case. For example the behaviors in an *adversarial* network where multiple firms reach out to same customer base would be different that those of supporting relations between immigrants. Regardless of the particulars, feedback from such common behavioral patterns works out and balances the micro-level structure of any network. In a sense they are the quantum mechanics of social networks, and useful in understanding the upper level of social structures.

These structural balances at play have a determining role in the similarity or difference between behaviors, languages, issues or opinions regarding basic concepts and so on.

DYADS: PAIRS OF INDIVIDUALS AND RECIPROCITY

We will refer to the small social entity consisting of two related individuals within a social network as "**dyads**". We will discuss the symmetry or, in other words, the **reciprocity**, of these dyads.

The relation we deal in a network with might be undirected, like a marital relation. In such a case, the relation is inevitably symmetrical and thus reciprocal. Marriage is a joint act. If the verb defining the social relation is transitive, the relation will be symmetrical, e.g. "meeting", "texting" and so on.

On the other hand, we also deal with directed relations on a frequent basis as far as social phenomena are concerned. An economic relation like "lending money", or a social relation like "liking someone", a relation as the one analyzed by Moreno, or a communicative interaction like "sending an e-mail" are among examples of such directed relations. In this case we can ask the question to what extent the dyad is symmetrical because asymmetry is now possible.

Social relations are almost always reciprocal to a great extent. In a sense, this is their *nature*. Moreno and Jennings asked the girls in the orphanage to what degree they considered other girls as their friends. Naturally, a considerable part of the answers to this question demonstrated reciprocity. In other words, if Individual A indicated Individual B as a close friend, in most cases B also counted A among her friends. Moreno then handled the following question: What kind of a network would we observe if individuals formed relations without expecting reciprocity and in a completely arbitrary manner? By doing so, they were able to compare the case where relations are placed randomly and the actual network. Therefore, they could answer the question of whether the behavior of reciprocity is too dominant to be regarded as exceptional. Moreno and Jennings, his colleague, attempted to come up with an answer to this question with statistics (Moreno, 1934; Moreno and Jennings, 1938) and proved that reciprocity is indeed too evident and frequent to be arbitrary. This line of thinking marks a considerable part of stochastic network models that we use. Today, we have a more systematic approach regarding this topic. We are able to measure the reciprocity levels of relations within different social networks and compare social phenomena and communities.

The level of reciprocity in a network is measured with an approach similar to the one adopted by Moreno, i.e. via the comparison of a hypothetical network formed with randomly placed ties with no reciprocity behavior at work, and the actual situation. For instance, let us suppose that we count the number of reciprocal dyads (ie. relations where if there is a tie from B to A there is also a tie from A to B) within a network of directed relations. Let M denote the number of reciprocal dyads. As the relations are bidirectional, the number of ties in them would be $2M$. Let us assume that the total number of dyads (including non reciprocal ones) is L. The M/L ratio, as the ratio of reciprocal dyads to the number of dyads, can give us a measure of the reciprocity level in the network. However, there is a problem here: The value is greater than 0 even if the relations are random, meaning that it does not permit an interpretation or comparison, because we do not have a *baseline*.

A simple method used to solve this measurement problem uses the sociomatrix notation of social networks we have described in the earlier chapters. A reciprocal tie will show up as two 1s (or non-zero values) that are symmetric around diagonal of the matrix; i.e. one nonzero value in the matrix cell corresponding to tie $A \rightarrow B$ and another in the symmetric cell corresponding to tie $B \rightarrow A$. The method for measuring reciprocity is based on finding the correlation of symmetric ties by diagonally folding the sociomatrix (Garlaschelli and Loffredo 2004). Let us call the numbers in the sociomatrix a_{ij}. Let us also assume an unweighted relation for the sake of simplicity. If there is a relation from i to j, the value in a_{ij} is 1; if not, it becomes 0. The **reciprocity level** in the network is thus calculated as follows using Pearson correlation (if you like, please refer to the appendix for its definition):

$$\rho \equiv \frac{\sum_{i \neq j} \left(a_{ij} - \bar{a} \right) \left(a_{ji} - \bar{a} \right)}{\sum_{i \neq j}}$$

Here $\bar{a}$ represents the average of a_{ij} values. This value is required for calculating correlation. Please note that it also is the density of the unweighted network. Think about it: it measures the average proportion of finding a value of 1 in the cells of the sociomatrix representing our netwotk. If there are N actors in the directed network, the density, as we have seen before, is calculated as follows:

$$\bar{a} \equiv \frac{\sum_{i \neq j} a_{ij}}{N(N-1)} = \frac{L}{N(N-1)}$$

Through this definition, we infer that there is a tendency of reciprocity in the social relation if the ρ value is greater than zero. Reversely the relation we are concerned may tend to be highly asymmetrical if ρ is smaller than zero. Furthermore, please note that its value is independent of the network size (unlike, e.g., density) because it is normalized with respect to density. Due to its scale-free nature, it allows us to compare networks of different sizes.

For some alternative measurement methods concerning reciprocity, see (Katz and Powell 1955). Please note that if the relation is a weighted relation we may need to revise the normalization part of the above formulation. The explicit formula allows you to reflect on ths problem. We leave it as an exercise.

You can calculate reciprocity using the statnet/sna library in R. Neither Gephi or the igraph package in R does not allow such a calculation. Please note that igraph is a generalized graph library whereas statnet and sna are libraries with a social science orientation. Thus it is necessary to switch libraries. One needs to be alert to namespace clashes and data object conversions in such switching.

The example for Krackhardt's network of advice-giving among high-level managers (directed) and the Florentine family marriages (undirected) is given below. Let us start by uploading necessary libraries and datasets:

```
require(igraph)
require(sna)
gFlorentine<-read.graph("data/Padgett-marital.dl",format="dl")
gHightech<-read.graph("data/HigTech-advice.dl",format="dl")
```

Now, let us look at reciprocity in the directed relation. To convert a graph uploaded by igraph to the unique datatype (network) of the sna package, we start by converting it to a matrix, a standard R format, and then transferring it to the library. Thus the n1 and n2 objects in the below code chunk are suitable for the sna library functions we use.

```
summary(gFlorentine)
## IGRAPH 174b6b5 DNW- 15 40 --
## + attr: name (v/c), weight (e/n)
nFlorentine <- network(get.adjacency(gFlorentine))
nHightech <- network(get.adjacency(gHightech))
dyad.census(nFlorentine)
##      Mut Asym Null
## [1,]  20    0   85
dyad.census(nHightech)
##      Mut Asym Null
## [1,]  45  100   65
```

In this code, the dyad.census() function reports us the number of dyads, and the number of those that are mutual and asymmetrical separately. The output here shows us that there are 45 mutual and 100 asymmetrical relations in the advice-giving network. There is no relation between 65 pairs of actors. Finally we can compute reciprocity:

```
grecip(nFlorentine)
## Mut
##   1
grecip(nHightech)
##       Mut
## 0.5238095
```

As you can see, the reciprocity in the marital network of Florentine families consisting of undirected relations is 1. This is obvious in the undirected network; simply note that one needs to be alert to such mistakes -of software function accepting what it shouldn't- when one sees and extreme output value such as 1.0. In contrast the reciprocity value is well below one in the managerial advice-giving network. This is not surprising as the act of giving advice depends on experience, meaning that it is directed/asymmetrical. In other words you are likely not to take advice from people you give advice to very often. The reciprocity would be different instead, for example, if this was a friendship network.

Triads: Balance and Transitivity

It may be emotionally awkward if two of our close friends do not know each other or are not in the best of terms. This can also be the case if your friend hangs out with someone that you do not necessarily like. Created with the addition of a third person to a relation between two individuals, **triads** are formed through such common dynamics. In order to simplify the argument presented here, we will imagine an undirected relation that can take positive or negative values. This could be a weighted relation, but for simplicity we assume that its weight can be +1 (positive) or -1 (negative). For the moment we will take the absence of a relation as negative while handling triads. Possible triad configurations are shown in Figure 1.

There would be 8 of these configurations and they depend on the positivity (+) or negativity (-) of each of the three relations. Some of them, however, are equivalent (think of flipping triangles). Thus the four cases here summarize all possible configurations.

Apart from completely balanced (all positive) example shown in the figure, it is also possible to see tensions like the ones mentioned previously. In the

Figure 1. Triad configurations.

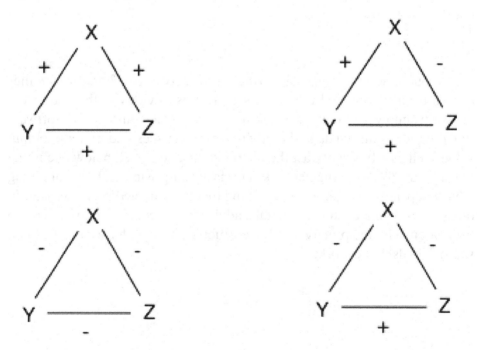

upper-right example, there is a tension that pushes either (1) for X and Z to become friends or (2) for the relation between X-Y or Y-Z to deteriorate. As for the lower-right case, there is no tension (The enemy of my enemy is my friend!). Generally, in a "circle" going between three individuals and returning to the first one, if there is an even number of negative relations (i.e. zero or two) the triad is balanced; if there is an odd number of negative relations it is not balanced. Think about the one in upper-right: friend of a friend is enemy, which is socially problematics. Similarry, in the lower left example enemy of an enemy is also an enemy, once again a socially awkward situation.

These configurations can be re-imagined for the case where absence of a relation is allowed. Such absence should be treated as negatives to understand the social tensions. For example if you remove one relation from the upper-left example then the friend of a friend is no more a friend (similar to the upper-right). Despite the lack of hostility/negativity there is a social tension of the same nature ("Uh, you two should meet some time!"). Therefore, most of what we have said about signed relations apply to unsigned relations in principle.

The elimination of such tensions via relations forming or dissolving in time is a fundamental dynamic in the formation of social groups. In the example given in Figure 2, you can see the formation of new relations in two steps, eliminating tensions in a network (and continuation of this pattern), i.e. how a group becomes tight after the "closure" of the triad. X-Z and Y-W become friends to close triangles with tensions. Then a new tension arises pushing X and W to become friends.

Of course, there is no rule necessitating that every triad with tensions should be closed. Particularly in weighted relations, the level of tensions between the triad might be high or low and may not require the closure of the triad, or that closure might happen in a much longer term. In Figure 3, it is possible for an X-Z relation to occur as both relations between Y-X and Y-Z are strong, but this new relation will start as a weak one. Moreover, it may remain so due to personal reasons not related to the network dynamics. Its existence, even if weak, is enough to eliminate tension on its own. On the other hand, as the relation between Z-W is weak, the presence and the power of the relation between Z-Y may not create enough enough tension to initiate a relation between Y-W. Similarly, as the newly-formed Z-X relation and Z-W relation are weak, tension they create for the initiation of the X-W relation is also weak.

Figure 2. Group formation in two steps with the elimination of tensions in triads

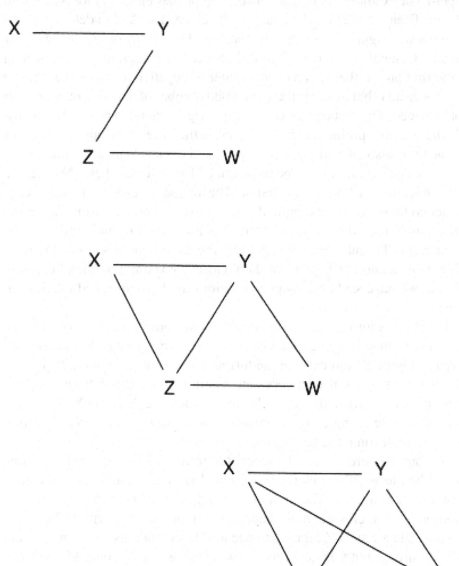

Triads in Directed Relations: Transitivity

In directed relations, the number of configurations increases because, in addition to the positivity/negativity (or presence/ absence) of the relations

Figure 3. Differences between triadic tensions in a weighted relation

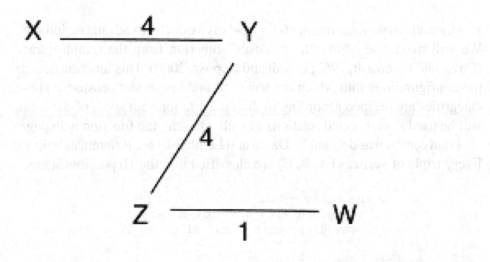

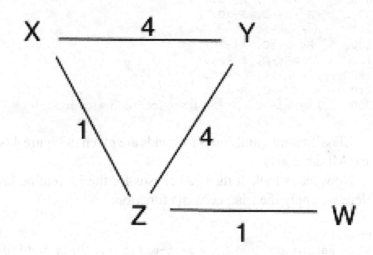

among the triad, their directions are also added to the configurations. If there is a relation from X to Y and from Y to Z, we expect a relation from X to Z as well. We call this expectation **transitivity**.

Triad Analysis

Here, we will make measurements for triads as we did for dyads and reciprocity. We will make use of the "triad.census" function from the igraph library (Davis and Leinhardt, 1967; Csardi and Nepusz, 2006). This function detects the configurations into which the triads fit and brings out censuses. These categories are defined according to directed relations but some of them can still be used in undirected relations as well. Quoting the function help page:

Triad census was defined by David and Leinhardt (see References below). Every triple of vertices (A, B, C) are classified into the 16 possible states:

```
003     A,B,C, the empty graph.
012     A->B, C, the graph with a single directed edge.
102     A<->B, C, the graph with a mutual connection between two
vertices.
021D    A<-B->C, the out-star.
021U    A->B<-C, the in-star.
021C    A->B->C, directed line.
111D    A<->B<-C.
111U    A<->B->C.
030T    A->B<-C, A->C.
030C    A<-B<-C, A->C.
201     A<->B<->C.
120D    A<-B->C, A<->C.
120U    A->B<-C, A<->C.
120C    A->B->C, A<->C.
210     A->B<->C, A<->C.
300     A<->B<->C, A<->C, the complete graph.
```

Classifications and codes for triads are given in Figure 4 (source: Batagelj and Mrvar, 2001).

Now, let us look at the triad census for the Florentine families example. Here we apply the triad.census() function:

```
require(igraph)
g1<-read.graph("data/Padgett-marital.dl",format="dl")
n1 <- network(get.adjacency(g1))
## <sparse>[ <logic> ]: .M.sub.i.logical() maybe inefficient
triad.census(n1)
##       003 012 102 021D 021U 021C 111D 111U 030T 030C 201 120D
120U 120C 210
## [1,] 239   0 175    0    0    0    0    0    0    0   0   38    0
0    0   0
```

Figure 4. Classification of triads and their code names used in analysis software.

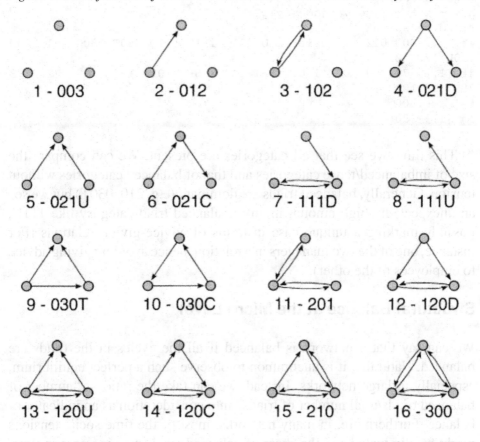

```
##        300
## [1,]    3
```

As the relation in question is undirected, we do not see certain configurations. For example, 012 is absent but 102 is present, and so on. The most frequent configuration is 003: triads with no relation. Here, only the configuration 201 includes unbalanced/tense triads; this is a figure regarding advantageous families due to their positions as bridges, the ones Padgett focuses on (Padgett, 2010). He counts this kind of positions. Not all of the bridges, of course, bear the same level of importance; this is only a local measure.

Let us do the same thing for Krackhardt's directed relation data (Krackhardt, 1987):

```
require(igraph)
g2<-read.graph("data/HigTech-advice.dl",format="dl")
```

```
require(sna)
n2 <- network(get.adjacency(g2))
triad.census(n2)
##       003 012 102 021D 021U 021C 111D 111U 030T 030C 201 120D
120U 120C 210
## [1,]  74 153  90  160   86   49   59  101  190    2  72   62
78   17 107
##       300
## [1,]  30
```

This time, we see that all categories are present. We can compare the size of imbalanced/tense categories and that of balanced categories without tension. Generally, balanced triads are dominant (e.g. 210, 030T) but we see an unexpectedly high amount in an imbalanced triad category like 111U, possibly marking a unique case in terms of advice-giving relations (For instance, one of the two managers in a relation, hence avoiding giving advice to employees of the other).

Structural Balance at the Micro Level

We can say that a network is balanced if all the cycles in the triads are balanced. Naturally, it is uncommon to observe such a perfect equilibrium, especially in large networks. Instead, we can take the ratio of "number of balanced triads/total number of triads" into consideration as an indicator of balance. Furthermore, in many networks, most of the time social tensions might be eliminated and the share of balanced triads may increase in time. On the other hand, political and organizational tensions or crises might result in the opposite situation.

CASE STUDY: ZACHARY'S KARATE CLUB

The data we will use in this case study comes from a research in the field of anthropology, collected by Wayne Zachary (Zachary 1977). The data includes several relations about members of a karate club in a university. Zachary studied a social duality what he labels as conflict and *fission*. There were two factions in this social group. Zachary have observed the group over some time and have found that the ties within factions became more intense (fission) whereas whatever ties existed between members from different groups has vanished over time (conflict).

This and some other datasets are available from an R library called igraphdata (Csardi, 2015), as igraph objects. Here we will first load and visualize this social network as seen in Figure 5. Please make sure you read the help page for the dataset using help(karate) function call before examining the following code chunks:

```
require(igraphdata)
data(karate)
require(igraph)
#help(karate) # Please read the explanations for the dataset
plot(karate)
```

We can now make a triad census for the club network:

```
require(igraphdata)
data(karate)
require(sna)
n <- network(get.adjacency(karate))
triad.census(n)
##          003 012  102 021D 021U 021C 111D 111U 030T 030C 201
120D 120U 120C
## [1,] 3971   0 1575    0    0    0    0    0    0    0 393
0    0    0
##       210 300
## [1,]   0  45
```

Figure 5. The network in Zachary karate club dataset. The two factions are visible in different colors

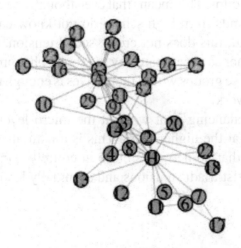

Her we see a lot of not-connected triads (003s) and dyads (102s) which is quite normal in social graphs and does not contain any tensions. We also see full connected triads (300s). But we also see triads with a missing link (201s). In this particular social setting this is normal because most of this configurations is between a master/trainer and several students of him. Thus the relation in these imbalanced configurations is only one of the many in this antropological research. The triadic tensions are not so high in the case of trainer-student relation, as it woul be in a friendship relation.

EXAMPLE OF HIGHER LEVEL BALANCE: PERSONAL FACEBOOK NETWORK

You can find the visual generated with Gephi using my personal data from Facebook in Figure 6, Generated using Gephi with YifanHu Multilevel layout at a time. (Unfortunately Facebook has since changed their rules and one can no longer download personal data network in this form. I find it utterly disturbing that I have voluntarily given away so much personal information but cannot make use of it myself as a social network researcher. This is just another case of *data* monopoly where valuable data is eventually slips away from us and commoditized.

In the network shown some groups such as work friends and family are visible, I avoid giving much details not to distract the subject from general structural features of the network.

Within the groups in this real network, structural dynamics are observed. Most of the triads in each group are closed and balanced. Yet this is not the case between the groups. This means that even though one of my work friends and one of my friends from high school do not know each other and thus create an open triad, this does not create social tension. Closure occurs in such a spatial manner as necessitated by the social phenomenon. Ultimately, the balancing of these groups within themselves is enough to alter the balance for the overall network.

Note that the balancing is at work at the micro level, but the network still has partitions at the higher level. This is a natural result of balancing social forces such that no networks close in entirely. Time, space, or class separations will resist triadic tensions and eventually lead to such partitions at the macro level.

Figure 6. My personal Facebook network (retrieved pre-2015)

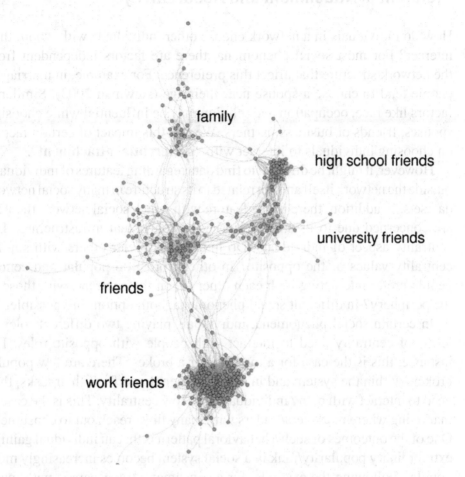

Structural Dynamics Related to the Power Asymmetries

Not everyone is equal in networks. We observed so far that some individuals are more popular or, if we are to use network-related terms, they have "higher centrality". differences within the network play an important role individuals select which individuals they interact (Newman 2002). In the following sections, we will examine some social dynamics and corresponding concepts that may explain such power asymmetries.

Preferential Attachment and Assortativity

How do individuals in a network choose other individuals with whom they interact? For most social phenomena, there are factors independent from the network structure that affect this preference. For example, in marriages, people tend to choose a spouse near their age (Newman 2003). Similarly, factors like race, occupation and religion may be influential while choosing spouses, friends or business partners. We call this impact of certain factors on choosing individuals to interact with "**preferential attachment**".

However, it might be difficult to find data regarding features of individuals, outside the network itself and not related to its structure in many social network datasets. In addition, there is one feature with which social network theories are concerned due to its structure-oriented conceptual infrastructure: The centrality aspect of individuals. Do individuals prefer others with similar centrality values or the opposite? In other words, do popular and central people prefer interacting with each other or, on the contrary, with those in the periphery? In different social phenomena, both options are possible.

In certain social phenomena, individuals playing two different roles in terms of centrality need to interact with people with opposite roles. For instance, this is the case for a mediator or a broker. There are few popular brokers within the system and in order for them to perform their tasks, they need to interact with many individuals with low centrality. This is the case in marketing where marketers/traders with many links reach out to consumers. One of the outcomes of such a behavioral pattern is that an individual gaining extraordinary popularity/rank in a social system becomes increasingly more popular. Following the example, for a consumer a tradesperson with many links (variety) is valuable, whereas a tradesperson will value customers with fewer links as profitable targets.

But in some other phenomena, individuals playing similar roles may prefer interacting with one another. Social relations among celebrities may be an example of such a case. We call this tendency to interact with individuals of similar popularity or rank as **assortativity**. One of the results of this is that, for example, individuals with high centrality interact with their ounterparts. In a sense, it corresponds to the tendency of celebrities to interact with other celebrities or that of wealthy people to befriend other wealthy people.

To measure such behavior, we take the baseline case of non-preferential, arbitrary relationship selection into consideration. Let us take the probability of the rank (degree) of a randomly-selected actor being k as p_k. While making the calculations below, we will use the term "added rank" signifying the rank obtained by the individual after the relationship is formed. Indeed, the given choice of a relationship is made before the relationship is actually formed. The added rank is the level information on the social network we already know, but here, we try to understand the choice before a certain relation is formed. In this case, the probability of the non-added rank of a selected actor being k is as follows:

$$q_k = \frac{(k+1)p_{k+1}}{z}$$

Here, $z = \sum_k kp_k$ denotes the average rank in the network.

Now let us consider the attachment rate of the actors with the ranks of j and k. These rates will form the basis for our preferential attachment calculation. Let us assume that e_{jk} represents the ratio of the ties connecting actors with the ranks of j and k. This estimate is also related to the definition above:

$$\sum_j e_{jk} = q_k$$

If there were no preferential attachments nor assortativity, and if the relations were selected randomly, the equatione $e_{jk}=q_j q_k$ would be true. The **assortativity coefficient** calculates the level of deviance from this randomness and is defined as follows:

$$r = \frac{\sum_{jk} jk\left(e_{jk} - q_i q_k\right)}{\sigma^2}$$

Here, the value σ^2 is the standard deviation of the q_k distribution.

The value r is 0 in a social network with no preferential attachment. With normalization, the value is in the intervalof $-1 \leq r \leq 1$. The value $+1$ signifies assortitative preferential relational behavior while -1 indicates a completely anti-assortitative preferential relational behavior.

The assortativity_degree() function in igraph makes this measurement possible. Its help page indicates that "The assortativity coefficient is positive is similar vertices (based on some external property) tend to connect to each, and negative otherwise." Let us examplify its use on Florentine families dataset:

```
require(igraph)
gFlorentine<-read.graph("data/Padgett-marital.dl",format="dl")
assortativity.degree(gFlorentine, directed=FALSE)
## [1] -0.3748379
```

The assortativity in this social setting is negative. This indicates that there are two roles in this social system. Larger, powerful families try to establish marriages with smaller families in order to form power conglomerates, and vice verse. The behavious could be much different in another setting.

EXERCISES

1. Consider the case of weighted relations. Do you think we can use the reciprocity measure as it is? Why or why not?
2. Create a random directed network similar to the following example. Then find its reciprocity. What do you expect the reciprocity of a random graph as such to be?:

```
require(igraph)
#create a network with 100 nodes and 120 directed ties
g<-erdos.renyi.game(100, 120, type="gnm", directed=TRUE)
plot(g)
```

Figure 7. A random graph

3. A dataset about social relations between faculty members is included in the igraphdata library with name UKfaculty (Nepusz et al. 2008). First visualize the network, and then make a reciprocity analysis. Finally make a triad census and analyse the results.
4. Compute the assortativity coefficient for Zachary's karate network. Does the result stand to your expectations for this type of social relation?

REFERENCES

Batagelj, V., & Mrvar, A. (1998). Pajek-Program for Large Network Analysis. *Connections*, *21*(2), 47–57.

Csardi, G. (2015). *igraphdata: A Collection of Network Data Sets for the'igraph'Package.* R Package Version 1.0, 1.

Csardi, G., & Nepusz, T. (2006). The igraph software package for complex network research. *InterJournal. Complex Systems*, *1695*(5), 1–9.

Davis, J. A., & Leinhardt, S. (1967). *The structure of positive interpersonal relations in small groups.* Academic Press.

Garlaschelli, D., & Loffredo, M. I. (2004). Patterns of Link Reciprocity in Directed Networks. *Physical Review Letters*, *93*(26), 268701. doi:10.1103/PhysRevLett.93.268701 PMID:15698035

Katz, L., & Powell, J. H. (1955). Measurement of the tendency toward reciprocation of choice. *Sociometry*, *18*(4), 403–409. doi:10.2307/2785876

Krackhardt, D. (1987). Cognitive social structures. *Social Networks*, *9*(2), 109–134. doi:10.1016/0378-8733(87)90009-8

Moreno, J. L. (1934). *Who shall survive? A new approach to the problem of human interrelations.* Academic Press.

Moreno, J. L., & Jennings, H. H. (1938). Statistics of social configurations. *Sociometry*, *1*(3/4), 342–374. doi:10.2307/2785588

Nepusz, T., Petróczi, A., Négyessy, L., & Bazsó, F. (2008). Fuzzy communities and the concept of bridgeness in complex networks. *Physical Review. E*, *77*(1), 016107. doi:10.1103/PhysRevE.77.016107 PMID:18351915

Newman, M. E. (2002). Assortative Mixing in Networks. *Physical Review Letters*, *89*(20), 208701. doi:10.1103/PhysRevLett.89.208701 PMID:12443515

Newman, M. E. (2003). Mixing patterns in networks. *Physical Review E: Statistical Physics, Plasmas, Fluids, and Related Interdisciplinary Topics*, *67*(2), 13. doi:10.1103/PhysRevE.67.026126 PMID:12636767

Padgett, J. F. (2010). Open Elite? Social Mobility, Marriage, and Family in Florence, 1282–1494. *Renaissance Quarterly*, *63*(2), 357–411. doi:10.1086/655230 PMID:20552737

Zachary, W. W. (1977). An Information Flow Model for Conflict and Fission in Small Groups. *Journal of Anthropological Research*, *33*(4), 452–473. doi:10.1086/jar.33.4.3629752

Chapter 6
Meso Dynamics:
Groups and Grouping

ABSTRACT

In social networks, an "inward gravitation" leading to a structure within which everyone is connected to one another does not occur. Instead, the network in question evolves into structural groups that are tightly connected within but with scarce ties between. An analogous situation is observed in all "complex" systems even if they are not social. We see a similar pattern in microbiological (concerning the interaction of molecular structures within the chemical system of the cell), macrobiological (regarding the interaction of species within an ecological system), and socio-economic (supply mechanisms and specialization of firms within a sector, organization of individuals in an office) systems. The factor underlying this pattern is the "specialization" of small systems through evolutionary processes. Owing to these relations, micro dynamics take place within the group while meso dynamics take place between groups. This chapter explores these groups and groupings.

So far, we have observed that small groups of individuals become tightly-attached groups by increasing the number of relations among each other (the opposite situation is also possible). Yet in social networks, an "inward gravitation" leading to a structure within which everyone is connected to one another does not occur. In other words networks do not "implode" due to micro level closure effects. Instead, the network in question evolves into

DOI: 10.4018/978-1-7998-1912-7.ch006

a structure that consists of parts that are tightly connected within but with scarce ties between.

An analogous situation is observed in all "complex" systems even if they are not social (Simon 1962). We see a similar pattern in microbiological (concerning the interaction of molecular structures within the chemical system of the cell), macrobiological (regarding the interaction of species within an ecological system) and socio-economic (supply mechanisms and specialization of firms within a sector, organization of individuals in an office) systems. The factor underlying this pattern is the "specialization" of small systems through evolutionary processes. In crowded systems, it is not possible for constituents to change and evolve in a mutual and compatible manner. Therefore, in all these systems there are groups having an intense volume of relations within themselves, specialized in certain functions. For instance, in professional communities, individuals are grouped based on their interests. Within a sector, firms are grouped according to their scopes and evolve into a specialized system by transforming something produced by someone else into an added value.

This frequent pattern is known as the small worlds phenomenon (Watts and Strogatz 1998). Within the scope of this pattern, there are scarce relations between tightly-connected groups, formed through the intermediation of one or two members of a group. Owing to these relations, micro dynamics take place within the group while meso dynamics take place between groups. At this point, think of each group as a component. These components will form groups among themselves through meso dynamics and follow a similar pattern.

Usually, we are able to determine individuals and the limits of the social network clearly, for example on the basis of some membership, geography, etc. However, defining and thus determining groups is not as easy. Yet it is important to determine groups to understand effects of structure on the homegeneity of behaviors and norms. While groups show a "closure" as far as the structure is concerned, they also develop unique cultures, languages and behavioral patterns. Conversely people of similar features (e.g. gender, religion, race) tend to socialize with each other. This social process called **homophily** stems from both imitation or mimetic behavior and social pressures. All these factors are vital for the functioning of the group and its commitment to tasks brought by its specialization.

GROUPING LEVEL OF THE NETWORK

The principles we have mentioned above indicate that every social network (generally speaking, all "natural" networks (biological, chemical etc.)) show a grouping pattern of **small worlds**: closely knit groups which have scarce relations between. But the grouping level of each network differs from one another. In a network, the level of inward closure of small groups and the scarcity/frequency of ties between the groups indicate the level of dominance of this pattern over the network structure. This criterion named **grouping level** might give us a much better idea regarding the network structure and its functioning when compared with individual-oriented estimates (centrality, even if non-local) or counting dyads and triads.

Watts and Strogatz (Watts and Strogatz 1998) use two terms while analyzing the grouping level in the structure. The first term is **characteristic path length** meaning the median of distances between any two actors in the network. This is a measure concerning the general structure of the network.

The second term is the **clustering coefficient**. This measure is computed as the mean of densities of ego networks of individuals in the network. Let us denote the graph representing the network of interest as $G(V,E)$. Then, for any component or actor, $v_i \in E$, let us define the set of other actors having a relation with it as its neighborhood:

$$N_i = \left\{ v_j : e_{ij} \in E, e_{ji} \in E \right\}.$$

Let k_i denote size of this set. he definition of neighborhood can be used for both directed or undirected networks. With this notation the ego network density of the focal actor, $v_i \in E$, is computed as follows if the network is directed:

$$C_i = \frac{\left| \left\{ e_{jk} : \upsilon_j, \upsilon_k \in N_i, e_{jk} \in E \right\} \right|}{k_i \left(k_i - 1 \right)}.$$

If the network is undirected the formula will be as follows:

$$C_i = \frac{2 \left| \left\{ e_{jk} : \upsilon_j, \upsilon_k \in N_i, e_{jk} \in E \right\} \right|}{k_i \left(k_i - 1 \right)}.$$

These formulas gives us the ego network density. These values can be considered as the clustering coefficient of a single individual. The median of these gives us the clustering coefficient of the whole network:

$$\bar{C} = \frac{1}{n}\sum_{i=1}^{n} C_i.$$

The clustering coefficient is zero for the example shown in Figure 1. Because none of the friends of actors having common friends have relations with one another. If there were relations between friends of an actor, triads would occur. Note that there's nothing wrong with this graph when we look at it. There are actors with varying degrees of centrality, there are circles and hubs. It is simply that the *micro* level patterns in the graph involves no triads. Therefore the absence of triads at the micro level is very common so that it results in a meso level clustering coefficient value of zero.

On the other hand, there is a triangle in the example given in Figure 2, making the clustering coefficient slightly different from 0.

CASE STUDIES ON NETWORK CLUSTERING

Let us see this measure at work on the Florentine families example. The igraph library is not specialized to social science so it uses a different name, transitivity for what we have defined above as clustering coefficient. The network was visualized before, but repeated below for your convenience. Please note that the format conversion problems are removed by simplify() operation here. It is a very typical case where data that you want to use is either not clean or is not in the proper format. It is a common task for the analyst to handle these situations.

A visual inspection reveals that there are a few triads, but most triples consist of two dyadic relations, thus lack ties that would make them triads:

```
require(igraph)
gFlorentine<-simplify(read.graph("data/PadgettMarital.
net",format="paj"))
plot(gFlorentine,
    displaylabels=T,
    layout=layout_with_kk,directed=F
  )
```

Figure 1. A network the clustering coefficient of zero

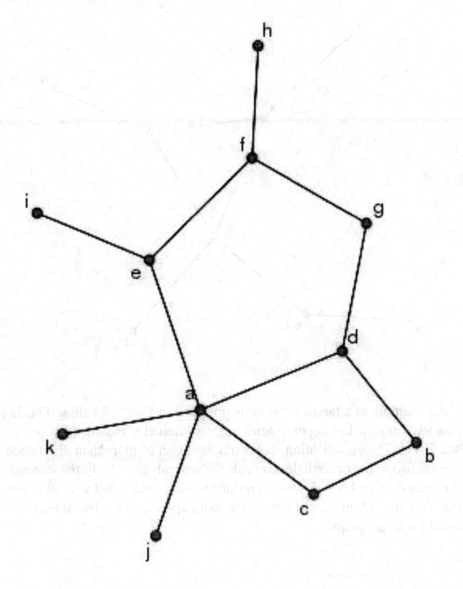

```
transitivity(gFlorentine)
## [1] 0.1914894
```

The transitivity (clustering-coefficient) value is 0.19 which is more on the "less clustered" side. This is consistent with our visual inspection. However, a visual inspection would be of much less use in larger networks.

Figure 2. A network the clustering coefficient of which is different from zero.

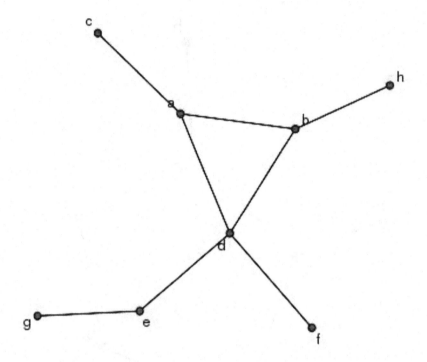

An example of a larger network is provided in Figure 3 below. This is a network composed of dependencies among Internet standards (Gençer and Oba 2011). The visualization shows only a subset of more than 4600 nodes in the network, but nevertheless reveals the general character of the structure. The code provided below would produce a full network, but will take some time. Try out if you have the patience, but expect a much less informative visual for larger graphs.

```
require(igraph)
d<-read.table("data/rfc.edges")
g<-graph_from_adj_list(d)
plot(g,
    displaylabels=T,
    layout=layout_with_fr,directed=F
  )
```

Apart from visualization we can compute the clustering coefficient of the full graph as follows:

Figure 3. İnternet standartları arasındaki bağıntılar

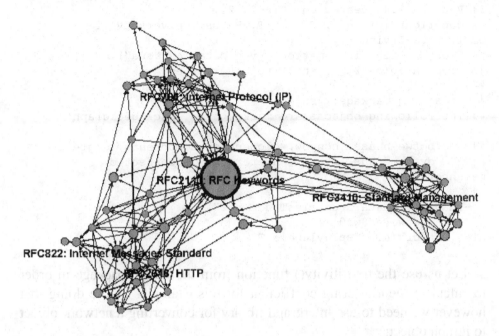

```
require(igraph)
d<-read.table("data/rfc.edges")
g<-graph_from_adj_list(d)
transitivity(g)
## [1] 0.0006431296
```

This is a very small value. This reveals an important characteristic of clustering coefficient measure: it depends on the size of the network. Therefore it cannot be used to compare networks of very different sizes.

Another example is the international trade network. You may consult the source for further explanation on this dataset and find some others.[1] The network is shown in Figure 4 and is much denser compared to similar size examples (such as Krackhardt's advice network, 1987). This time we will use the network library (Butts, 2008) to read the graph dataset because the pajek file contains multiple graphs (for different trade markets). This is just another example showing how important it is to prepare data for an analyst, before proceeding to analysis:

```
require(network)
require(sna)
## Loading required package: sna
```

```
## sna: Tools for Social Network Analysis
## Version 2.4 created on 2016-07-23.
## copyright (c) 2005, Carter T. Butts, University of
California-Irvine
##  For citation information, type citation("sna").
##  Type help(package="sna") to get started.
##
## Attaching package: 'sna'
## The following objects are masked from 'package:igraph':
##
##      betweenness, bonpow, closeness, components, degree,
##      dyad.census, evcent, hierarchy, is.connected,
neighborhood,
##      triad.census
n<-read.paj("data/CountriesTrade.net")
n1 <- n$networks$ws0
plot.network(n1,displaylabels=T)
```

Let us use the transitivity() function from the igraph package in order to calculate the clustering coefficient for this example. Before doing that however we need to use intergraph library for converting a network object to igraph object:

```
require(intergraph)
require(igraph)
```

Figure 4. Clustering in the international trade network.

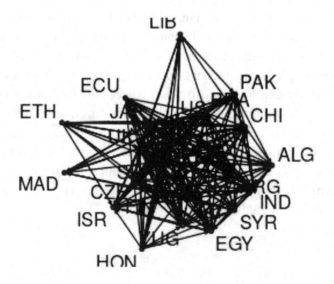

```
require(network)
require(sna)
n<-read.paj("data/CountriesTrade.net")
n1 <- n$networks$ws0
g1<-asIgraph(n1)
transitivity(g1)
## [1] 0.7990654
```

The high clustering coefficient in this example is once again consistent with visual features. the value makes sense as most pairs of countries have some level of trade between.

Varieties in Structure and Their Interpretation

Despite the popularity of the phenomenon of small worlds, the main aspect concerning us is probably the manner of differentiation (e.g. market specialization) of the network structure. This seems to be the most striking difference between network research within the scopes of social sciences and physics/natural sciences (Borgatti et al. 2009). Because physics and natural sciences analyze similar networks using probabilistic methods. As for social sciences, they are concerned with the reasons and outcomes of significant differences and varieties occurring in the global or local structure of the network.

Let us consider software programmers working together online as an example. These programmers exchange information via e-mail. One may ask a variety of *social* question regarding the structural variations and its social effects. For example, how does the position of a programmer within this information exchange network affects or affected by their productivity? Our study regarding this phenomenon (Gençer and Oba 2011) puts forward that the local centrality of a programmer is directly proportionate to their problem-solving performance and that this factor concerning the network structure has an additional effect on the performance regardless of the experience of the programmer.

This is similar to the correlation between centrality and wealth we observed in Padgett's Florentine families. Please note that our examples throughout demonstrate very different social systems. The value of social network analysis lies exactly in its potential to provide a consistent set of measurement apparatus independent of the inherent features of networks. In return, the researcher must develop an understanding of the abstractions used in network metrics to interpret them is various research settings.

Finding Groups: Agglomerative Methods

We have discussed how *grouped* a network is and developed the clustering coefficient to measure that. The measure essentially averages ego-network properties. Thus it was a fiest step from micro level to meso level. In this section we will take another step upwards. To do this we must focus on the level of "groups".

In the most strict sense, a group can be defined as the set of individuals all of which are connected to one another (this corresponds to the "strongly connected component" in graph algorithms). Yet we rarely see such ideal groups in real networks. We need to widen the scope of this definition for real-life scenarios (Wasserman and Faust 1994). A more sensible definition of a group could be "a set of actors whose ties between are more dense compared to their ties with others". In other words a group is an island of ties in a sea of rarity of ties. Research has developed several mathematical notions to develop this understanding of groups into graph based definitions. Some graph-based definitions used frequently in this respect are as follows:

- **Clique** (the strictest definition): Subgraph the members of which are all connected (fully-connected).
- **n-Clique**: Subgraph within which the longest distance between members is *n*. For values bigger than 2, this definition is not socially much meaningful. Furthermore, ties can cross actors outside the group.
- **n-Clan**: n-cliques with a diameter of *n*. This limitation ensures that the geodesy between each couple of actors crosses only group members. Each n-clan is an n-clique.
- **n-Club**: A contrastingly looser clique definition. A subgraph with a diameter of *n*.

All these methods are based on finding groups by connecting individuals with others with whom they are related or, in other words, going upwards.

An example is given in Figure 5, reproduced from Mokken's example (Mokken 1979).

In this example, the following groups consistent with our definition are present:

```
Clique: (a,b,c)
2-Cliques: (a,b,c,d,e) and (b,c,d,e,f)
```

Figure 5. Cliques, clans and clubs.

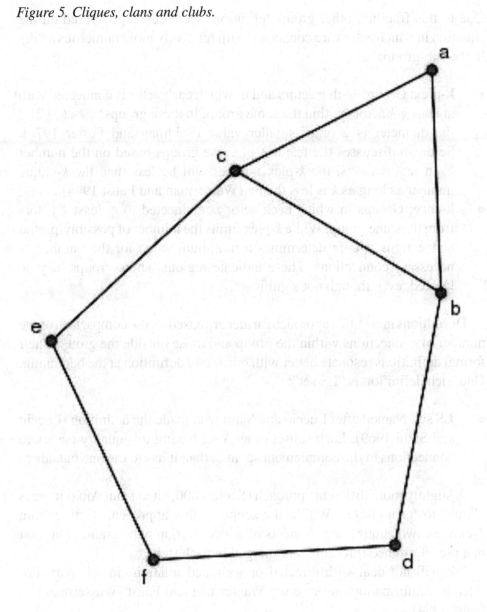

```
2-Clan: (b,c,d,e,f)
2-Clubs: (a,b,c,d), (a,b,d,e), and (b,c,d,e,f)
```

Cliques and other group definitions derived from cliques are more fragile compared to our fuzzy but socially sound definition at the beginning. For example adding a tie between c and d will change the resulting groups entirely.

Due to this fragility, other group definitions were developed based on the situation in which actors are connected with relatively more numerous actors in the sub-group:

- **k-plex**: Groups with g actors and in which each actor is connected with at least g-k actors within the same group. In these groups, if $k<(g+2)/2$ the diameter is 2 or of smaller value (Seidman and Foster 1978). Seidman discusses the features of these groups based on the number k. In real datasets, the k-plex number will be less than the k-clique number as long as k is less than g (Wasserman and Faust 1994).
- **k-core**: Groups in which each actor is connected to at least k actors from the same group. While k-plex limits the number of possibly-partial connections, k-core determines a minimum value for the number of necessary connections. These indicate regions where groups may be located, even though not significant.

Definitions taking this approach further are based on the comparison of the number of connections within the group and those outside the group. Their formal definitions resonate better with our *social* definition at the beginning. One such definition is "LS set":

- **LS set**: Named after Luccio and Sami who made the definition (Luccio and Sami 1969). Each subset of an S set having this quality has more connections to the complement set in S. than it has to the one outside S.

A slightly more different approach (Scott, 2000, cited from Alba) merges cliques to form circles. Within the scope of this approach, starting from 1-cliques, two cliques, the elements of which overlap with a ratio of at least p, a predetermined threshold, are merged in each step.

We will not deal with directed or weighted relations in this part. For reference information on those see Wasserman and Faust (Wasserman and Faust 1994).

Case Studies

We will start with Krackhardt's advice giving network example to apply some of the group finding techniques above. let us remember how we import and convert the dataset. The network was visualized in Chapter 4, Figure 5:

```
require(NetData)
data(kracknets)
edgelist <- as.matrix(  # turn data into edgelist suitable for
igraph
    advice_data_frame[advice_data_frame[3]==1,1:2])
    #a 1 in the third column of data indicates a tie
require(igraph)
g<-graph_from_edgelist(edgelist)
```

We can now use the cliques() function from igraph library to find cliques in this network. Please note that the function treats directed graphs as undirected ones. Also, the function has a different design than our descriptions abov. It finds not *n*-cliques but cliques with number of nodes in the given range. For example to find cliques of size four (slightly more interesting than triads) use the folloqing call. The code chunk limits the output for practical purposes, using head() function:

```
head(
   cliques(g,min=4,max=4),
   n=3)
## [[1]]
## + 4/21 vertices, from c893c68:
## [1]  1  2 15 17
##
## [[2]]
## + 4/21 vertices, from c893c68:
## [1]  1  2 15 18
##
## [[3]]
## + 4/21 vertices, from c893c68:
## [1]  2 14 15 18
```

A related function, largest_cliques() reports the largest size clique(s) in the network:

```
largest_cliques(g)
## [[1]]
## + 10/21 vertices, from c893c68:
##   [1] 15  2 18  1 10 11  3  8  4 20
```

In the Krackhardt example the largest clique has 10 nodes. There is also a function to find maximal cliques, ie. cliques which cannot be extended with another node. For example, now that we know that the largest clique has 10 nodes we can find those with at least nine nodes:

```
maximal.cliques(g, min=9)
## [[1]]
## + 9/21 vertices, from c893c68:
## [1]  5  2 15 20 18  1 11 10 19
##
## [[2]]
## + 9/21 vertices, from c893c68:
## [1]  5  2 15 20 18  1 11 10  8
##
## [[3]]
## + 9/21 vertices, from c893c68:
## [1]  8  1 18 15  3  2  9 11 10
##
## [[4]]
## + 9/21 vertices, from c893c68:
## [1]  8  1 18 15  3  2 20  4 21
##
## [[5]]
## + 10/21 vertices, from c893c68:
##  [1]  8  1 18 15  3  2 20  4 11 10
##
## [[6]]
## + 9/21 vertices, from c893c68:
## [1] 10  1 20 15  3  2 18 11 19
```

Another method in the igraph library attempts a generalized group finding. The method is an agglomerative one (Clauset, Newman, and Moore 2004). In order to demonstrate this algorithm we will use a dataset about the "scene co-appearance" network of the characters in Victor Hugo's famous novel "Les Miserables". The original data is retrieved from the Stanford network database (Knuth 1993). You may apply the group finding algorithm using the fastgreedy.community() function as follows. The function produces a community object, which facilitates querying membership of nodes to communities as demonstrated below:

```
require(igraph)
g <- read.graph("data/lesmiserables.gml", format="gml")
gu<-simplify(as.undirected(g))
comm<-fastgreedy.community(g)
length(comm) #number of communities
## [1] 5
sizes(comm) #sizes of communities
## Community sizes
##  1  2  3  4  5
## 17 13 26 15  6
membership(comm) #vertex membership of communities
```

```
##  [1] 3 3 3 3 3 3 3 3 3 3 3 3 3 3 3 3 3 2 5 5 5 5 5 5 4 4 4 2 4
3 4 4 4 3 3 3
## [36] 3 3 3 3 2 4 4 4 2 3 3 1 1 1 2 2 2 2 2 2 2 2 1 1 1 1 1 1
1 1 1 1 4 4
## [71] 4 4 2 1 1 4 1
modularity(comm)
## [1] 0.5005968
```

Note that the measurement of modularity is somewhat similar to that of transitivity (also called the clustering coefficient):

```
modularity(comm)
## [1] 0.5005968
transitivity(gu)
## [1] 0.4989316
```

The advice here is to use the same method for comparing across different networks. The subtleties between definitions of the two are beyond the scope of our discussion in this text.

Finding Groups: Divisive Methods

Generally speaking, finding groups is computationally exhaustive. We have defined a group as a sub-graph with "more internal connections than external ones". Some concrete estimations corresponding to this general definition were created. However, we need to try all possible sub-graphs in a graph to see if they are compatible with this definition. If there are n nodes in the graph, the number of potential candidates for groups is $n!$. This number exceeds computational capacity in most cases.

For this reason, finding groups is a topic of many studies and many approaches are tried in other to solve this problem. Apart from bottom-up methods combining individuals, as in the previous section, some other methods decipher the network with a top-down approach, i.e. through separation aimed to detect groups. In the method proposed by Newman and Girvan (Newman and Girvan 2004), we start by finding the "betweenness" level of the ties connecting two groups will have the highest values. Betweenness of a tie is defined similar to betweenness of a node in the graph: it is the count of how many times the ties is on the shortest path between any pair of nodes. A tie with a high betweenness is very *connective* in the network. If we leave such ties out, it is very likely that the remaining network will break apart into independent groups. There are also other separation methods (Moody and White 2003) using a similar **divisive** approach.

Dynamics of Intergroup Relations

In addition to both micro-dynamics and the "specialization" dynamic in the network acting as an impetus for withdrawal and isolation of groups, other dynamics cause intergroup relations to be formed. For instance, even though rare in social phenomena, if an individual changes their location/setting (e.g. graduating from high school and enrolling in college, changing cities, changing jobs etc.) they become a part of another group but maintain ties with their former group. Therefore, these individuals moving within such a social network form intergroup networks. In socio-economic phenomena, groups form relations on the basis of inevitable environmental needs such as being supplier and buyer.

Thus, dynamics causing withdrawal/intensification of social clusters (i.e. intra-cluster tie formation) and those forming inter-cluster relations work at the same time. Yet the latter is always limited, meaning that they do not result in the dissolution of groups. Think of it this way: An individual may form relations outside the group from which they get all their social support. But if the number of those relations increase and cause them to neglect in-group relations, this will have a high social cost. For that reason, some feedback mechanisms are present that balance the relations within and outside the group.

EXERCISES

1. Consider the UKfaculty dataset (Nepusz et al., 2008) from igraphdata library.

```
require(igraph)
require(igraphdata)
data(UKfaculty)
plot(UKfaculty)
```

Find the triad census in the network. Then find the clustering coefficient. Are the two results compatible? Compare the coefficient to other examples in the chapter.

Figure 6. UK faculty data set visualization

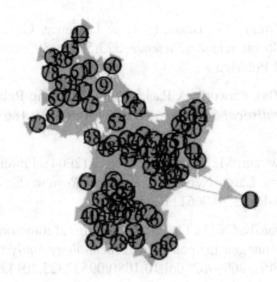

2. Find the clustering coefficient in Zachary's karate club example, which was covered in the previous chapter (Zachary, 1977), and provided by the igraphdata library.
3. Find the largest clique in th UKfaculty network.
4. There are many data sets at http://www-personal.umich.edu/~mejn/ netdata/ . Choose one of them and find the following features for each, then write a commentary comparing the general grouping structure of the network:
    a. Network density
    b. Reciprocity (if directed)
    c. Triad counts
    d. Local centrality distributions
    e. General centrality (betweenness) distributions
    f. Clustering coefficient

REFERENCES

Borgatti, S. P., Mehra, A., Brass, D. J., & Labianca, G. (2009). Network Analysis in the Social Sciences. *Science, 323*(5916), 892–895. doi:10.1126/science.1165821 PubMed

Butts, C. T. (2008). network: A Package for Managing Relational Data in R. *Journal of Statistical Software, 24*(2), 1–36. doi:10.18637/jss.v024.i02 PubMed

Clauset, A., Newman, M. E. J., & Moore, C. (2004). Finding Community Structure in Very Large Networks. *Physical Review. E, 70*(6), 066111. doi:10.1103/PhysRevE.70.066111 PubMed

Gençer, M., & Oba, B. (2011). Organising the digital commons: A case study on engagement strategies in open source. *Technology Analysis and Strategic Management, 23*(9), 969–982. doi:10.1080/09537325.2011.616698

Knuth, D. E. (1993). *Les miserables: coappearance network of characters in the novel les miserables. The Stanford GraphBase: A Platform for Combinatorial Computing.* New York, NY: Springer.

Krackhardt, D. (1987). Cognitive social structures. *Social Networks, 9*(2), 109–134. doi:10.1016/0378-8733(87)90009-8

Luccio, F., & Sami, M. (1969). On the decomposition of networks in minimally interconnected subnetworks. *IEEE Transactions on Circuit Theory, 16*(2), 184–188. doi:10.1109/TCT.1969.1082924

Mokken, R. J. (1979). Cliques, clubs and clans. *Quality & Quantity, 13*(2), 161–173. doi:10.1007/BF00139635

Moody, J., & White, D. R. (2003). Structural cohesion and embeddedness: A hierarchical concept of social groups. *American Sociological Review, 68*(1), 103–127. doi:10.2307/3088904

Nepusz, T., Petróczi, A., Négyessy, L., & Bazsó, F. (2008). Fuzzy communities and the concept of bridgeness in complex networks. *Physical Review. E, 77*(1), 016107. doi:10.1103/PhysRevE.77.016107 PubMed

Newman, M. E., & Girvan, M. (2004). Finding and evaluating community structure in networks. *Physical Review. E, 69*(2), 026113. doi:10.1103/PhysRevE.69.026113 PubMed

Scott, J. (2000). *Social Network Analysis*. Atlanta, Ga.: Sage.

Seidman, S. B., & Foster, B. L. (1978). A graph-theoretic generalization of the clique concept. *The Journal of Mathematical Sociology*, *6*(1), 139–154. doi:10.1080/0022250X.1978.9989883

Simon, H. A. (1962). The architecture of complexity. *Proceedings of the American Philosophical Society*, *106*(6), 467–482.

Wasserman, S., & Faust, K. (1994). Social network analysis: Methods and applications (Vol. 8). Cambridge university press. doi:10.1017/CBO9780511815478

Watts, D. J., & Strogatz, S. H. (1998). Collective dynamics of 'small-world' networks. *Nature*, *393*(6684), 440. doi:10.1038/30918

Zachary, W. W. (1977). An Information Flow Model for Conflict and Fission in Small Groups. *Journal of Anthropological Research*, *33*(4), 452–473. doi:10.1086/jar.33.4.3629752

ENDNOTE

[1]   Retrieved on June 23, 2019, from http://vlado.fmf.uni-lj.si/pub/networks/data/WaFa/default.htm

Chapter 7
Macro–Level Analyses and Dynamics

ABSTRACT

There are few studies on the macro-level dynamics of networks. These dynamics affect the whole network and concern non-local changes. Macro-level changes almost always stem from reasons outside the network. We observe this in its most typical form when the network population increases or decreases in an unusual manner. We cannot correlate such a population change with the relations of actors or the dyad, triad, or intergroup behaviors within the scope of these relations as it was the case in microo r meso-level dynamics. Sudden changes in population in a social network may "disturb" the established order and, therefore, may affect individual communicative relations. Population growth, on the other hand, might result in a revival in terms of other aspects. This chapter these macro-level dynamics.

There are studies which use data for a whole population, thus uncovering features at the macro level. In particular research on populations of organizations fit this level very well. These research focus on clusters of firms, board interlocks of firm management boards, etc.(Gulati, 1995; Kogut, 2012;). Most of these studies, however, are exploratory in its nature. There are much fewer studies on the macro-level dynamics of networks compared to other levels. For this reason this chapter covers a relatively shorter content and examples. Recent availability of extensive and temporal data presents research opportunities at this level.

DOI: 10.4018/978-1-7998-1912-7.ch007

The dynamics at the macro level affect the whole network and concern non-local changes. Due to its nature macro level impact on networks is often caused by dynamics that are beyond the structure of the network itself. In other words they are non-structural, and in a sense fall off the methodological and epistemological interest of network studies easiliy. Nevertheless, it is quite instructive to investigate the macro level as it offers an understanding of the whole network as a system, interacting with other systems.

Macro-level changes almost always stem from reasons outside the network. We observe this in its most typical form when the network population increases or decreases in an unusual manner. We cannot correlate such a population change with the relations of actors or the dyad, triad or intergroup behaviors within the scope of these relations as it was the case in micro or meso-level dynamics.

Sudden changes in population in a social network may "disturb" the established order and, therefore, may affect individual communicative relations. Population growth, on the other hand, might result in a revival in terms of other aspects.

Each social network develops its unique culture and language (Lave and Wenger 1991). The culture and language in question are, in the most basic sense, transferred from the old to the new through processes we name as socialization. This is also valid for a business organization, as it is valid for a family or a neighborhood. For example in a business organization, there are institutionalized points of view and behavioral patterns in success or failure stories told to new employees. The terms used, the meanings attached to words and even the jargon used in the organization form the unique culture of the business. In most cases, there is also a professional culture intertwined with this culture. Similarly, professional culture is indoctrinated both by trainers during vocational education and by "seniors" during internships or the initial years of professional life.

Population changes, such as the admission of a large number of new members into the social group, can cause changes in behavior, hence in structure. For example an increase in population may cause an unexpected decrease in the "communication" skills of the social group. It takes time for newcomers to be integrated into the existing culture. Therefore, in such a case, more communicative efforts, like taking more time to address an issue within the group, may be required. As the literature regarding this topic is limited, in this chapter, I will carry out a discussion over a study of our own that may help us understand the general features of the issue of macro level.

A CASE STUDY: NETWORK OF SOFTWARE DEVELOPERS

Our study with my co-author, Beyza Oba, analyzes the growth stages of a social network for software developers (Gençer and Oba 2011). The social network in focus was created as a result of the strategic decisions and actions of certain software firms. Some trust issues arose in the creation stage; then, some agreements were made to address these problems and some agencies were created for the management of the network. Thus, it is a suitable case to analyze the growth and shrinkages of the network on a macro scale in terms of both (1) the changes in the network sourcing from its relations with the outside world and (2) the impacts of these changes on the social processes within the network.

The Eclipse software was a small commercial project, when it was bought by IBM and turned into an open source software project. Open source software tools are available for everyone. In return, users contribute their own improvements and updates to the software. A technology development model based on such an exchange process, the open source model was seen to be suitable for and then was used in many software projects (e.g. the Android operating system in cell phones, or Mozilla internet browser). IBM found the project to be suitable for development using an open source model and created an online social platform in which developers and users outside its own human resources can be included in the development (see http//www.eclipse.org for info on project and its history).

The part of this network with which the partner companies of IBM are concerned is visualized in Figure 1. I would like to underline that in this case, we use the term "social network" for a network between companies and not between individuals. Ultimately, we can use this term as long as the relations creating the connections within a network are of socio-economic nature.

Inherently, these developments occured outside the social network, e.g. in IBM headquarters. Nevertheless these actions outside the social network directly influence the social network itself. As a result of the steps taken by IBM, the number of people in the professional software development community interested in the Eclipse project increased after a certain point. Some events occurring within the scope of the project, the number of newcomers in the

Figure 1. The Eclipse software technology ecosystem

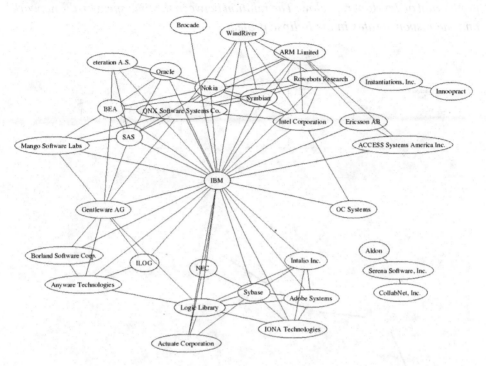

project over the same timeline and, finally, the changes in the total population of the social network are shown in the graphic in Figure 2.

In this graphic, we can see the changes in the population resulting from certain milestones. The graphic on the bottom shows the changing population of the social group over time. We observe that the increases and decreases in the focal population stem from some critical events (in our case, these include the establishment of the Eclipse Foundation, the launch of new versions and the successful communication). Although initially limited, the participation rate in the project sped up following some steps taken by IBM marking that the software will not remain under its control and that it will be accessible by all (e.g. establishing a foundation, giving voting rights to other companies in the foundation etc.). The initial versions of the software were acclaimed by professionals, resulting in a further increase in the number of participants. Naturally, at a certain point, the software reached its peak and shown moderate progress after that point.

The analysis we have made during the study of this social network concerned the contribution level to communicative processes by individuals, the length

Figure 2. Above: The timeline of decisions regarding Eclipse project; middle: The population of developers; below: The relation between the time spent on the network and the response rates in the Eclipse project

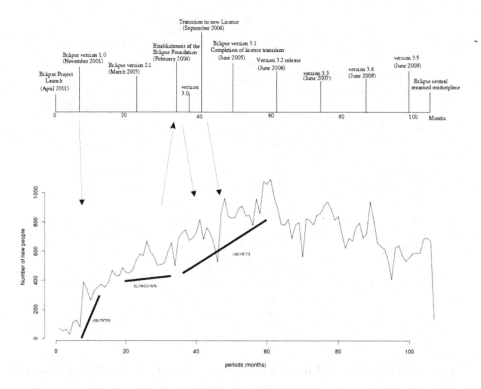

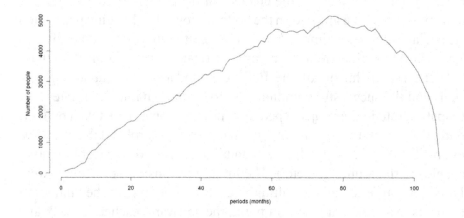

of conversations and the response rate of the messages, in relation to the macro level population changes. The dialogs in question are made via e-mail, therefore they are registered. The responses to an e-mail and the responses to those etc. form a sequence branching like the roots of a tree. We can examine the number of participants in a discussion on a certain topic, the number of reciprocal correspondences (i.e. dialog depth) and whether the correspondences receive any answers (response rate) by looking at these records.

Table 1 shows the results of the analyses regarding whether these measures about communication quality vary in accordance with the macro-level changes, i.e. the changes in population. The outcome was generated using the social network population, as an explaining datum, and the number of individuals joining or leaving the network in every time period on general linear modeling. If the impact of the explaining factor on the participation rate, dialog depth or response rate is shown with an asterisk (*), it means that the impact is supported by the data.

The data above show that the measured parameters are mostly related to changes in population. For example, the dialogs become longer and deeper as the rate of newcomers increase. Because newcomers need to devote more effort and to make more communicative moves to express themselves until they are accustomed to the language of the social group. In contrast, departures from the group cause the communication density to decrease. Newcomers, on the other hand, result in the opposite case. The considerable difference between the blank deviation and surplus deviation show that population changes alone are primary factors affecting communication quality.

Problem-solving performances are also handled within the scope of the same study. Software developers use "bug tracking" systems regarding the product. Many developers contribute efforts and devote some time before a

Table 1. Communication problems arising with the increase in the network population and admissions/departures. Results of linear regression models

Factors	Particip.Lev.	Dialog Depth	Response rate
Population	0.18396***	0.03151**	0.48507***
Participation	0.18362*	0.03863*	0.03760
Departures	-0.42307***	-0.04713*	0.02671
(Coefficient)	0.42706***	0.25498***	1.08455***
(Null deviance)	1.75179	0.11053	0.92148
(Residual dev.)	0.96251	0.08449	0.52658

Table 2. The impact of population change variables on the time spent for problem-solving, shown as coefficients of a linear regression model

Factors	Average problem solving time
Population	-0.010274***
Particip.	0.011281**
Departure	-0.010450**
Contrib.	-0.034462***
(Coeff.)	0.052734***
Null Err.	14.8810
Resid.Err.	4.4532

problem is solved. The results concerning the average problem-solving times are shown in Table 2.

Here, the problem-solving performances of individuals suffer from departures. In contrast, new members increase the performance. However, surprisingly, the performance decreases as the total population increases. The reason for this is thought to be the increasing difficulty of coordination in a larger group.

As another example of macro dynamics, the same study examines the behavior towards newcomers. The graphic below in Figure 3 shows the possibility of responses to newcomer's messages. We can see that the possibility of receiving a response is higher than older members. This means social group behaves kindly towards new members in order to integrate them into the group and try to answer all their questions.

ECONOMIC STRUCTURE ANALYSES AND GIANT COMPONENTS

Some macro-level studies in the research literature are about economic networks. One of the topics of such studies is to reveal the economic structures of countries (Kogut 2012). In these studies, one type of the datasets used is the information on companies in the stock market. Such a study encompasses the main actors directing the national economy.

Economic networks are, of course, intertwined with politics and power relations. Relations in such networks such as partnerships or executive board

Figure 3. The relation between the time spent on the network and the response rates in the Eclipse project

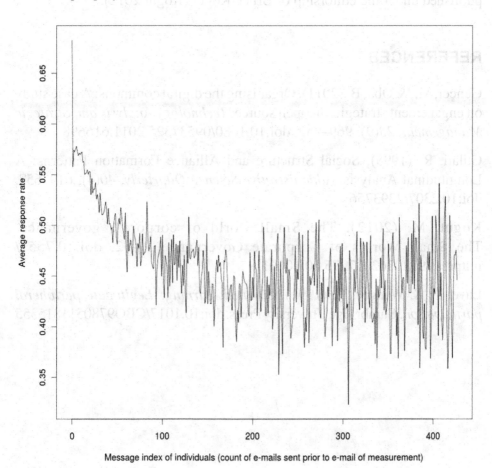

memberships may indicate the functioning of an economy and the level of representation of different stakeholders in the country among other features.

One of the methodical tools used in these analyses is the giant component analysis. The largest group composed of actors all of which are (in)directly connected is called a **giant component**. Sometimes this giant component covers the whole network, possibly signifying an inclusive case with nobody being left behind. However, depending on the features of the network, this might also indicate a monopolistic clique.

In most real networks, there is one giant component covering a significant portion of the network along with other smaller components. A comparison among countries is interesting in terms of understanding to what extent

143

national economies function properly. An ambitious study on this topic was published under the editorship of Bruce Kogut (Kogut 2012).

REFERENCES

Gençer, M., & Oba, B. (2011). Organising the digital commons: A case study on engagement strategies in open source. *Technology Analysis and Strategic Management, 23*(9), 969–982. doi:10.1080/09537325.2011.616698

Gulati, R. (1995). Social Structure and Alliance Formation Patterns: A Longitudinal Analysis. *Administrative Science Quarterly, 40*(4), 619–657. doi:10.2307/2393756

Kogut, M. (2012). The Small world of corporate governance. The Small Worlds of Corporate Governance, 1–52. doi:10.7551/mitpress/9780262017275.001.0001

Lave, J., & Wenger, E. (1991). *Situated learning: Legitimate peripheral participation.* Cambridge University Press. doi:10.1017/CBO9780511815355

Chapter 8
Modeling Network Dynamics:
Random Networks

ABSTRACT

Social relationships and the social networks over these relationships do not occur arbitrarily. However, the random networks dealt with in this chapter are important tools for modeling the networks of these systems. The authors use random networks to understand and to model dynamics regarding the whole social structure. Random network models became the topic of several studies independently from social network analysis in the 1950s. These models were used in the analysis of a wide range of social and non-social phenomena, from electrical and communication networks to the speed and manner of disease propagation. This chapter explores the modeling network dynamics of random networks.

Social relationships and the social networks over these relationships do not happen arbitrarily. But to the extend that they capture general characteristics of a social structure, stochastic models can be very helpful to uncover the social dynamics. Thus, the random networks we will deal with in this chapter are important tools for modeling the networks of social systems.

At this point, we should focus on the concept of being "random". Distribution is one of the fundamental concepts of statistics and the "normal distribution" is its most frequently-used type. Let us first start with remembering some basic concepts that underlie the discussion further below. For instance, let us assume that we weigh the body masses of a sample group selected from

DOI: 10.4018/978-1-7998-1912-7.ch008

a human population. In a "normal" population, these measures form a so called normal distribution. Within this context, we answer the question "what would be the weight of a randomly selected individual from this population" by using a stochastic, or random, distribution. At the individual level, the weight of this individual, naturally, depends on their dietary habits along with genetic and other bodily features; therefore, it is not random at all. Here, stochastic distribution is used to comprehend the features not at the individual level but at the community level, or properly called as the population level. A stochastic model in this case consists of the general shape of distribution ("normal" or "Gaussian" in this case), its location (the mean value) and further particulars of its shape, such as how spread it is (variance, standard deviation) or its deviations (kurtosis, skewness). Overall, a distribution provides us the likelihood of a value of interest (the body weight) of an idividual randomly selected from the population. The plot in Figure 1 shows the distribution in the form of a frequency histogram from a real data set of tree heights in R. Most trees are "normal" as they are around the center, with fewer being extremely tall or very short. The summary values below provide measures for the location and shape of the distribution. A random normal distribution, it turns out, is a good approximation for real phenomena like this one.

```
hist(trees$Height,breaks=)
```

```
summary(trees$Height)
##     Min. 1st Qu.  Median    Mean 3rd Qu.    Max.
##       63      72      76      76      80      87
```

Similar to the example, we use random networks to understand and to model dynamics regarding the whole social structure. In one of the first examples of modeling effort, Moreno and Jennings developed graph-based estimations in order to show that reciprocity in relationships is not arbitrary and that it is a dominant type of social behavior (Moreno and Jennings 1938). In other words they have calculated how much more reciprocity was actually there in a network compared to the baseline of ties (and hence reciprocating ties) being entirely random. Such a way of estimation allows us to indicate whether there is a different kind of reciprocity behavior in a certain social network when compared with others.

Figure 1. A normal distribution

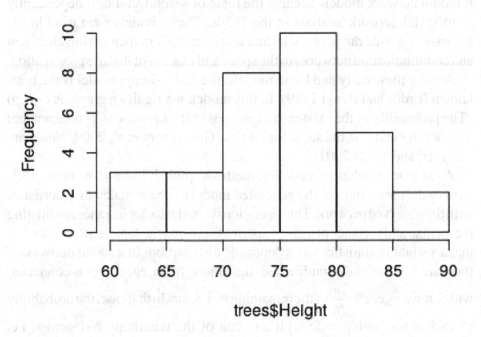

HIstogram of trees$HeIght

BASIC MODELING CONCEPTS AND EARLY
STUDIES ON RANDOM MODELS

Let us name the data collected for a social network as "observed network". In random network modeling, this network is the occurrence of a random event in a probability space (we can say that we are dealing with a non- Bayesian branch of probability). Random network modeling assumes that we know some characteristics of the network (for example, and especially, the number of actors), but we do not know how the network pattern is generated randomly. The purpose of the modeling is to create and test hypotheses concerning this random process (Robins et al. 2007). A variety of models were proposed in the literature.

Erdös-Rényi Model: Scale-Free Networks and the Giant Component

Random network models became the topic of several studies independently from social network analysis in the 1950s. These models were used in the analysis of a wide range of social and non-social phenomena, from electrical and communication networks to the speed and manner of disease propagation.

Among these early and basic models, the Erdös-Rényi model is the best-known (Erdös and Rényi 1959). In this model, we signify a graph as $G(N,p)$. The probability of the existence of any ties in the network, p, is independent of other ties and it is the same for all ties (Goldenberg et al. 2009; Newman, Strogatz, and Watts 2001).

As in other stochastic modeling methods, probabilistic networks models require the parameters of the generated model to be estimated in accordance with the observed network. This operation is similar to, for instance, estimating the median and variance of a given distribution using the sample after assuming that a variant in statistics has a "normal" distribution. In a social network, if there are N actors and n -undirected- ties among them, each actor is connected with, on average, $z = \dfrac{2n}{N}$ of the remaining N-1 actors In that case, the probability of each actor having a tie with any one of the remaining N-1 actors, i.e. probability of any tie being present is calculated as:

$$p = \frac{z}{N-1} = \frac{n}{\binom{N}{2}}$$

A variant of this model is called the Erdös-Rényi-Gilbert model and it uses a formalism in which the number of ties is constant rather than the probability being constant. This model is symbolized as $G(N,E)$. Here, E represents the number of ties. Each of the E ties is selected randomly from the possible $\binom{N}{2}$ ties.

How can we test the hypothesis stating whether such a model corresponds to the real network? Comparing actors and ties and looking at whether the ties in the real network also exist in the random network would not be appropriate. Because the claim regarding the random network we generated and the model parameters are related to the overall distribution of the ties and not to specific ties. Thus, the hypothesis test can only be conducted regarding the features of the whole network.

The most important feature among these is the degree distribution of the actors in the network. In the model mentioned above, the possibility of the degree of an actor being k is p^k. The observed degree distribution is represented as the ratio, or probability of the number of actors with a degree of k (Newman, Strogatz, and Watts 2001):

$$p_k = \binom{N}{k} p^k$$

This distribution is known as the Poisson distribution. The interesting aspect of this degree distribution is that it does not depend on the figures n and N but exclusively on their ratio. Therefore, as long as this ratio remains the same, the degree distribution, one of the basic qualities of the network, does not change. Such random networks are called **scale-free** networks.

One of the most significant results obtained by Erdös and Rényi concerns the **giant component**, another element regarding the quality of the overall network. They used the value $\lambda = pN$ to analyze one of the asymptotic features of the network structure. As the value of λ increases, the density of the ties in the network also increases. The analysis of Erdös and Rényi shows that when the density reaches a certain level, a giant component is formed among the little groups/islets in the network. This change occurred for the threshold value of $\lambda = 1$. We can express this outcome in a more specific manner as follows (Goldenberg et al. 2009). The $O(.)$ notation denotes the order of computaional complexity in computational sciences.

- If $\lambda < 1$ then no component of the network will have a size exceeding $O(\log N)$ for the asymptotic case $N \to \infty$.

- If $\lambda = 1$ then the largest component will have size $O\left(N \cdot \frac{2}{3}\right)$ for the asymptotic case $N \to \infty$.

- If $\lambda > 1$ then there will be a single giant component with size at least $O(\log N)$ for the asymptotic case $N \to \infty$ and there will be no component larger than that.

Although these results are not directly related to social phenomena, they have played a vital role in the analysis of phenomena like disease propagation and paved the way for statistical models in the field of social networks.

Applications and Examples

The igraph package in R can be used to generate Erdös-Rényi networks. The sample_gnp()function in the package is for creating a network denoted as $G(N,p)$. The plots produced by the below code in Figure 2 and 3 show the network and its degree distribution:

```
require(igraph)
g<-sample_gnp(1000,0.0011) #100 actors and p=0.2, pN=2>1
#degree_distribution(g)
plot(degree_distribution(g),type="l",xlab="Degree",ylab="Proba
bility")


plot(g)
```

Figure 2. Random GNP graphs

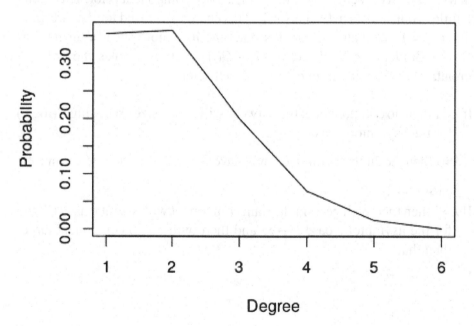

Degree

   To estimate and test the models on the networks we deal with, we can use the ergm library (Hunter et al. 2008) included in the statnet suite (Handcock et al. 2008a). You can practice using the Sampson dataset in the ergm library. This dataset collected in 1969 is the outcome of one of the first studies estimating the change of a social system in time. The data concerns the relations among a group of monks (Sampson 1969), and the network is shown in Figure 4, along with summary information display below the code:

```
require(ergm)
data(sampson)
#help(sampson)
samplike
##   Network attributes:
##     vertices = 18
##     directed = TRUE
##     hyper = FALSE
##     loops = FALSE
##     multiple = FALSE
##     total edges= 88
.##     missing edges= 0
##       non-missing edges= 88
##
##   Vertex attribute names:
##       cloisterville group vertex.names
##
##   Edge attribute names:
##       nominations
plot.network(samplike, displaylabels=TRUE)
```

Figure 3. Random GNP graphs

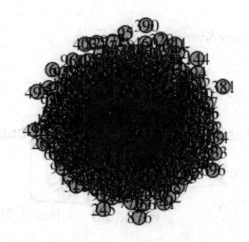

In this directed network, there are 18 actors and 88 ties. Thus, the coefficient in the Erdös-Renyi model can be calculated as $p=88/(18 \cdot 17)=0.2875817$.

```
require(ergm)
data(sampson)
model1 <- ergm(samplike ~ edges)
model1$coef
##      edges
## -0.9071582
```

The ergm function does not give us the expected result, which we have calculated as $p=0.2875817$, but the logit/log-odds value $\log \dfrac{p}{1-p}$. We can reverse this as follows using a function from the boots package.[1]:

```
require(boot)
inv.logit(model1$coef)
##      edges
## 0.2875817
```

1.1 p_1 model

Known as the p1 model in the literature and directly aiming to model networks regarding social phenomena, this model was put forward by Holland and Leinhardt (Holland and Leinhardt 1981). Focusing on directed relationships, it uses the following parameters regarding social behaviors within the context of dyad formation:

Figure 4. Network among Sampson's monks

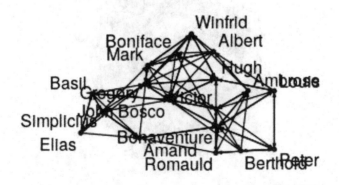

- θ: Base probability of the formation of any tie,
- α_i (diffusion): Tendency of the actor i to form ties with others,
- β_j (popularity): Tendency of other actors to form ties with i,
- ρ_{ij} (reciprocity): Tendency of the relationship between i and j to be reciprocal.

We will use the probability $P(0,0)$ to denote this model. In this notation, $P_{ij}(0,0)$ denotes the probability that there is *not* a relation in any direction between the actors i and j. Similarly, $P_{ij}(1,0)$ denotes the probability of a relationship directed from i to j but not the other way around; $P_{ij}(1,1)$ denotes the probability of a relationship in both directions. The p_1 model denotes these probability statements as follows:

- $\log P_{ij}(0,0) = \lambda_{ij}$,
- $\log P_{ij}(1,0) = \lambda_{ij} + \alpha_i + \beta_j + \theta$,
- $\log P_{ij}(0,1) = \lambda_{ij} + \alpha_j + \beta_i + \theta$,
- $\log P_{ij}(1,1) = \lambda_{ij} + \alpha_i + \beta_i + \alpha_j + \beta_j + 2\theta + \rho_{ij}$,

Since probabilities are denoted as logarithmic functions, tendency parameters essentially give us the probability value when multiplied with one another. In this model λ_{ij} signifies the normalization constant necessary fothe sum of probabilities to be 1.

There are many parameters in the model and the number of parameters increases as the number of actors and dyads increase. It is quite difficult to estimate such a model using an observed network. However, some simplifications within this parameter space are possible (Goldenberg et al. 2009):

1. If all the parameters are set to zero as in $\alpha_i=0$, $\beta_j=0$, $ve\rho_{ij}=0$ it becomes the same as the Erdös-Rényi model apart from the relationship being a directed one.
2. $\rho_{ij}=\rho$, the constant reciprocity model. This is the original p_1 model worked on by Holland and Leinhardt.

Despite constant reciprocity simplification, there are still too many parameters, making estimation and hypothesis verification impossible. Yet the model can only be used to confirm hypotheses regarding reciprocity. It can, of course, also be used to create experimental random networks.

Application We Can Use the ergm Package to Apply the Model as Well

```
require(ergm)
data(sampson)
model2 <- ergm(samplike ~ edges + sender + receiver + mutual)
summary(model2)
##
## ===========================
## Summary of model fit
## ===========================
##
## Formula:   samplike ~ edges + sender + receiver + mutual
##
## Iterations:  2 out of 20
##
## Monte Carlo MLE Results:
##             Estimate Std. Error MCMC %  z value Pr(>|z|)
## edges        -1.1967    0.7143      0   -1.675  0.093872 .
## sender2      -0.2281    0.8970      0   -0.254  0.799251
## sender3       1.4717    1.0055      0    1.464  0.143298
## sender4       0.3984    0.9950      0    0.400  0.688890
## sender5       0.1650    0.9222      0    0.179  0.858020
## sender6       1.2750    1.0253      0    1.243  0.213702
## sender7       0.6450    0.9559      0    0.675  0.499852
## sender8       1.4195    0.9728      0    1.459  0.144514
## sender9       0.6750    1.0171      0    0.664  0.506923
## sender10      2.1157    0.9871      0    2.143  0.032081 *
## sender11      1.4687    0.9918      0    1.481  0.138647
## sender12     -0.1439    0.9375      0   -0.153  0.878009
## sender13     -0.2103    1.0410      0   -0.202  0.839940
## sender14      0.6523    0.9709      0    0.672  0.501686
## sender15      1.9193    0.9725      0    1.973  0.048441 *
## sender16      1.4570    0.9803      0    1.486  0.137201
## sender17      1.2640    1.0108      0    1.251  0.211097
## sender18      1.9185    0.9888      0    1.940  0.052342 .
## receiver2    -0.1932    0.8358      0   -0.231  0.817173
## receiver3    -3.0617    1.0243      0   -2.989  0.002797 **
## receiver4    -1.7898    0.8944      0   -2.001  0.045387 *
## receiver5    -0.8723    0.8500      0   -1.026  0.304754
## receiver6    -3.4633    1.1200      0   -3.092  0.001986 **
## receiver7    -1.6126    0.8853      0   -1.821  0.068534 .
## receiver8    -2.3306    0.9373      0   -2.487  0.012895 *
## receiver9    -2.2268    0.9512      0   -2.341  0.019235 *
## receiver10   -3.9674    1.1129      0   -3.565  0.000364 ***
## receiver11   -3.0687    0.9829      0   -3.122  0.001796 **
## receiver12   -0.9695    0.8638      0   -1.122  0.261706
```

```
## receiver13   -1.4928      0.8771       0  -1.702 0.088762 .
## receiver14   -1.6242      0.8959       0  -1.813 0.069841 .
## receiver15   -3.3264      1.0179       0  -3.268 0.001084 **
## receiver16   -3.0612      0.9957       0  -3.074 0.002109 **
## receiver17   -3.4317      1.1092       0  -3.094 0.001977 **
## receiver18   -3.3338      1.0029       0  -3.324 0.000887 ***
## mutual        3.7183      0.6646       0   5.595  < 1e-04 ***
## ---
## Signif. codes:  0 '***' 0.001 '**' 0.01 '*' 0.05 '.' 0.1 ' '
1
##
##       Null Deviance: 424.2  on 306  degrees of freedom
##  Residual Deviance: 280.0  on 270  degrees of freedom
##
## AIC: 352   BIC: 486    (Smaller is better.)
```

Let us simplify the model and try to focus on estimating the effect of reciprocity:

```
model3 <- ergm(samplike ~ edges + mutual)
summary(model3)
##
## ============================
## Summary of model fit
## ============================
##
## Formula:   samplike ~ edges + mutual
##
## Iterations:  2 out of 20
##
## Monte Carlo MLE Results:
##        Estimate Std. Error MCMC % z value Pr(>|z|)
## edges   -1.7570     0.2042      0  -8.605   <1e-04 ***
## mutual   2.3083     0.4133      0   5.585   <1e-04 ***
## ---
## Signif. codes:  0 '***' 0.001 '**' 0.01 '*' 0.05 '.' 0.1 ' '
1
##
##       Null Deviance: 424.2  on 306  degrees of freedom
##  Residual Deviance: 332.3  on 304  degrees of freedom
##
## AIC: 336.3   BIC: 343.8    (Smaller is better.)
```

Here, you can see that the model is stronger since the AIC value is lower than the previous one. This shows us that the excessive number of parameters creates a serious problem during estimation. Apart from this, we can see that the reciprocity tendency is a strong value of 2.31. Let us convert this logit value into a probability value:

```
require(boot)
inv.logit(2.3107)
## [1] 0.9097593
```

In other words, the probability of a connection in a certain direction being reciprocal is 0.9097593.

p_2 Model

In the p_1 model, values signifying features like diffusion and popularity are considered to be *fixed effects*. These are taken to be determined and estimated through methods such as regression using the observed network. As for the p_2 model (Snijders, Bunt, and Steglich 2010; Brandes, Lerner, and Snijders 2009) these are considered to be random effects. In this model, these values are random, generated from a certain stochastic distribution. In addition to being more suitable and realistic for more scenarios than the previous model, it also allows the use of estimation methods. However, its theory is well beyond the scope of this text.

Exponential p Random Network Model

Since exponential random network models have a complex theoretical framework in terms of probability use and estimation, we will only be able to provide a brief summary in this chapter. You can refer to the article written by Newman et al. for a detailed explanation of such models (Newman, Strogatz, and Watts 2001).

Before describing this model, let us determine a notation. Let Y_{ij} denote a random variable that represents the probability whether there is a relationship between two actors. This variable will take the value $Y_{ij}=1$ if there is a relation between actors i and j and $Y_{ij}=0$ if there is not. Now, let us assume that y_{ij} denotes whether the relation is observed in reality. With this notation let the random and observed variables be denoted as Y and y respectively. In addition let Y denote the set of all possible values y can take.

Unlike the previous models, the p model generalizes the assumption that all possible ties in the network stem from a stochastic distribution. This generalization is formulated as follows:

$$P_{\Theta,Y}(Y=y) = \frac{\exp\{\Theta^T g(y)\}}{\kappa(\Theta,Y)}$$

In the equation above, Θ is the vector consisting of model coefficients and $g(y)$ is the statistics vector examining the features of the observed matrix (Hunter et al. 2008). The denominator $\kappa(\Theta,Y)$ is a normalization coefficient making the sum of the statistical distribution equal to 1:

$$\kappa(\Theta,Y) = \sum_{x\in Y}\exp\{\Theta^T g(y)\}$$

What makes this generalization suitable for real phenomena and interesting is that the observed network, y, is present in both sides of the equation. Therefore, the probability of a network occurring in a certain form depends on the structural features of that particular form.

The size of the value space Y in this model grows rapidly along with the number of actors and reach up to $N=2n(n-1)$. Furthermore, as it is a model with both sides connected to each other, it can only be used with certain simulation methods. The use of an effective simulation in this respect has an extensive literature dedicated to it and will not be covered here.

Use of Models for Random Network Generation

We have seen how models expressed with ergm notation before in this chapter, and how the parameters of these models are estimated on the observed network. Such models can be used later to generate similar artificial networks. Let us begin by creating a model, once again using the Sampson dataset:

```
require(ergm)
data(sampson)
model4 <- ergm(samplike ~ edges + sender + receiver + mutual)
```

Now, with the fitted model in hand we can generate a network out of the model. The result is shown in Figure 5:

```
artificial4 <- simulate(model4)
plot(artificial4)
```

157

Note the face similarity of the artificial network to the original one in Figure 4. Beyond visual similarity, we can also compare network statistics. The example below produces the edge count, mutual edge count, part of degree distribution and triangle statistic using the R ergm package. These statistics are produced for both the original Sampson network and the artificial random network created using its model. The rbind function below binds the two to each other for better visual inspection:

```
rbind(
  summary(samplike ~ edges + mutual + idegree(0:3) + triangle),
  +
  summary(artificial4 ~ edges + mutual + idegree(0:3) +
triangle)
)
##      edges mutual idegree0 idegree1 idegree2 idegree3
triangle
## [1,]  88     28      0        0        3        5
193
## [2,]  69     16      2        1        6        1
103
```

The output of this example demonstrates both strengths and weaknesses of this modeling technique. The dyadic level statistics (edge and mutual edge count) are very similar. However in the remainder of these statistics the similarity is more limited than one would expect. The dyadic level lends itself much better to modeling in a relatively small network like this one. Triad count is less precise. However, higher level (i.e. global level) features such

Figure 5. Random network created from a fitted model

as degree distribution is not approximated well at all by the model. Problems regarding the way the estimation quality of the estimated model is quantified are the topics of discussion in the literature (Hunter et al. 2008; Handcock et al. 2008a). Generally, if detecting and developing the estimation quality are necessary, a control like the one above is required. The key problem in these modeling efforts is that the conditions for estimation quality is not theoretically well understood as in the case of conventional statistics, e.g. for linear regression. Furthermore the estimation becomes computationally complex quickly as the size of the modeled network grows.

Dynamic Models

The random network models discussed in the previous sections are usually static. This means that they are the models of a social network structure that is stationary over time, or it represents only a certain instance of it. They do not concern the changes of the social structure over the course of time. More precisely, as random network ties are generated one-by-one in all the models, we can characterize this as pseudo-dynamic. Yet none of these static models describe the compatibility of the observation data on a real social system collected over time and the model that represents it. They only attempt to explain the structural features in a given instance.

The dynamic models to be discussed here take random modeling further and claim to explain social dynamics. For example, one of the primary concerns regarding static models in the previous chapter is that they ignore the fact that relations in real social networks can terminate just like they start. However, none of the static models take this into consideration. Besides, most of these static models are not able to generate scale-free networks as observed in real social networks (Barabási and Albert 1999).

In the sections below, some of the mathematical articulations of the discussed models are presented without much explanation of their trace of development. This is due to the scope of our text. The aim of including the formulas here is merely to give the reader a sense of similarities and differences of their conceptualizations, rather than engage in the mathematical theories that underlie them. Such a sense should be sufficient for making informed decision regarding the models to use in social research.

Barabasi-Albert Preferential Attachment Model

One of the first examples of dynamic models, the Barabási and Albert model (Barabási and Albert 1999) is based on modeling of preferential features in tie establishing behavior. This model is specifically designed to generate a scale-free network. According to the model, there are N_0 non-connected actors in the network in the beginning. In each temporal stage, a new actor is added to the network and this new actor has $m \leq N_0$ ties with other actors. The key behavioral assumption in this model is that the probability of this new actor being connected with an existing other is correlated with the degree centrality of the other actor. Therefore, the other actors with whom those m ties of the new actor will be established is selected based on the following probability distribution:

$$p_i = \frac{\sigma_i}{\sum_j \sigma_j}$$

Here, σ_i denotes the degree of the other actor. Essentially, this model represents a social network starting with a small group and then growing with a behavioral pattern such as "the rich getting richer" or "the popular becoming ever more popular".

The Barabasi-Albert model generates a network in which the degree centralities of actors have a **power law distribution**. In different studies (Goldenberg et al. 2009), the power distribution coefficient of the networks created according to the original model was calculated as $\gamma_{BA}=2.99\pm0.1$. Other variants of this model that can take the power distribution coefficient as a parameter were also developed in the literature.

The following example shows the way such a random network can be generated, shown in Figure 6. You can try the same with a larger network and see when the network is large and dense, how visualization algorithms fail to produce a much useful result. Degree distribution is also shown and exposes stuctural features much decisively.:

```
require(igraph)
g <- sample_pa(1500)
plot(g,vertex.label=NA)
hist(log(degree_distribution(g)))
```

Many variations of the Barabasi-Albert model emerged later on. For instance, one of these variations called the RTG model provides a significant part of the features observed in real networks (Goldenberg et al. 2009).

Figure 6. A random network created with Barabasi-Albert model

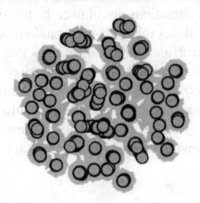

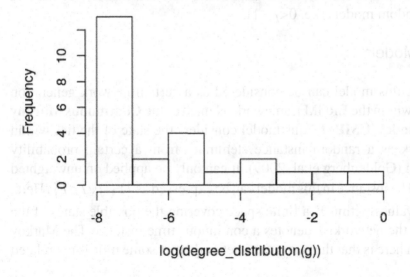

The Small Worlds Model

Proposed by Watts and Strogatz (Watts and Strogatz 1998), this model can be considered as pseudo-dynamic. Essentially, it is a random network generation model developed to prove that the *clustered* structure of real networks cannot be observed in random networks.

This model starts with a **regular network** structure and makes random alterations on it. These alterations disconnect the ties in the network shaped like a regular ring and places them between random actors. We start with a ring-shaped network structure with N nodes and k ties per node. Then, each tie is disconnected with a probability of p and rewired to a new and random place (i.e. pair of actors). If p increases from 0 towards 1, this becomes an Erdös-Rényi-Gilbert model because then all ties would be rewired randomly. The code below produces a regular network using the make_lattice() function in igraph library, then rewires the ties with rewire() applied with each_edge() modifier function:

```
require(igraph)
g <- make_lattice(c(16,1,1), circular=TRUE) # make_
ring(10)#sample_smallworld(1, 10, 5, 0.05)
g2<-rewire(g, each_edge(p = .2, loops = FALSE))
plot(g,layout=layout_in_circle)
plot(g2,layout=layout_in_circle)
```

Watts and Strogatz used this model in order to prove that real networks are not random and can be placed somewhere between entirely-regular and entirely-random models (i.e. $0<p<1$).

Markov Models

Essentially, this model can be considered as a certain network generation procedure within the ERGM framework. Named as the **Continuous Markov Process Model (CMPM)**, this model considers the state of the ties within the network as a random instance stemming from a certain probability distribution (Goldenberg et al. 2009). It can only be applied on unweighted networks. The instance in this model can be expressed as $\{Y(t) \lor t \in T\}$. Here, $Y(t)$ takes values within Y, a finite space covering the possible states of the ties within the network. T denotes a continuous time instance The Markov assumption here is that the state of the network after some time is not related

Figure 7. A demonstration of Wattz and Strogatz rewiring

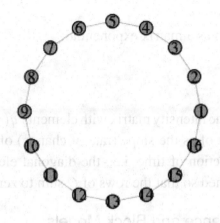

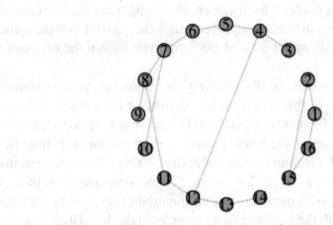

to the past but to the current state and the time period following this current state. If t_a is the present time and t_b is a future time instance, probability of transition to a certain state is expressed as:

$$Pr(t_b - t_a) = Pr\{Y(t_b) = \tilde{y} \vee Y(t_a) = y\}_{y, \tilde{y} \in Y}$$

This can be written as a matrix exponential:

$$Pr(t) = e^{tQ}$$

where Q is known as the intensity matrix with elements $q(y, \tilde{y})$. The elements $(y, \tilde{y})$ can be thought of as the slope (rate of change) of the probability of state change as a function of time, i.e., the diagonal elements $q(y, \tilde{y})$ are negative and are defined so that the rows of Q sum to zero.

Structural Equivalence and Block Models

All networks discussed throughout the book were based on the ties between components (i.e. actors). However, in some branches of social sciences, we concern ourselves with certain social positions (roles) and the relationships formed among these roles rather than particular individuals and their relationships. For example, in economics, we deal with the relationships between enterprises and the investment capital financing them; in political economy, we concern ourselves with the relationships between employers and employees. In this context, for instance, there might not be a structural connection between two different employers since they do not hire the same workers, but we can talk about a tie of the same type within the economic system.

Ties between individuals expire relatively more quickly, yet ties among social roles are related to the long-term functioning of the system and they change relatively less frequently (Scott 2000). The structure between roles do not change much even if the actors change, only the actors fulfilling the said roles are altered (Cross and Prusak 2002; Burt 2005). Naturally, systems are also subject to changes in the long term. For example, the roles of taxi drivers, plate owners, and customers within the urban transport system are completely altered with the entrance of an e-trade model like Uber.

Structural Equivalence

The presence of roles within a social systems indicate the structural equivalence of different individuals in the same roles. This equivalence reveals itsel in that two individuals in the same roles form similar relations with individuals with similar roles.

Structural equivalence is, of course, closely connected with the cultural or organizational norms and institutions, as the source of the equivalence. If there are no norms regarding a certain role or if such norms are weakened, equivalence may not be observed in the relationships of the individuals playing the role in question.

For example, in the 1960s, the changes in the role of women, as it was the case for many societal roles, altered the socio-economic role of women in Western societies. Meanwhile, while gender roles were disintegrated (at least to some extend), labor-capital relations or class roles were strengthened further in the same period.

In contrast, finding patterns in relationships is important in order to determine developing social roles and conduct more profound studies. Rising values and systemic relations might not have become cultural or organizational norms yet, but the path created by change will create a certain pattern, a trace on the structure.

Proposing one of the best descriptions of structural equivalence and the term block-model, the study of Lorrain and White (Lorrain and White 1971) gives a description of the matrix configuration. According to the study, if the sociomatrix containing data regarding a social system can be formed with relationships (e.g. values of 1) remaining on certain blocks within the matrix and gaps (e.g. values of 0) on other cells by reorganizing its rows and columns. By this way we can uncover blocks and their structural equivalence for the social structure in question.

An example of this phenomena is given in the study of Glückler and Panitz (Glückler and Panitz 2016). Within the scope of their study, data concerning the creation, collection, and use stock images were collected and parallelisms between systemic roles and the structure were examined. The visuals they provide demonstrate that there is a systemic connection between distributors and collectors. However, editors tend to form ties among themselves while distributors and collectors do not form any relationships with each other as they are competitors. Glückler and Panitz' work demonstrates these role relations in the form of a network as well as a graph.

Another good example is provided by a study on partisanship (Lazer et al. 2009). This study provides and example concerning the network of links between opposing political blogs in the USA. The network demonstrates a structure where two political camps tend to clamp into themselves, with few bipartisan blogs abridging the two groups.

As you can see from these examples, block structure is specific to the social system. The strength of roles (e.g. how clearly separated the matrix blocks are) can be very useful in undestanding the strength of the roles.

Block-Model Definitions and Methods Application

In light of the explanations above, we can speak of two concepts and two corresponding structural features in order to define block-models:

- (Roles) a fragmentation in which actors are separated into isolated clusters, and
- (Relationships among roles) a description regarding whether there is a tie for each dyad in the fragment

Moving from the description here, we can consider a block- model as a hypothesis concerning the macro-level tie structure of the social network, i.e. the structure among the roles in the network. There are many methods for finding this structure. Some of these methods include the CONCOR algorithm and Non-negative Matrix Factorization (NMF).

Applications

Our first application below is creating an artificial network with predefined roles. A synthetic network which has two roles is produced with the code below and shown in Figure 8. The code uses a hand coded 2 by 2 matrix containing preferences of tie formation within or between the two roles. In this example the individuals in each role tend to form ties with individuals from their own role, with differing tendencies of 0.1 and 0.05 for the two roles. They are less likely to form ties with other roles (each 0.002). the two roles show up in the visualized graph as two lumps. Note that the sample_sbm() function explicitly sets the populations of the roles as 30 and 70 respectively in the example below:

```
require(igraph)
## Two groups with not only few connection between groups
pm <- cbind(c(.1, .002), c(.002, .05))
g <- sample_sbm(100, pref.matrix=pm, block.sizes=c(30,70))
plot(g,vertex.label=NA)
```

Note that in this example the strength of role division or segregration of roles is inscribed into network generation and very strong.

The second example below does the reverse: it finds the blockmodel from a real network. Our example here is Krackhardt's advice giving network we have examined before (Krackhardt, 1987). The code first uses the equiv.clust() function from the sna library to form a hierarchical clustering of network nodes. This clustering by default uses correlation of two nodes' rows in the adjacency matrix as the similarity value in clustering. The clustering shown in Figure 9 shows the two clusters nicely, corresponding to roles in the network: the advice givers and advice takers.

```
require(sna)
require(igraph)
g2<-read.graph("data/HigTech-advice.dl",format="dl")
n2 <- network(get.adjacency(g2))
eq<-equiv.clust(n2)
plot(eq)
```

The blockmodel() frunction can be used to find and display the matrix representation of relations between roles as below, producing the matrix visual in Figure 10. By inspecting the clustering dendrogram, it is appropriate to cut it at around 25, producing two blocks indicated by dotted lines in the blockmodel matrix. We can see in the matrix that most ties are from role 2 to role 1 (the dark area on bottom-left):

Figure 8. A random graph using a a blockmodel

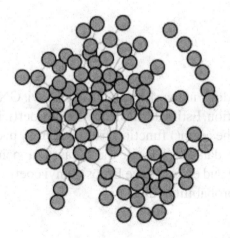

Figure 9. Clustering of individuals in Krackhardt's dataset

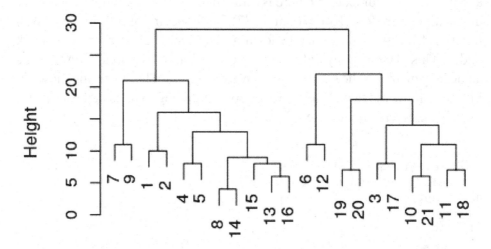

Cluster Dendrogram

as.dist(equiv.dist)
hclust (*, "complete")

```
#Form a blockmodel cutting the clustering at height=5
b<-blockmodel(n2,eq,h=25)
plot(b)
```

EXERCISES

1. Produce a random network with Erdös-Rényi GNP model. Find its degree distribution. Estimate the Erdös-Rényi coefficient of your random network with the ergm() function from the ergm package.
2. Use the karate dataset (consult the datasets appendix for finding it; Zachary, 1977) and estimate the Erdös-Rényi coefficient. Convert from logit value to probability value.

Figure 10. A blockmodel visualized in the sociomatrix

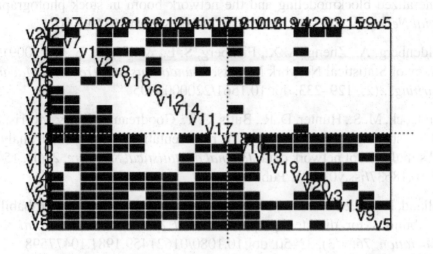

Relation - v1

3. Estimate the *p* model for the karate dataset. Then make a simulated random network from your model. Plot and identify similarities nad differences. How do ypu interpret the differences, if any?
4. Create a random network using Barabasi-Albert model.
5. Find and plot a clustering for the karate dataset. Then choose a clustering height cutoff and produce a blockmatrix.

REFERENCES

Barabási, A. L., & Albert, R. (1999). Emergence of scaling in random networks. *Science, 286*(5439), 509–512. doi:10.1126/science.286.5439.509 PubMed

Brandes, U., Lerner, J., & Snijders, T.A.B. (2009). Networks Evolving Step by Step: Statistical Analysis of Dyadic Event Data. 2009 Advances in Social Network Analysis and Mining, 200–205.

Burt, R. S. (2005). *Brokerage and Closure*. Oxford University Press.

Cross, R., & Prusak, L. (2002). The people who make organizations go–or stop. Networks in the Knowledge Economy, 248-260.

Erdös, P., & Rényi, A. (1959). On Random Graphs, I. *Publicationes Mathematicae (Debrecen)*, *6*, 290–297.

Glückler, J., & Panitz, R. (2016). Unpacking social divisions of labor in markets: Generalized blockmodeling and the network boom in stock photography. *Social Networks*, *47*, 156–166. doi:10.1016/j.socnet.2016.07.002

Goldenberg, A., Zheng, A. X., Fienberg, S. E., & Airoldi, E. M. (2009). A Survey of Statistical Network Models. *Foundations and Trends in Machine Learning*, *2*(2), 129–233. doi:10.1561/2200000005

Handcock, M. S., Hunter, D. R., Butts, C. T., Goodreau, S. M., & Morris, M. (2008). statnet: Software tools for the representation, visualization, analysis and simulation of network data. *Journal of Statistical Software*, *24*(1), 1548. doi:10.18637/jss.v024.i01 PubMed

Holland, P. W., & Leinhardt, S. (1981). An exponential family of probability distributions for directed graphs. *Journal of the American Statistical Association*, *76*(373), 33–50. doi:10.1080/01621459.1981.10477598

Hunter, D. R., Handcock, M. S., Butts, C. T., Goodreau, S. M., & Morris, M. (2008). ergm: A package to fit, simulate and diagnose exponential-family models for networks. *Journal of Statistical Software*, *24*(3).

Kogut, M. (2012). The Small world of corporate governance. *The Small Worlds of Corporate Governance*, 1–52. doi:10.7551/mitpress/9780262017275.001.0001

Krackhardt, D. (1987). Cognitive social structures. *Social Networks*, *9*(2), 109–134. doi:10.1016/0378-8733(87)90009-8

Lazer, D., Pentland, A., Adamic, L., Aral, S., Barabási, A. L., Brewer, D., ... Jebara, T. (2009). Computational social science. *Science*, *323*(5915), 721–723. doi:10.1126/science.1167742 PubMed

Lorrain, F., & White, H. C. (1971). Structural equivalence of individuals in social networks. *The Journal of Mathematical Sociology*, *1*(1), 49–80. doi: 10.1080/0022250X.1971.9989788

Newman, M. E., Strogatz, S. H., & Watts, D. J. (2001). Random graphs with arbitrary degree distributions and their applications. *Physical Review. E*, *64*(2), 026118. doi:10.1103/PhysRevE.64.026118 PubMed

Robins, G., Pattison, P., Kalish, Y., & Lusher, D. (2007). An introduction to exponential random graph (p*) models for social networks. *Social Networks*, *29*(2), 173–191. doi:10.1016/j.socnet.2006.08.002

Sampson, S. F. (1969). *A Novitiate in a Period of Change: An Experimental and Case Study of Social Relationships*. Academic Press.

Scott, J. (2000). *Social Network Analysis*. Atlanta, Ga.: Sage.

Snijders, T. A., Van de Bunt, G. G., & Steglich, C. E. (2010). Introduction to stochastic actor-based models for network dynamics. *Social Networks*, *32*(1), 44–60. doi:10.1016/j.socnet.2009.02.004

Watts, D. J., & Strogatz, S. H. (1998). Collective dynamics of 'small-world'networks. *Nature*, *393*(6684), 440. doi:10.1038/30918

Zachary, W. W. (1977). An Information Flow Model for Conflict and Fission in Small Groups. *Journal of Anthropological Research*, *33*(4), 452–473. doi:10.1086/jar.33.4.3629752

ENDNOTE

[1]   http://www.wiki-zero.net/index.php?q=aHR0cHM6Ly9lbi53aWtpcG VkaWEub3JnL3dpa2kvTG9naXQ accessed on 19 June 2018

Section 3
Contemporary Applications and Methods

Chapter 9
Social Capital and Social Embeddedness

ABSTRACT

The term social capital embodies a concept that emphasizes recent acknowledgement of how important social structure is to business life and how economic and business activity is embedded within the social structure. This rather theoretical chapter summarizes and exemplifies these concepts. This theory proves important in interpreting structural features whose analysis are covered in other chapters.

The dynamics we have discussed so far show that the structure of social networks typically consists of several relatively closed groups. We have seen in the chapter concerning microdynamics that the internal ties of these groups tend to increase and get stronger in time, making the group even more closed.

Some individuals, on the other hand, belong to multiple groups due to their tasks or personal inclinations. These individuals act as bridges connecting groups. A bridge connecting two groups usually goes through two individuals, one from each group in question. Sometimes, however, a third person or an intermediary might also be present. Figure 1 shows an example where there are two groups and two connections between them. One of these connections passes by n11, an intermediary. This intermediary does not belong to any of the two groups. The other connection is a direct one going through n11 and n2, both of whom belong to one group.

DOI: 10.4018/978-1-7998-1912-7.ch009

The structural features of these connections can be revealed to an extent using measurement methods we have seen before, such as betweenness centrality. For example one can measure betweenness of a tie, similar to betweenness of individuals, in order to find out ties that connect groups in a network. There are also some alternative measurement methods based on topographic analogies such as "peaks" and "bridges" (Scott 2000).

Social and economic processes are not independent of this structure, thus the term **social embeddedness** of socio-economic activity. This can be seen in a variety of cases: brokers exploiting market opportunities, or implications of (not)fulfilling a verbal commitment embedded into an actor's structural position. Numerous social norms such as cultural stereotypes concerning the limits of gender roles manifest themselves in accordance with the position of the individual within the social structure and influence socio-economic processes. In other words, these socio-economic processes are not independent of the social structure surrounding the individual; in fact, they are embedded within this structure (Granovetter 1985).

In this chapter, we will examine social embeddedness based on certain theories, some of which are controversial, mainly related to the functioning and nature of the processes. We will not introduce new quantitative metrics

Figure 1. Connections between groups

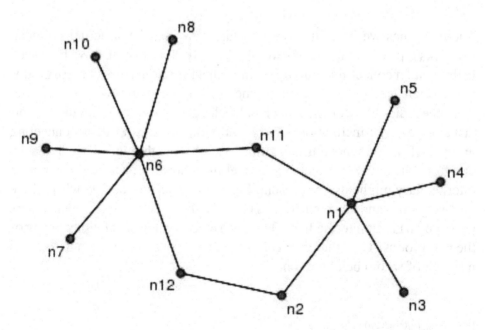

or measurement methods. But measurement methods we have previously analyzed may be used to that end, depending on the focus of examination, and we will be pointing to these uses. While the concept of social capital which we introduce below is very useful, there is no consensus on its measurement. Here we suggest uses of measures we have seen in the previous chapters but there are many ways discussed in the literature (Täube, 2004).

Social Embeddedness

How and to what extent structural patterns affect individuals living and working within the social structure? As far as this question goes, there are disagreements and polarizations gradually becoming more evident between economics, one of the oldest and most significant disciplines among social sciences, and other fields such as anthropology, social psychology, and sociology. Despite such differences, the common point of view is that the position within the social structure definitely affects socio-economic behaviors (Granovetter 1985; Borgatti et al. 2009). Discordances mainly concern the degree of this effect.

Let us consider Moody and White's study (Moody and White 2003) as an example research on social embeddedness. One of the datasets used within the their study consists of information on more than 4000 high school students. An outcome of the study is that "if the student is well connected to the social network, they have an increased sense of belonging to the school". This shows us that the perception of the student regarding the quality of their school is reltively independent of educational quality or physical facilities; rather, it is a matter of social integration, i.e. a configuration of embeddedness.

An important inference based on such findings is that a "community" like, for instance, a school is not a uniform social space. Individuals are connected to the community to varying extents. Therefore, we cannot perceive such a social mass as a homogeneous group within the boundary separating the network from the outside world. In terms of belonging, there are significant differences between the individuals in a central position within the social group and those on the periphery.

Similarly, informal social networks within a company should not be regarded as homogeneous structures (Cross and Prusak 2002). Instead, it would be appropriate to consider the center as a stricter, more closed and stationary structure while the periphery as an more transient one that is more sensitive to external factors. For instance, this becomes more apparent as far as innovation, a crucial factor for corporate success, is concerned. Individuals that are on the "periphery" of the informal network of a company are more prone to hearing about or coming up with innovative ideas. Some name these people as "idea scouts" (Whelan et al. 2011). However, these ideas, no matter how valuable they are, will not have any effect unless they are transferred to the decision makers in the central positions. If there are individuals capable of making this transfer and having connections with both innovative younger people on the periphery and the decision makers at the center (called idea connectors by Whelan), it becomes possible to sustain the innovative process successfully and consistently. Thus, such an outlook indicates that successful innovation management is not only about keeping a topic on the agenda and allocating resources but also about understanding the informal social network and devoting necessary efforts to transform the structure accordingly.

Social Embeddedness and Economic Theories

One of the fundamental assumptions of classical economic theories beginning with Adam Smith (Smith 2006) is that individuals act rationally in terms of their economic activities. According to this view the individual (including company managers) makes economic decisions solely based on their own interests: where to work, which product to purchase... As a result of this assumption, it is presumed that one acts independently of their social environment and circumstances. Hoever, common cases in which one purchases a product from a close relative even though the sale price is higher than the average, or an employer who hires fellow townspeople although they are not qualified for the job contradict this theoretical assumption. The main function of this assumption in Smith's theory is as follows: if everyone looks after one's interests, the economic system (or the "invisible hand" as described by Smith) will allow the allocation of resources to be in the way that satisfies everyone the most.

However, field research regarding economic systems disproves the unconditional validity of this general assumption. Coleman (Coleman 1988) gives the example of New York diamond market in this respect. The market in question is entirely dominated by the Jewish community. There is a huge volume of marital connections among the economic actors in the market and most of these actors live in the same neighborhood or go to the same synagogues. This means a closed and intensely connected social group. The diamond market of the city can only function on this social ground. Because these traders send valuable gemstones to one another without any written contracts. They exchange expertise and mediate among each other; these gemstones are then sent back to their rightful owners without any hindrances (e.g. stealing, swapping with less valuable ones). This process is sustained only through the trust brought about by the social fabric. The execution of such processes without this social background would frequently require legal contracts, resulting in a slowed down and more expensive and inefficient form of "trade". The market works on a communitarian basis as much as it does on a selfish basis.

Many individuals in managerial roles in economic life can recall similar experiences. For instance, the gold market in Istanbul functions in a similar way: with an increased facility stemming from a nuclear social structure usually consisting of certain religious communities. Likewise, in most economic sub-systems, if not all, religious or ethnic communities are integrated with the way the market works. Therefore, Adam Smith's assumption of absolute and universal rationality begs for a comprehensive review. On the other hand, as Granovetter reminds us (Granovetter 1985), one must be careful while moving towards the other end of the critical scale. In other words individuals should be considered as operating on a calculated balance of rational self-interest and social consequences of economic acts.

A second assumption used alongside economic rationality concerns "the possession of all relevant knowledge" required for a rational decision. This assumption claims that, for instance, a businessperson is familiar with every possible method for producing a machine and chooses the most logical one among them. A serious critique of this was made by Hayek (Hayek 1945). Hayek states that the information necessary to calculate what is the best course of action is never entirely accessible by a single individual, firm, or organization. He mainly elaborates on this as a critique of communism: he alleges that the structure based on the central management of an entire economy as in the Soviet system is not feasible and will fail. On the other hand, he comes up with the principle of "local administration" as a crucial outcome of his critique. Decisions within the economic system (e.g. decisions regarding production in a factory) should be taken by those that are the closest to the issue. According to Hayek's argument, every decision is "incomplete", but leaving these decisions to the upper management who is not quite close to the problem and, consequently, to relevant information about it will result in less rational decisions. Indeed, especially in innovation-oriented companies where each problem is a novel one, this becomes common practice and brings about success.

Transforming this critique into a comprehensive framework, Simon and March theorize the phenomenon of **bounded rationality** (Simon 1955; March and Simon 1958; Cyert and March 1963; Cyert, Kumar, and Williams 1993). Economic rationality is always bounded and economic decisions are made based on incomplete information. Simon takes the same critique and comes up with the concept of "**satisficing**": if a manager is not able to access to all the necessary information for the "best" solution, they must settle with any solution eliminating the problem. When we render this theoretization back to structure we see that management structure of organization must be evaluated on the basis of its qualities to inform the manager, and not only to simplify power transfer structure.

Furthermore, apart from Hayek's critique, it is imperative to address the effect of "institutionalism". Behaviors institutionalized based on the local factors and the culture significantly determines what is acceptable. For example, when compared with Anglo-Saxon countries where hiring and firings on the grounds of "necessity" are considered to be usual practice, such decisions will be heavily biased on the culture and and social structure in countries like Japan and France where a different employment institution works.

DISTANT TIES: SOCIAL CAPITAL AND STRUCTURAL HOLES

One of the most cited studies concerning the impacts of individuals living in closed social islets, particularly regarding economic life, was conducted by Mark Granovetter (Granovetter 1973). Focusing on the employment-seeking process of individuals, the study unexpectedly showed that "distant ties" (in Granovetter's words, **"weak ties"**) are more influential in this economic phenomenon. One's close ties are usually within the same closely-knit environment(s). Thus, for example, there will not be any significant differences between the information provided by two or five of your friends from the same group. Because all of them gather their knowledge from the same information circulating within the group. It is not quite possible to obtain much novel information from a third friend after consulting two friends from the same group. In contrast, seeking the help of a distant acquaintance might prove to be useful in discovering brand new information. Such a person with completely different connections to different social groups will provide you "new" information more so than your close friend circle.

Generally speaking, observations regarding the impact of the presence or absence of social ties on economic success (performance) have lead to the frequent use of the concept of **"social capital"** (Coleman 1988). The preference for the word "capital" is very significant since it underlines a necessity for a "capital" similar to financial capital or human resources in order for the economic process in social relationships to function correctly. Indeed, research studies on Silicon Valley (Castilla et al. 2000), for instance, reveal that the success of the industrial region in question stems from the presence of a closely-connected partnership and acquaintance network among the companies and their founders as much as from other factors. If, for example, some individuals in Silicon Valley are founders of and consultants for two or more companies, they act as a bridge of trust among these companies. It is due to the high number of these bridges that Silicon Valley companies are able to develop supplier or collaborative partnerships between themselves. Such a "network of trust" cannot be formed through incentive programs. In the Silicon Valley example, the initial development of the network of trust has been a result of events and structures organized by Stanford University that gather Silicon Valley actors together.

One of the definitive studies in this field was conducted by Burt (Burt 1992, 2005). Burt associates one's professional success with their position within the social network and clearly demonstrates this association with field studies. He uses the term "structural hole" while doing so. According to this account, the absence of ties within a social network is as significant as their presence and positions. Burt names the regions where ties are absent or scarce as **structural holes**. Structural holes block the movement of information and opportunities; similar to a pile of earth blocking the flow of water, they prevent mobility. If - certain- ties formed by an individual go through structural holes, such ties become more valuable when compared with others. A connection in the middle of a structural hole results in an intense flow from this position, just like a canal. The actor serving as a "gatekeeper" gains advantage from this passage. This is similar to Granovetter's perspective of distant ties. A tie formed in an area where connections are already dense does not provide exclusive access to opportunities. However, if you have ties reaching, for instance, actors such as clients and suppliers known to none of your colleagues, this will prove useful for your career advancement.

Therefore, ties traversing structural holes where other actors have none or few connections create economic opportunities for actors.

Business and Industry Networks

Like individuals, companies also form networks among themselves. These networks can shape a national or regional economy or a global industry. Companies contradict the assumption of rationality of classical economics in the following respect: they might prefer remaining loyal to their strategic partners instead of purchasing the ostensibly most advantageous product in the market. Edith Penrose traces this behavior back to the search of companies for stability in a tumultuous economic environment (Penrose 2008). Within the framework of this phenomenon named as **virtual organizations** by Penrose, owing to the ties formed among companies, firms form a relatively stable network of supply and support in unreliable market conditions.

Despite most of the examples used to illustrate the topic, discussions within economic theory regarding social structure are not only about competition. They can also be handled in terms of collaboration. Firms within a sectoral economic system that are not competitors but suppliers of each other are highly co-dependent (Kogut 2000). A firm's focusing on a certain business area in such an economic system and the consequential specialization is only possible when another firm or firms concentrate on complementing areas that act as suppliers or customers to the focal firm. Thus, they evolve together. This is called *"co-evolution"* or *"co-specialization"* (Kogut and Zander 1992; Walker, Kogut, and Shan 1997). During the course of this transformation, the technological knowledge forming the sector, although necessary for proper functioning in its entirety, is distributed among different actors in the sector and the functioning is maintained through continuous relationships between them. Therefore, for instance, the release of a novel product by a company requires that one of the suppliers change a component or produce a brand new one. This means that actors within such a system "know" and "learn" together to a considerable extent. As a result, you can think that such companies do not give up on each other because of small price differences. Findings of this kind, once again, begs a substantial critique of classical economic assumptions of price based rationality. Such new points of view in economics encompassing social networks indicate that price based competition is not the sole dominant factor in the functioning of economic systems and that collaboration almost always precedes competition. In fact, sometimes rivals might be obliged to collaborate at some point, a mix of competition and collaboration labeled as **co-opetition** (Nalebuff and Brandenburger 1997). This is the exact case when you come across a television advertisement of "X Producers Association". Consisting of firms producing the same goods and, therefore, competitors, an association as such works together in order to expand the X market and to change consumer perceptions.

In the general sense, this theory is compatible with economic network theories. Also present in Kogut's studies, this way of thinking underlines that the trust formed based on economic ties and the continuity of such ties allows a company to specialize in its own field thanks to the relationships with other suppliers and clients (Kogut and Zander, 1992; Kogut, 2000). Overall these studies underline the systemic and social nature of economic relations that may resist market fluctuations in a way that contradicts superficial and price based economic reasoning.

REFERENCES

Barabási, A. L., & Albert, R. (1999). Emergence of scaling in random networks. *Science, 286*(5439), 509–512. doi:10.1126/science.286.5439.509 PubMed

Brandes, U., Lerner, J., & Snijders, T.A.B. (2009). Networks Evolving Step by Step: Statistical Analysis of Dyadic Event Data. 2009 Advances in Social Network Analysis and Mining, 200–205.

Burt, R. S. (2005). *Brokerage and Closure*. Oxford University Press.

Cross, R., & Prusak, L. (2002). The people who make organizations go–or stop. Networks in the Knowledge Economy, 248-260.

Erdös, P., & Rényi, A. (1959). On Random Graphs, I. *Publicationes Mathematicae (Debrecen), 6*, 290–297.

Glückler, J., & Panitz, R. (2016). Unpacking social divisions of labor in markets: Generalized blockmodeling and the network boom in stock photography. *Social Networks, 47*, 156–166. doi:10.1016/j.socnet.2016.07.002

Goldenberg, A., Zheng, A. X., Fienberg, S. E., & Airoldi, E. M. (2009). A Survey of Statistical Network Models. *Foundations and Trends in Machine Learning, 2*(2), 129–233. doi:10.1561/2200000005

Handcock, M. S., Hunter, D. R., Butts, C. T., Goodreau, S. M., & Morris, M. (2008). statnet: Software tools for the representation, visualization, analysis and simulation of network data. *Journal of Statistical Software*, *24*(1), 1548. doi:10.18637/jss.v024.i01 PubMed

Holland, P. W., & Leinhardt, S. (1981). An exponential family of probability distributions for directed graphs. *Journal of the American Statistical Association*, *76*(373), 33–50. doi:10.1080/01621459.1981.10477598

Hunter, D. R., Handcock, M. S., Butts, C. T., Goodreau, S. M., & Morris, M. (2008). ergm: A package to fit, simulate and diagnose exponential-family models for networks. *Journal of Statistical Software*, *24*(3).

Kogut, M. (2012). The Small world of corporate governance. The Small Worlds of Corporate Governance, 1–52. doi:10.7551/mitpress/9780262017275.001.0001

Krackhardt, D. (1987). Cognitive social structures. *Social Networks*, *9*(2), 109–134. doi:10.1016/0378-8733(87)90009-8

Lazer, D., Pentland, A., Adamic, L., Aral, S., Barabási, A. L., Brewer, D., ... Jebara, T. (2009). Computational social science. *Science*, *323*(5915), 721–723. doi:10.1126/science.1167742 PubMed

Lorrain, F., & White, H. C. (1971). Structural equivalence of individuals in social networks. *The Journal of Mathematical Sociology*, *1*(1), 49–80. doi:10.1080/0022250X.1971.9989788

Newman, M. E., Strogatz, S. H., & Watts, D. J. (2001). Random graphs with arbitrary degree distributions and their applications. *Physical Review. E*, *64*(2), 026118. doi:10.1103/PhysRevE.64.026118 PubMed

Robins, G., Pattison, P., Kalish, Y., & Lusher, D. (2007). An introduction to exponential random graph (p*) models for social networks. *Social Networks*, *29*(2), 173–191. doi:10.1016/j.socnet.2006.08.002

Sampson, S. F. (1969). *A Novitiate in a Period of Change: An Experimental and Case Study of Social Relationships*. Academic Press.

Scott, J. (2000). *Social Network Analysis*. Atlanta, Ga.: Sage.

Snijders, T. A., Van de Bunt, G. G., & Steglich, C. E. (2010). Introduction to stochastic actor-based models for network dynamics. *Social Networks*, *32*(1), 44–60. doi:10.1016/j.socnet.2009.02.004

Watts, D. J., & Strogatz, S. H. (1998). Collective dynamics of 'small-world' networks. *Nature*, *393*(6684), 440. doi:10.1038/30918

Zachary, W. W. (1977). An Information Flow Model for Conflict and Fission in Small Groups. *Journal of Anthropological Research*, *33*(4), 452–473. doi:10.1086/jar.33.4.3629752

Chapter 10
Varieties of Networks and Their Characteristics

ABSTRACT

Contemporary social network analysis deals with network data of varying nature. An important source of this variety comes from availability of continuous, temporal data from online and digitalized interactions between actors. E-mail exchanges or Twitter activity are some examples of such data. This chapter introduces terminology to classify network data according to its content. In addition, it exemplifies research on temporal data and methods used in analysis of such data.

VARIETIES OF NETWORKS AND THEIR CHARACTERISTICS

We have provided many examples of networks in the previous chapters. Some of them being generated artificially, these networks have quite different structural features. At the same time, while defining many structural measures, we have talked about how to or how not to use them for comparing different networks. In real social networks, many structural features have similarities. Within the scope of this chapter, we will examine some similarities encountered during contemporary field studies. We will also look at the interpretations of differences.

Social scientists are not the only ones dealing with networks. Physicists and biologists are also interested in the subject. Non-social issues such as attractive

DOI: 10.4018/978-1-7998-1912-7.ch010

interactions among protein molecules and their impact on protein folding, networks of enzyme or gene interaction might be analyzed using graphs, an abstract mathematical concept suitable for representing relational structure of all these networks. Therefore, social and non-social network studies show certain parallelisms and make use of common mathematical methods and criteria (Borgatti et al. 2009; Lazer et al. 2009). However, significant variations arise from time to time due to the dissimilarity of phenomena. Indeed, complex and dynamic nature of social systems may require certain extensions to basic graph representation, such as for representation of temporality.

Can the structure of human social groups, as it is the case for natural/biological phenomena, be the reflection of the basic behavioral features? Jacques Monod, a natural scientist, gives the example of snowflakes and discusses how all of them differ from one another while showing the features of their main component (i.e. the water molecules) (Monod 1997). While this view may lean towards somewhat mechanistic determinism, it is useful in exploring how complexity of a whole emerges from the nature of its components. In a similar vein, Moreno notes that he looks for the universal features of human communities in his studies (Moreno, 1934). Do social groups bear similarities? To what extent they are similar? Can the same mathematical models represent variations as different as snowflakes and social systems? What are the reasons and meaning of differences in the social patterns?

Like the relationships forming them, social networks also display remarkable variety. For that reason, social network research approaches similarities and dissimilarities in a different way than that of natural sciences. We have explored the basic types of graphs and exemplified the types of social networks they can represent, in earlier chapters. In this chapter we will extend this exploration and give examples of more rich graph representations that are used in representing contemporary empirical data encountered in social network research.

Types of Relations and Networks

We have seen many phenomena analyzed in social network studies: liking, marriage, professional advice-giving, etc. Looking at this variety, we can classify them into certain relation categories and technical feature profiles. Here, using the classification partially cited from the study of Borgatti and colleagues (Borgatti et al. 2009) will help us to pick the methods to be used in our applications. A summary of this classification is given in Table 1.

Similarity Relations and Bipartite Datasets

Similarity ties are ties that are not necessarily found as direct connections between actors. Instead, tie definitions like "living in the same neighborhood" and "similar alcohol/ substance use habits" are often used in social research, although they require some caution. In some cases these ties are often for comparing to what extent they correspond to networks of real ties (e.g. friendship). On other cases, ties such as "being members of the same club" are close enough to real ties such that we can safely assume that they signal a real interaction among people, such as in the case of members of the same club.

An example of this category was compiled by Galaskiewicz (Galaskiewicz et al. 1985). This dataset consists of data concerning membership of a sample of 26 managers of large companies and their spouses to corporate executive boards and city clubs. In this example, due to the nature of the boards and clubs in question, "membership to the same club" is very likely to signify an interaction between two people. This dataset is a **bipartite dataset**. In the dataset, there are individuals on one side and clubs on the other; ties are always between the components of the former to those of the latter. Thus, components forming the social network dataset create two groups that are completely different in terms of relations. This is why we use the term "bipartite" to denote two disctinct partitions each containing different types of entities. Graphs can also be tripartite and so on. However, this is not common in social networks.

Table 1. Types of relations encountered in social network research and features of corresponding datasets

Tie type	Examples	Graph/dataset features
Similarities	Living at the same place, going to the same club/event, being of the same gender, having similar habits.	Bipartite data. Conversion is required before use. Conversion result is an undirected relation, mostly unweighted.
Relations	Being relatives, marriage, being friends or colleagues, liking, disliking.	Mostly undirected, mostly unweighted
Interactions	Getting together, helping, giving advice	mostly directed and unweighted
Flows	Information flow employee flows between companies international trade	directed and weighted,

Almost all analyses in social network studies are only suitable for **monopartite networks**, i.e. all the networks we have mentioned so far where ties are between a set of actors of the same type, such as Florentine families, or friendship networks. Thus, we almost always need to convert bipartite datasets into monopartite ones. Indeed, the aim behind Galaskiewicz's dataset is to reveal the relations (in terms of clubs and indirectly) among individuals. We can make the conversion easily using matrix algebra. Let us illustrate this with an example. Think of club memberships as a matrix as given below. These matrices are different from the adjacency matrices we have discussed in the previous chapters: they are directed not from one actor towards another but from a set of actors/components to another set. Therefore, sizes may differ as the two dimensions of the matrix corresponds to the sizes of the two sets:

```
              Club-1 Club-2
Individual-1    1       1
Individual-2    1       0
Individual-3    0       1
```

In this small-scale example, we can see that individual-1 has a relationship (from club-1) with individual-2 and (from club-2) with individual-3. It is important to underline that the matrix is asymmetrical. The size of the matrix is 3x2 because, in our bipartite social network, one set of components has 3 individuals while the other has 2 clubs. This is called an **incidence matrix**. As the incidence matrix is asymmetrical, it is not suitable for the social network analysis methods we have mentioned previously. We multiply the matrix with the transpose matrix to convert it into a matrix of individual-to-individual relations. Therefore, if we name an incidence matrix with a size of $n \times m$ as A, the matrix $S = A \cdot A^T$ will be a sociomatrix showing us relations among individuals.

```
1 1       1 1 0       2 1 1
1 0   X   1 0 1   =   1 1 0
0 1                   1 0 1
```

The resulting 3x3 matrix is now the sociomatrix showing relations between individuals.

Now, we need to set the diagonal cells of the matrix to zero: naturally, the strongest relationships seem to be there because of the state of being at the same club with oneself, but these are not social and therefore can be excluded.

```
            Individual-1 Individual-2 Individual-3
Individual-1    0             1            1
Individual-2    1             0            0
Individual-3    1             0            0
```

If we had done the opposite, meaning that if we multiplied the transpose matrix with the original one, we would have got a 2x2 matrix giving us the relationships among clubs.: $S' = A^T \cdot A$.

```
1 1 0   1 1     2 1
1 0 1 X 1 0  =  1 2
        0 1
```

Even though the second operation is not quite meaningful as far as our small example goes, it is helpful in illustrating the method. Therefore, we can continue by setting the diagonal to zero.

Let us consider what it would mean to use the first and second matrix operation above for the corporate executive boards example. Some managers are members of multiple executive boards. This means that we have a bipartite dataset in our hands. A conversion of the first kind given above will reveal the relationships among managers (i.e. in how many executive boards two managers work together?). As for the second conversion, it will provide us with the relationships among companies (i.e. how many members do two corporate executive boards have in common?).

In a real dataset, it is sufficient to transpose and multiply the matrices to conduct these operations on R. In the code below I have used the statnet library (Handcock et al., 2008) since it worked better on the dataset in hand. The resulting graph in the code below is shown in Figure 1 (plotted with Kamada Kawai graph layout mode; Kamada and Kawai, 1989). Th operation denoted as %*% in the code below means matrix multiplication in R. The transpose is so common an operation that its function name is simply t(). Part of the matrix is printed out to demonstrate the structure of a real bipartite example:

```
require(statnet)
##              Installed  ReposVer  Built
## ergm         "3.9.4"    "3.10.4"  "3.5.1"
## ergm.count   "3.3.0"    "3.4.0"   "3.5.1"
## network      "1.13.0.1" "1.15"    "3.5.1"
## networkDynamic "0.9.0"  "0.10.0"  "3.5.1"
## statnet      "2018.10"  "2019.6"  "3.5.1"
```

```
## statnet.common "4.1.4"    "4.3.0"  "3.5.1"
## tergm            "3.5.2"    "3.6.1"  "3.5.1"
## tsna             "0.2.0"    "0.3.0"  "3.5.1"
ceo <- read.paj("data/GalaskiewiczCEOs.net")
ceoMatrix <- as.matrix(ceo)
head(ceoMatrix[1:7,1:7],n=7)#print only part of matrix
##        club-1 club-2 club-3 club-4 club-5 club-6 club-7
## CEO-1      0      0      1      1      0      0      0
## CEO-2      0      0      1      0      1      0      1
## CEO-3      0      0      1      0      0      0      0
## CEO-4      0      1      1      0      0      0      0
## CEO-5      0      0      1      0      0      0      0
## CEO-6      0      1      1      0      0      0      0
## CEO-7      0      0      1      1      0      0      0
ceoMatrixTransposed <- t(ceoMatrix)   #matrix transpose
ceoUnipartiteMatrix<-ceoMatrix %*% ceoMatrixTransposed # matrix
multiplication
head(ceoUnipartiteMatrix[1:7,1:7],n=5)#print only part of
matrix
##        CEO-1 CEO-2 CEO-3 CEO-4 CEO-5 CEO-6 CEO-7
## CEO-1     3     1     1     1     1     1     2
## CEO-2     1     3     1     1     1     1     1
## CEO-3     1     1     2     1     1     1     1
## CEO-4     1     1     1     3     1     2     1
## CEO-5     1     1     1     1     3     2     1
ceoGraph<-as.network(ceoUnipartiteMatrix)
plot(ceoGraph, mode="kamadakawai",displaylabels=TRUE)
```

In this similarity relationship, the original dataset contains an unweighted relationship, but we obtained a weighted dataset after the conversion because

Figure 1. Finding the network between managers from the bipartite dataset

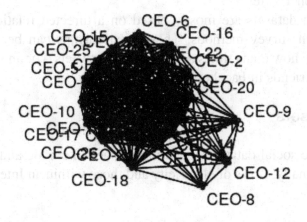

there might me multiple indirect relationships between two components. For example CEO-1 and CEO-7 have a tie strength 2 because they have overlapping membership to two clubs: club-3 and club-4.

Monopartite Datasets

Monopartite or **unipartite** datasets are those we already have been using throughout the book. Unless otherwise stated a network dataset is given in this form, i.e. as adjacency information. The monopartite data can be encountered in various cases discussed below.

Relational Datasets

We have dealt with these datasets extensively in our previous examples, therefore we will not examine them again. These are dataset about direct relations. In cases like the relation is "being relatives" or "marital relations", the dataset is unweighted and undirected. However, in cases such as "liking one another", it might be directed and even weighted. This differentiation must be made in accordance with the defined relationship. These datasets almost always use monopartite component sets.

Interaction Datasets

Most of the time, interpersonal interactions can be measured objectively. Particularly, interactions taking place online nowadays have made it possible to obtain such rich datasets. For instance, there are many studies on datasets such as e-mail interactions in an office or in a virtual space, or retweeting interactions on Twitter.

Interaction datasets are mostly based on a directed relationship when collected with survey methods. These relationships can be measured as weighted (e.g. how many times A retweeted B's tweets?) or unweighted (e.g. are A and B friends in Facebook?).

Flow Datasets

These include social datasets concerning issues like trade and information flow. Additionally, flows of electricity and those within an Internet network in the field of engineering, and transportation flows with a logistics fleet in the field of business management can also be included under this category.

One of the most frequently cited datasets from this group is the one created by Wasserman and Faust concerning international trade relations (Wasserman ve Faust 1994). The flow/relationship in question is an economic one, but it employs the same methods with social network analysis. You need to pay attention to its content if you wish to use this dataset: the data in this set consists of the recollection of the same data a couple of years in a row. This means that there are multiple networks (an international trade network for each year) in the dataset. The use of this dataset with R is illustrated below. Use of multiple datasets in a single file required to use the network library below. If you consult the data file you will see that ws2 corresponds to Crude materials. You can experiment with trade networks of other types of goods such as ws0 (Food and live animals), and so on:

```
require(network)
trade<-read.paj("data/CountriesTrade.paj")
#summary(trade)
#trade$networks # list the networks in the data file
plot(trade$networks$ws2,displaylabels=TRUE) # The "crude
materials" network
```

```
network.vertex.names(trade$networks$ws2)
##  [1] "ALG" "ARG" "BRA" "CHI" "CZE" "ECU" "EGY" "ETH" "FIN"
```

Figure 2. An example of network including data on flows: A trade network

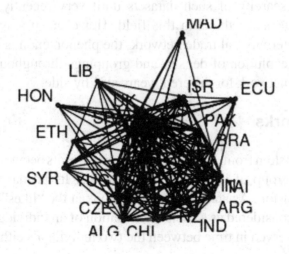

```
"HON" "IND"
## [12] "ISR" "JAP" "LIB" "MAD" "NZ"   "PAK" "SPA" "SWI" "SYR"
"TAI" "UK"
## [23] "US"   "YUG"
degree(trade$networks$ws2)
##   [1] 19 23 25 30 25 12 28 15 33  9 26 22 39 12  6 27 23 41
38 16 28 41 43
## [24] 33
network.density(trade$networks$ws2)
## [1] 0.5561594
```

The measurements in this example show that the United States (US) has the greatest trade volume. A visualization of this network is given in Figure 2. Even though the tags of components in the middle are problematic, this visual shows some countries like Honduras and Madagascar as peripheral ones while showing countries like the US as central ones. All of the bigger countries have trade relations with all the remaining countries regardless of their volumes; this creates a dense network. The density of this network consisting of 24 countries is 0.56, quite a high value for its size.

Temporal Analysis in Monopartite Datasets

Generally, the evolution of a social system in the course of time is vital for social research on its dynamics. However, it was rarely possible to observe a social system continuously. For that reason, temporal datasets were mostly acquired by recollecting social network data periodically. Recently however, it is more an more common to find real time data about many types of networks due to digitalization of many activities in our lives.

Due to the scarcity of such datasets until very recently, there are no specialized analysis methods in this field. However, in a system like, for instance, the international trade network, the phenomenon is interpreted by examining the evolution of density and groupings throughout the years by comparing the network for different years side by side.

Event Networks

Event networks stem from, as the name suggests, events occurring throughout time within a group of individuals/components. Its primary feature is its temporal dimension. As an example, let us look at the "likes" on Facebook. Liking can be considered as a social affirmation of an individual by another. "Likes" are observed in time between the two individuals either unilaterally or reciprocally. However, how can we understand their effects as time goes by? In other words if a like is not "forever" how long it lasts? How do we interpret the sentiment between actors on an ongoing basis?

Studies on this newly emerging field calculate the impact of these events through chemical analogies based on "half-life" (Snijders, Bunt, and Steglich 2010; Butts 2008). This means that the impact of an event fades in time, but new events between the two individuals might bring about a revitalization to their relationship.

EXERCISES

1. Use the Galaskiewicz network to find the relation between clubs. Although clubs are not actors themselves, the network between the clubs may hint how the institutional structure is.
2. Use a different network from the world trade network and find degree centralities of countries. Then compare centralities in two different trade networks, for example by computing correlation of degree centralities from two different networks.

REFERENCES

Borgatti, S. P., Mehra, A., Brass, D. J., & Labianca, G. (2009). Network Analysis in the Social Sciences. *Science*, *323*(5916), 892–895. doi:10.1126cience.1165821 PMID:19213908

Butts, C. T. (2008). A relational event framework for social action. *Sociological Methodology*, *38*(1), 155–200. doi:10.1111/j.1467-9531.2008.00203.x

Galaskiewicz, J., Wasserman, S., Rauschenbach, B., Bielefeld, W., & Mullaney, P. (1985). The Influence of Corporate Power, Social Status, and Market Position on Corporate Interlocks in a Regional Network. *Social Forces*, *64*(2), 403–431. doi:10.2307/2578648

Handcock, M. S., Hunter, D. R., Butts, C. T., Goodreau, S. M., & Morris, M. (2008). statnet: Software tools for the representation, visualization, analysis and simulation of network data. *Journal of Statistical Software*, *24*(1), 1548. doi:10.18637/jss.v024.i01 PMID:18618019

Kamada, T., & Kawai, S. (1989). An algorithm for drawing general undirected graphs. *Information Processing Letters, 31*(1), 7–15. doi:10.1016/0020-0190(89)90102-6

Lazer, D., Pentland, A., Adamic, L., Aral, S., Barabási, A. L., Brewer, D., ... Jebara, T. (2009). Computational social science. *Science, 323*(5915), 721–723. doi:10.1126cience.1167742 PMID:19197046

Monod, J. (1997). *Rastlantı ve Zorunluluk-Modern Biyolojinin Doğa Felsefesi Üzerine Bir Deneme*. Dost Kitabevi.

Moreno, J. L. (1934). *Who shall survive? A new approach to the problem of human interrelations*. Academic Press.

Snijders, T. A., Van de Bunt, G. G., & Steglich, C. E. (2010). Introduction to stochastic actor-based models for network dynamics. *Social Networks, 32*(1), 44–60. doi:10.1016/j.socnet.2009.02.004

Wasserman, S., & Faust, K. (1994). *Social network analysis: Methods and applications* (Vol. 8). Cambridge University Press. doi:10.1017/CBO9780511815478

Chapter 11
Network Visualization

ABSTRACT

Visual inspection of networks is a powerful tool in exploratory analysis of social networks. However, visualization of graphs has inherent problems that may result in misleading visualizations. This chapter first introduces basic theory behind these inherent problems. Then it introduces features of common layout algorithms used in visualization. Through applied examples, the chapter explores the use of layout parameters to obtain visualizations appropriate for the research focus.

NETWORK VISUALIZATION

Conventional datasets are placed in tables with few columns corresponding to variables and rows corresponding to observations. We have many advanced tools in our disposal to see, examine, and summarize such tables. Examining raw data before diving into analysis is an indispensable necessity for many statisticians, just like a doctor needing to see and examine a patient. Advanced medical technology can provide the doctor with many indications concerning the patient, meaning that the doctor is able to examine the patient in many "indirect" ways. Nevertheless, seeing a patient and examining them directly remains as the primary means of diagnosis for a doctor. A stethoscope remains an important tool despite sophisticated devices such as MRI scanners Similarly, for a statistician, analyzing raw data and the tools necessary for doing so are as essential as advanced analysis algorithms or software.

DOI: 10.4018/978-1-7998-1912-7.ch011

The tools required for exploration of conventional table data are not suitable for examining relational data representing social networks. Even if you present the data as a sociomatrix (which is essentially a table), there are different structures and patterns. Therefore, network visualization has been a vital instrument for social network researchers for many years. Analyzing a graph visual representing an entire network is the closest way to examining raw data all at once. For that reason, choosing the appropriate visualization method for different types of social networks (in terms of size and structural features) is a critical step for a researcher.

Challenges of Visualizing Graphs

Graph visualization has certain fundamental challenges. We have a three-dimensional visual perception and many visuals we deal with for practical reasons are on a two-dimensional paper or screen. This is the primary source of these difficulties because, in order to visualize the social distances between n actors accurately, we need a coordinate system with n-1 dimensions or degrees of freedom.

Let us illustrate this with an example and assume that we have measured the distances between the actors in a social network; now, we want to visualize these values. We can place two points corresponding to two of these actors in any way we want on a straight line or a coordinate system with one **degree of freedom**. But we are more restricted when we want to place the third point as it is the case in Figure 1. The figure shows the social "distances" between pairs of actors as a matrix. In the figure, points A and B are placed at a certain distance meaning that their distance correlated with the strength of their tie in the social network. Now one needs to place C as well. We first place the point C with a certain distance to A according to their tie strength. But then we have no freedom to choose its distance from B. Here the problem is related to degrees of freedom. The degrees of freedom is "two" in this example since we have freedom to place two points on a one dimensional coordinate system. But it is one shorter than we need since we have three points in the social system at hand and need two degrees of freedom. The same thing happens for A when we try a certain distance from B. We can, of course, also consider placing C in the middle of A and B, but this time both distances will be wrong.

The same problem can be demonstrated for the case of a social network of 4 or more actors and a two-dimensional coordinate system to draw the

Figure 1. Degrees of freedom and challenges encountered while creating a social network graph, an example in a one-dimensional system

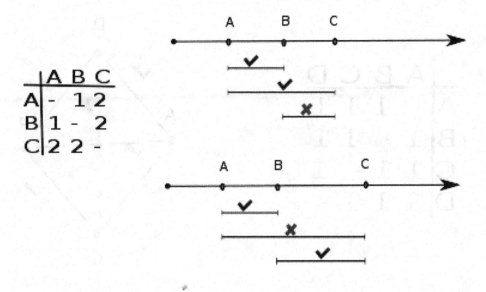

network. After placing the first three points in the example shown in Figure 1, it is impossible to choose the right social distance while placing the point D. The problem will worsen as the number of actors increases.

Taking this into account, placing a graph with more than three actors (regardless of the relationship is either weighted or binary/unweighted) on a plane (e.g. a computer screen) will never reflect actual social distances between the actors in the visualization accurately. In other words visualization of any social network with more than 3 actors is almost always *distorted* in the sense that it cannot be drawn to show line lengths between actors corresponding to actual social distances. However, we still need visualization just like we need a stethescope, and there are some studies concerning the ways of minimizing the distortion in this process.

Methods regarding the way in which graph visualization can be made with minimum distortion, or in general to obtain most informative visualizations, attempt to obtain certain characteristics:

1. Considering the restrictions mentioned above, the distance between points in the two-dimensional system should be as proportionate to the social distance as possible, but points must not coincide. Furthermore, unrelated points should be far from one another.
2. There should be as few intersections between connection lines as possible.

Figure 2. Degrees of freedom and challenges encountered while creating a social network graph, an example from a two- dimensional system

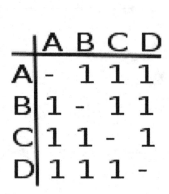 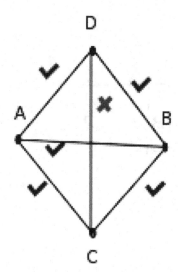

3. Basic features of social network actors should be reflected by, for instance, showing more central actors with larger dots.
4. Structural features of complex and large networks (e.g. groupings) should be shown visually. For this, the visual must be **multi-scale**, meaning that it highlights and places the most important actors and ties as accurately as possible and to do this pushes the distortion towards less significant actors, if necessary.

Obtaining these qualities almost certainly involves conflicts, thus becomes difficult especially in large networks. For this reason researchers attempt to use a wide range of methods, each of which is suitable for different social networks in terms of types and sizes. These methods should also be computationally efficient meaning that they have to produce results in a reasonable time and using reasonable memory capacity on a computer.

Force-Directed and Spring Model Drawing Methods

Force-directed methods are one of the initial methods meeting some of the desired criteria above and still being frequently used. These methods follow analogies to physical objects and forces between them. Within the scope of these methods, network components are considered to be physical objects in a two dimensional space, such as atomic particles attracting and repulsing one another (Eades et al. 2010). There is a force of attraction between two objects commensurate with the strength of their social relationship. Furthermore, repulsion is also observed -although less evidently- among all objects. Computer algorithms applying this approach first scatter the points randomly over the plane. Then, they adjust the places of the points through these forces of attraction/repulsion by calculating and incrementally imposing them onto the objects. Thus, as unrelated objects diverge through repulsion, related objects remain in a distance in which the totality of the forces came to a balance as much as possible. The visualization is then completed by drawing lines between related objects when the aforementioned placement is transferred to a screen or piece of paper.

This method is, in a way, similar to a cluster of physical objects normally repulsing each other but some attacting each other by having strings between them. Consider pairs of actors without a tie repulsing each other and pairs of tied actors as having a string between them. Repulsion will sweep disconnected actors away from each other, just like in a physical cosmos of mixed forces. But in the process some of the strings will be tangled in a complex system. This corresponds to unrelated yet intersecting connecting lines in network visuals.

The restrain in the strings in this approach correspond to irreconcilable constraints that stem from the degrees of freedom problem. Through the course of time, improvements were introduced into these methods to ease this problem. Some methods are based on random alterations aimed at surmounting these obstacles and disentangling such knots. One of the most frequently used variation is the algorithm developed by Fruchterman and Reingold (Fruchterman and Reingold 1991).

Another variation of this basic approach was developed by Kamada and Kawai (Kamada and Kawai 1989). This approach not only places attractive forces between neighbors but also takes the social distances between all pairs of actors into account while making the placements accordingly.

The majority of the examples provided in this book were generated using these two visualization algorithms. The phase of deciding where to put points and lines in a graph visualization is called **graph layout**. Each of the plotting functions we have used have some sensible defaults for the choice of **graph layout algorithm** they use. In the case of igraph you can examine the algorithms provided for its plotting function by reading the help manual for layout_ generic function. In particular read the help for layout_nicely regarding how the software makes a choice of layout algorithm automatically according to size.

Let us now make the choice of this algorithm explicit, for example in the case of Florentine families. This is a moderate size network with 16 nodes. The example below uses four different layout algorithms whose results are shown in Figure 3. Note that each named layout also corresponds to a function. In the last case where Davidson-Harel algorithm is used (Davidson and Harel 1996), the call demonstrates how the layout function can be called directly instead of giving it as a parameter:

```
require(igraph)
g <- read.graph("data/PadgettMarital.net", format="pajek")
gu<-simplify(as.undirected(g))
V(gu)$size <- 20
plot(gu, layout=layout_in_circle,main="Circular layout")
plot(gu, layout=layout_with_fr,main="Fruchterman-reingold
layout")
plot(gu, layout=layout_with_kk,main="kamada-Kawai layout")
plot(gu, layout=layout_with_dh(gu,cool.fact=0.9), vertex.
size=10, main="Davidson-harel layout")
```

Note that in visualizing this particular network some algorithms produce similar results. The true nature of algorithms, however, ususally surface in more difficult visualizations, i.e. when there are more nodes and ties. Let us see how the network size makes a difference using a larger example. Our next example uses the data about the "scene co-appearance" network of the characters in Victor Hugo's famous novel "Les Miserables". The original data is retrieved from the Stanford network database (Knuth 1993). This network has 77 actors/nodes, that appear throughout this voluminous novel. The visualizations shown in Figure 4 uses the same algorithms as in Figure 3. But this time the results are considerably different from each other. The plotting stage also demonstrates some advanced features. For example the size of each vertex is different and proportional to degree of the vertex. Also the example shows labels for most important characters only. You can try otherwise and see how cluttered the plot would turn out. In this larger graph the layouts produce different results according to their tolerance of size.

```
require(igraph)
g <- read.graph("data/lesmiserables.gml", format="gml")
gu<-simplify(as.undirected(g))
V(gu)$size <- 10
plot(gu, layout=layout_in_circle, main="Circular layout")
```

Figure 3. Four different layouts of Florentine families network

Circular layout

Fruchterman-reingold layout

Davidson-harel layout

kamada-Kawal layout

```
plot(gu, layout=layout_with_fr,main="Fruchterman-reingold
layout")
plot(gu, layout=layout_with_kk,main="Kamada-Kawai layout")
degrees<-degree(gu)
labels<-ifelse(degrees>11,vertex.attributes(gu)$label,NA)
plot(gu, layout=layout_with_dh, vertex.size=degrees/2,vertex.
label=labels,label.cex=0.9,main="Davidson-Harel layout")
```

Multi-Scale Drawings

After around 20-30 actors, the size of a social network might start to render the rather classical visualization methods mentioned in the models above unusable. We have already discussed the primary reason behind this: as the number of actors increases the degree of freedom required to draw the network accurately also increases, but we are still drawing on a two-dimensional surface.

A solution for this problem is using **multi-scale methods** while drawing large networks. Essentially, this means that we apply the aforementioned force-directed drawing method firstly on a couple of central actors only, then fix their positions. Then, we apply the layout algorithm to the remaining (less significant) groups of actors to which each central actor is tied through the same algorithm one-by-one, without moving the main actors fixed in the previous stage (Hu 2006; Harel and Koren 2001). Drawings generated in this way are preferred as they distribute the errors stemming from the degree of freedom limitations unequally among "significant" and "insignificant" actors. This is because significant actors are placed with less distortion of their actual social place and our visual identification regarding the network structure focuses on more important actors. However, more distoritons are imposed while placing actors of secondary importance.

Figure 5 demonstrate the difference between these drawing methods. This example uses Les Miserables dataset above. The first visualization is a force-directed one which produces an acceptable visual identification despite the size of the network. The second and third ones use two different multi-scale methods called Distributed Recursive Layout (Kolaczyk and Csárdi 2014) and Metric Multidimensional Scaling (Cox and Cox 2000). The juxtaposition highlights potential effectiveness of each method as far as the objective of visual diagnostics is concerned.

```
require(igraph)
g <- read.graph("data/lesmiserables.gml", format="gml")
gu<-simplify(as.undirected(g))
```

Figure 4. Different layouts of coappearance network of characters in Victor Hugo's Les Miserables

Circular layout

Fruchterman-reingold layout

Kamada-Kawal layout

```
degrees<-degree(gu)
labels<-ifelse(degrees>11,vertex.attributes(gu)$label,NA)
plot(gu, layout=layout_with_dh, vertex.size=degrees/2,vertex.
label=labels,label.cex=0.9,main="dh layout")
plot(gu, layout=layout_with_mds, vertex.size=degrees/2,vertex.
label=labels,label.cex=0.9,main="mds layout")
plot(gu, layout=layout_with_drl, vertex.size=degrees/2,vertex.
label=labels,label.cex=0.9,main="drl layout")
```

Our next example is suitable to demonstrate the case where a much larger network is at stake. The Air Traffic network used below comes from the Koblenz Network Collection (see Appendix A on datasets and data sources). It contains the data about the airline connection between US airports, with 1227 airport in the data. The visualization in Figure 6 reveals how different a network can look depending upon your choice of layout algoritm, thus leading to different diagnosis. The mds method seem to work better in this particular case, but drl method still has the potential of revealing the 'hubs' in the network. Therefore, it is up to the user to choose the method most approrpiate for the question at hand.

```
require(igraph)
g<-read.graph("data/maayan-faa/out.maayan-
faa",format="edgelist")
gu<-simplify(as.undirected(g))
plot(gu, layout=layout_with_mds, vertex.size=1, vertex.
label=NA)
plot(gu, layout=layout_with_drl, vertex.size=1, vertex.
label=NA)
```

Visual Effects Facilitating Diagnosis

We have used an additional effect in Figure 7 in order to make visual identification easier: the sizes of actors differ from one another. The sizes are proportionate with the centrality of the actor. It is also possible to use other visual information such as colors to make network visualizations convey more information in inspections

A common way colors are used in graph visualization is indicating groups. The groups within the social network can be identified and each group can be colored with a different color. Such visual reflections are possible in all drawing layout methods. If the social network size permits, other kinds of labels or colors can also be used on actors and/or relationships. The example

Figure 5. Multi-scale layout of Les Miserables network

dh layout

mds layout

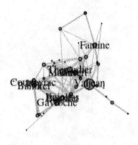

drl layout

Figure 6. US air traffic network visualized with two different multi-scale layouts

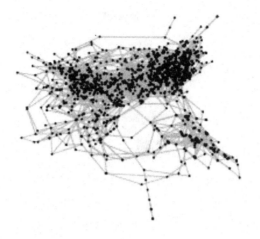

below produces the visual in Figure 7 where each group in the graph is in different color. The code uses a few tricks. First of all it uses the vertex. color parameter in the plot function. To make the example as general as possible it uses the rainbow() function which produces as many contiguous colors as needed. In our case the number of colors is equal to the number of communities. The color for each vertex is given as a vector in vertex. color parameter of the plot function. The color of vertices is chosen using the group membership function. Vertex and label sizes use some arithmetic to make the plot more appealing. Overall, these also demonstrate that graph visualization is as much a design it is a science, since it has to be interpreted according to the visual needs.

```
require(igraph)
g <- read.graph("data/lesmiserables.gml", format="gml")
gu<-simplify(as.undirected(g))
l <- layout_with_fr(gu)
comm <- fastgreedy.community(gu)
colors <- rainbow(max(membership(comm)))
plot(gu, layout=l, vertex.color=colors[membership(comm)],
  vertex.size=5, vertex.label=NA)
degrees<-degree(gu)
labels<-ifelse(degrees>11,vertex.attributes(gu)$label,NA)
plot(gu, layout=l,
  vertex.color=colors[membership(comm)],            #set the
vertex colors
  vertex.size=2*sqrt(degrees),vertex.label=labels, #set the
vertex sizes
  vertex.label.cex=log(degrees)/max(log(degrees))) #set the
vertex label sizes
```

New Generation Graph Visualization Libraries for R

Those who use R for analytics are very likely to be familiar with the library named ggplot2 (Tyner et al., 2017). This library was an important addition to R ecosystem that elevates the graphics quality to contemporary standards. ggplot2 have its particular style of expressing graphical constructs, which is somewhat beyond the scope of our text. Nevertheless, I would like to give some pointers and examples for the curious reader.

The ggplot2 library itself allows user to control many visual aspects quite easily. In addition it has a very rich variety of visual capabilities one can choose from. The following simple example demonstrates ggplot2 capabilities on a

Figure 7. Les Miserables network with actors sized according to their degree centralities

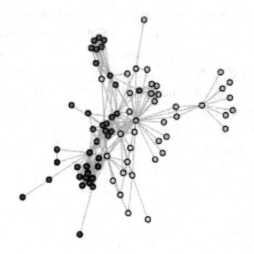

conventional R data set about cars' features and their fuel consumption. The resulting plot is shown in Figure 3 where you can see features such as a nice legend, control on output plot aspect ratio and so on; capabilities which are considerably more cumbersome in older R libraries:

```
library(ggplot2)
qplot(x=mpg, y=disp, color=cyl, size=hp, data=mtcars
    , main="ggplot2 example", asp=1/2)
```

The above example uses a simplified function called quick plot (qplot) from the ggplot2 library. Most tutorials on the ggplot2 library use its own style of expression where a graph is constructed by adding up data and aestethic layers, actually with a "+" operator. The following is the same graph produced with this ggplot2 style code instead of the more concise but limited qplot():

```
library(ggplot2)
ggplot(mtcars) + #the data layer
        aes(x=mpg, y=disp, color=cyl, size=hp)+
        geom_point()+
        theme(asp=1/2)+
        labs(title = "ggplot2 example")
```

Figure 8. An example of ggplot2 library capabilities on a conventional dataset

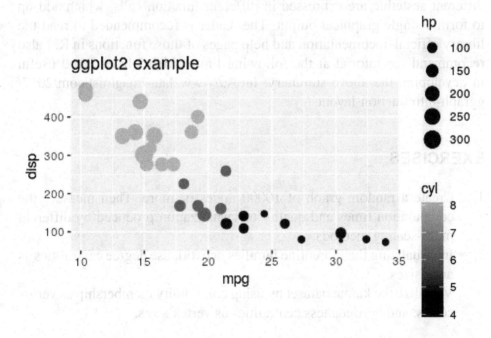

The particular labrary that uses ggplot2 for graph visualization is ggraph (see https://cran.r-project.org/web/packages/ggraph/index.html. The following code demonstrates its output shown in Figure 4. The example uses a dataset collected by Coleman (Coleman, a 1964) and it shows the friendship ties between high school boys as assessed by the question: "What fellows here in school do you go around with most often?". The measurement was repeated twice, in 1957 and 1958 and the plot shows the change in friendship network between the two years. Years are color coded and node size denotes degree centrality:

```
library(ggraph)
library(igraph)
graph <- graph_from_data_frame(highschool)
years<-factor(highschool$year)
layout <- create_layout(graph, layout = 'drl')
degrees<-degree(graph)
ggraph(layout) +
    geom_edge_link(aes(colour = years)) + #use color to code
years
    geom_node_point(size=degrees/5)+  # use degree for vertex
sizes
    geom_node_point()
```

The code is similar to the ggplot2 style of expression in the sense that different aestethic are expressed in different function calls, which add up to form a single graphical output. The reader is recommended to read the library official documentation and help pages of those functions in R. I also recommend the tutorial at the following link, which I have found useful in developing the above summary: https://www.data-imaginist.com/2017/ggraph-introduction-layouts/.

EXERCISES

1. Create a random graph of 10000 nodes or more. Then measure the computation times and quality of visualization produced by different multi-scaling methods.
2. In visualizing the Florentine families network use degree centralities as node sizes.
3. Visualize the karate dataset by using community membership as vertex colors, and betweenness centralities as vertex sizes.

Figure 9. An example of ggraph library for plotting graphs

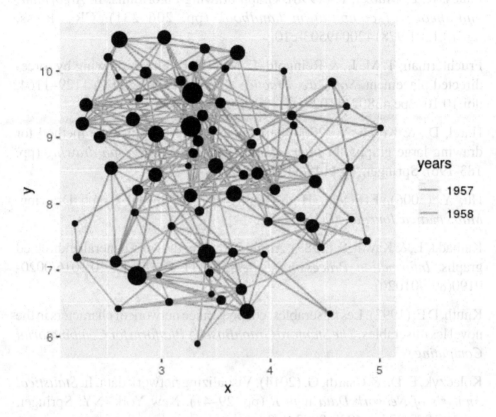

4. Use the ggraph library to visualize the karate dataset with the requirements in the previous question.

REFERENCES

Coleman, J. S. (1964). *Introduction to Mathematical Sociology*. Glencoe.

Cox, T. F., & Cox, M. A. (2000). *Multidimensional Scaling*. Chapman Hall/CRC. doi:10.1201/9781420036121

Davidson, R., & Harel, D. (1996). Drawing graphs nicely using simulated annealing. *ACM Transactions on Graphics*, *15*(4), 301–331. doi:10.1145/234535.234538

Eades, P., & Mutzel, P. (1998). Graph drawing algorithms. In *Algorithms and theory of computation handbook* (pp. 206–231). CRC Press. doi:10.1201/9781420049503-c10

Fruchterman, T. M. J., & Reingold, E. M. (1991). Graph drawing by force-directed placement. *Software, Practice & Experience, 21*(11), 1129–1164. doi:10.1002pe.4380211102

Harel, D., & Koren, Y. (2000, September). A fast multi-scale method for drawing large graphs. In *International symposium on graph drawing* (pp. 183-196). Springer. 10.1145/345513.345353

Hu, Y. (2006). Efficient, High-Quality Force-Directed Graph Drawing. *Mathematica Journal, 10*(1), 37–71.

Kamada, T., & Kawai, S. (1989). An algorithm for drawing general undirected graphs. *Information Processing Letters, 31*(1), 7–15. doi:10.1016/0020-0190(89)90102-6

Knuth, D E. (1993). Les miserables: coappearance network of characters in the novel les miserables. *The Stanford GraphBase: A Platform for Combinatorial Computing*.

Kolaczyk, E. D., & Csárdi, G. (2014). Visualizing network data. In *Statistical Analysis of Network Data with R* (pp. 29–41). New York, NY: Springer. doi:10.1007/978-1-4939-0983-4_3

Tyner, S., Briatte, F., & Hofmann, H. (2017). Network Visualization with ggplot2. *The R Journal*.

Chapter 12
Social Media Analysis

ABSTRACT

With merely more than a decade since its birth, social media has become a huge area of our socialization. With more social interaction shifting to social media, it becomes an important source for research in different social sciences. This chapter looks at typical pipelines for social media analysis and introduces specialized R packages for these tasks, such as Twitter.

INTRODUCTION

Throughout the development of the field of social network analysis, traditional and cumbersome data collection methods such as questionnaires have been the basis of the data obtained by researchers. Nowadays, quickly becoming popular, social media technologies and platforms offer a substantial source of data. Facebook, Google+, Twitter, LinkedIn, WhatsApp, Pinterest, Instagram, and YouTube are the most prominent examples of such platforms. These platforms, becoming the primary media of communication for the majority of the global population, are naturally an exciting source for social science researchers.

Following are some examples of social media research that demonstrate the usage potential of these sources within the scope of different disciplines of social sciences:

- Social or natural emergencies can be spotted by detecting sudden and excessive activities arising from a particular place through the

DOI: 10.4018/978-1-7998-1912-7.ch012

monitoring of Twitter feeds (Sakaki, Okazaki, and Matsuo 2010; Atefeh and Kreich, 2015).

- A US-based study examined the connections among web blogs supporting different political parties (Adamic and Glance 2005, Lazer et al. 2009). The results of the study exhibit the extent of political division and the role of moderate web blogs in maintaining the connections between two political camps in the US. Such a study provides a dataset that cannot be collected with traditional methods of political science and makes a theoretical phenomenon measurable in a concrete manner.
- Certain firms make use of social media posts of their clients for product innovation (Ghazawneh 2011).

These studies and other similar ones show how data on social media use can be utilized to create added value for research or business. On the other hand, social media studies have some challenges since it is a multi-disciplinary field where knowledge from the fields of data mining, textual analysis, and social network analysis is used. This chapter focuses on social media, particularly on how to obtain social network data from Twitter, one of the most popular social networking platforms, and the analyses making use of these data.

Applications of Social Media Analysis

All the social media platforms mentioned above were initially targeted for personal use. However, as a result of a social media applications becoming more popular, many companies regard social media as a crucial communication channel to reach out to their clients and vice versa. Today, providing customer support not only via telephone but also through WhatsApp or making corporate announcements on Twitter are among the practices aimed at improving communication with clients and increasing customer satisfaction. Therefore, popular social media platforms are vital for enterprises.

Some of these business practices focus on the content of social media posts, generally on the text content but recently including analysis of images as well. As the examination and constant monitoring of a huge body of texts are not a task to be accomplished merely through reading of content by humans, textual analysis algorithms are used. Using algorithms developed by computer engineers, these analyses help us classify social media posts under thematic titles based on keywords in them. This method might be employed in order to, for instance, develop customer support services or eliminating problems in a timely manner by detecting publications made by unhappy clients.

Another group of studies concentrates on the structure of social media interactions rather than their posted content. Interactions such as likes, retweets, mentions, or hashtags on platforms like Facebook and Twitter are useful in detecting the interactive network among users. As a result, if, for example, a company or brand is to conduct promotional or public relations efforts, they can focus their efforts on the most influential (central) users or on the users giving the most positive/negative feedbacks; all of which can be revealed by social network analysis. In my own experience, the short courses nd workshops I have offered on this rather technical field was surprisingly popular among executives who work in the field of marketing or public relations.

Similar studies can also be conducted by institutions providing public services. Public protection and support services for people with high priority are among the areas open for development through such analyses. One example of this is a project (of which I had the chance of being a part) jointly conducted by a communication company and public institutions in Turkey aiming to understand the demographic movements and problems of refugees using mobile communication data (see http://d4r.turktelekom.com.tr/).

Transforming Social Media Data Into a Social Network

A considerable part of social media interactions consists of actions such as users liking and sharing posts by another user and following that other user. Therefore, "directed" social network data stems from such actions. For example, a user named A likes/retweets a post/tweet written by a user named B, creating a directed connection from A towards B.

As we have discussed in the chapter concerning network dynamics, there is a considerable level of social reciprocity in such networks, meaning that user B is also expected to like or share posts by user A. Of course, as stated in the section regarding preferential relationships, popular individuals receive likes from many people but not all of these people receive some kind of feedback.

We have previously discussed the structure of Facebook networks and interpreted their implications in the network dynamics part, in chapter 5. Here, however, we will see the stages of gathering and processing network data directly. We will start with Twitter data first. Twitter was so popular among social network analysis practice that there are R packages and functions dedicated to collecting and transforming Twitter data.

Extracting Twitter Data

NodeXL (Smith et al., 2009) is one of the tools you can use to extract Twitter data (see https://archive.codeplex.com/?p=nodexl). Having a free edition as well, this software tool works as an add-on of Excel, Microsoft's spreadsheet. Therefore, it can only be run using the Windows operating system. Although its setup is easy, as far as I see, further development of the software tool is halted and is not continued by a community since no open source is available. The latest free version, although a bit outdated, might still be useful for simple analysis.

An alternative I prefer is the R package named twitteR. It uses an API (Application Programming Interface) provided by Twitter, a standard interface provided by the company itself, ensuring communication with third party computer software as well as their own. However, you need to create a developer account on the Twitter system to connect to this interface (https://developer.twitter.com/). A code you will generate using this account will be necessary to connect to the Twitter system before downloading data with the twitteR package. In all of the following examples I have used my own account in producing the results but concealed them in the code chunks shown.

```
require(twitteR)
setup_twitter_oauth(
# Following info from your own Twitter developer account
  "XXX", #consumer key
  "XXX", #consumer secret
  "XXX", #access token
  "XXX" #access secret
)
```

The parts indicated as XXX that I did not make public due to security concerns are the information titled consumer_key, consumer_secret, access_token, and access_secret, respectively, that you will obtain from your Twitter developer account.

Once you log in to Twitter, you can conduct searches available to free accounts. Twitter people have an elegant solution that they provide a small sample of all the traffic to everyone, whereas they sell the full tweet flow to enterprise customers. Here we will use the free service. In the example below, we will examine the tweets from the "Greenpeace Mediterranean" Twitter account. We will search for tweets sent from this account, but you can reproduce the code for whichever account you desire. I first conduct a search using the sender account name, limiting the results to 1000 tweers only:

```
tweets<-searchTwitter('@@Greenpeace_Med',n=1000)
1000 tweets were requested but the API can only return 871
```

Here you can see that there were a little less number of tweets than we have requested. You can inspect the tweets as follows, if you like

```
head(tweets, n=3)
[[1]]
[1] "yesilpostaorg: RT @Greenpeace_Med: Sevdiğin
tehlike altındayken ne yaparsın?\n\nDünyadaki tüm yaşamı
okyanuslarımıza borçluyuz ve şimdi onları koruma sırası…"

[[2]]
[1] "YusufCimbom: RT @Greenpeace_Med: Avrupa Birliği'nde
plastik çatal, bıçak ve kaşıklar yasaklandı. Üye ülkelerin bu
kuralı uygulamaya başlamak için iki yı…"

[[3]]
[1] "tascio02: RT @Greenpeace_Med: Avrupa Birliği'nde plastik
çatal, bıçak ve kaşıklar yasaklandı. Üye ülkelerin bu kuralı
uygulamaya başlamak için iki yı…"
```

Most likely you should store the search results in a data file, because you shouldn't repeat the same query when you repeat the analysis. A first alternative is to use CSV files for storage, as in the following example. In this case the data is stored as a standard R data frame:

```
df<-twListToDF(tweets)
write.csv(df, "./tweets.csv")
Thus the data can be restored with conventional functions:
df<-read.csv("./tweets.csv")
```

Another method, recommended for larger data sets, is using the simple SQLite interface provided by the library:

```
sql_lite_file="./tweets-sqlite"
register_sqlite_backend(sql_lite_file)
store_tweets_db(tweets)
```

In this case you can later reload such tweets as follows:

```
sql_lite_file="./tweets-sqlite"
register_sqlite_backend(sql_lite_file)
tweets<-load_tweets_db()
head(tweets,n=3)
```

Now, it is time for further analysis. My choice as first step is to make visualization, by creating a graph using our tweets. There are more than one type of interaction and corresponding relations in Twitter, such as like, retweet, reply etc. In the example below, I included only the "retweeted" tweets as analyzing multiple relationships in the same graph might not give reliable results. First let's check if we have enough data by looking at the `isRetweet variable of tweets data frae:

```
df<-read.csv("./tweets.csv")
summary(df$isRetweet)
##    Mode    FALSE    TRUE
## logical    120     751
```

Now we separate the retweets from others as follows:

```
sp = split(df, df$isRetweet)
```

The split() function requires a categorical vector, in our case a logical vector telling whether the tweet is a retweet. The given data frame is split into multiple data frames, each corresponding to a unique value of the factor. We can access and display the splits for each factor using a notation as follows:

```
summary(sp[["TRUE"]]$retweetCount)
##    Min. 1st Qu.  Median    Mean 3rd Qu.    Max.
##     1.0    44.0    90.0   152.9   300.0  2107.0
```

We will use several new packages here for manipulating strings in Twitter's own format. This process is technically complex as we will dissect Twitter's unique information format and convert it into graph data. If you require further information, you can look at the following documentation and tutorials:

- https://www.rdocumentation.org/packages/twitteR/versions/1.1.9
- https://rpubs.com/cosmopolitanvan/twitternetworks

The example below is complete in the sense that it runs from loading data from file to processing it into a graph:

```
df<-read.csv("./tweets.csv")
require(qdap)
require(networkD3)
require(stringr)
require(dplyr)
#We will create a network relationship by looking at retweets
excluding other types of intractions
sp = split(df, df$isRetweet)
#The following row adds a computed column named 'sender' to the
dataset
rt = mutate(sp[['TRUE']], sender = substr(text, 5, regexpr(':',
text) - 1))
el = as.data.frame(cbind(sender = tolower(rt$sender), receiver
= tolower(rt$screenName)))
el = count(el, sender, receiver) #substract the number of
tweets and create graph
require(igraph)
rt_graph <- graph_from_data_frame(d=el, directed=T)
rtu<-simplify(as.undirected(rt_graph))
#Visualize the retweet network
degrees<-degree(rtu)
plot(rtu,layout=layout_with_mds)
```

The mutate function from the dplyr library adds a computed column to the dataset. The columön extracts the sender from the text, field of tweets data frame, by following Twitter's encoding that puts sender before a column, ":". Then the code takes sender and receiver of the retweet action and uses it ingraph_from_data_frame()` to produce an igraph object. The rest of the code should be familiar from the previous chapters. The plot produced in

Figure 1. Retweet interactions around @Greenpeace_Med account on Twitter

Figure 1 can be improved visually, but here we focus on Twitter data retrieval and leave it as an exercise.

Network Analysis and Interpretation

Naturally, the network data and visual we generated in the example above requires further study. However, at the very least, it shows us that there are at least four groups of different sizes that do not interact with one another. Actors like central individuals in each group can be analyzed using the methods we have discussed before. Ultimately, this initial outlook indicates that activists of Greenpeace Mediterranean should foster the interaction between these four groups. They can achieve this by contacting central figures in groups, resulting in a better and more integrated activism network.

In conclusion, only on certain occasions, such data will be completely surprising. However, in any case, they contain detailed information that can change the course of decision- making processes. Having an estimate regarding the effective individuals in this activism network and being able to measure this clearly have huge differences in terms of the effective use of resources. The same principle applies to public administration or businesses.

EXERCISES

1. Use the Greenpeace Turkey data as in the chapter example but build a network from "reply" relations instead of "retweet" relations. In doing so make sure you investigate the variable in the tweet data set.
2. Repeat the Greenpeace exercise for an international celebrity of your choosing. Do you see country or language groups in the network?

REFERENCES

Adamic, L. A., & Glance, N. (2005). The political blogosphere and the 2004 U.S. election. *Proceedings of the 3rd International Workshop on Link Discovery - Linkkdd '05*, 36–43. 10.1145/1134271.1134277

Atefeh, F., & Khreich, W. (2015). A survey of techniques for event detection in twitter. *Computational Intelligence, 31*(1), 132–164. doi:10.1111/coin.12017

Ghazawneh, A. (2011). The power of platforms for software development in open innovation networks. *International Journal of Networking and Virtual Organisations*, *9*(2), 140–154. doi:10.1504/IJNVO.2011.042415

Lazer, D., Pentland, A., Adamic, L., Aral, S., Barabási, A. L., Brewer, D., ... Jebara, T. (2009). Computational social science. *Science*, *323*(5915), 721–723. doi:10.1126cience.1167742 PMID:19197046

Sakaki, T., Okazaki, M., & Matsuo, Y. (2010, April). Earthquake shakes Twitter users: real-time event detection by social sensors. In *Proceedings of the 19th international conference on World wide web* (pp. 851-860). ACM. 10.1145/1772690.1772777

Smith, M. A., Shneiderman, B., Milic-Frayling, N., Mendes Rodrigues, E., Barash, V., Dunne, C., ... Gleave, E. (2009, June). Analyzing (social media) networks with NodeXL. In *Proceedings of the fourth international conference on Communities and technologies* (pp. 255-264). ACM. 10.1145/1556460.1556497

Wasserman, S., & Faust, K. (1994). *Social network analysis: Methods and applications* (Vol. 8). Cambridge university press. doi:10.1017/CBO9780511815478

Appendices

APPENDIX A. NETWORK DATASETS

Network data of certain research institutions are available publicly. You can find network datasets of varying natures in the following links:

- http://moreno.ss.uci.edu/data.html
- http://konect.uni-koblenz.de/networks/
- http://networkdata.ics.uci.edu/index.html
- http://www.casos.cs.cmu.edu/computational_tools/datasets/index.html
- https://snap.stanford.edu/data/
- https://sparse.tamu.edu/Pajek

Datasets Used in the Book

A significant majority of the datasets used in the book are the ones mentioned in the primary reference book by Wasserman and Faust (Wasserman and Faust 1994). They are explained in detail below. You may download most of them from the book website at http://appliedsna.mgencer.com/data/

Padgett's Florentine Families

This dataset was compiled by John F. Padgett (2010). He collected the relationships between medieval Florentine families. The original study notes are available on the following website: http://home.uchicago.edu/jpadgett/papers/unpublished/maelite.pdf. The complete dataset is available in the following link: http://www.casos.cs.cmu.edu/computational_tools/datasets/external/padgett/index2.html

Among these relational datasets, the one used in the book concerns marriages among the families. The data is available on the website of the book for easy use: http://appliedsna.mgencer.com/data/Padgett-marital.net provides the marriage network data and http://appliedsna.mgencer.com/data/ PadgettWealth.csv provides the wealth vector of families.

Read the dataset and wealth information as follows, using read.graph() function from the igraph library.

```
require(igraph)
g <- read.graph("data/PadgettMarital.net", format="pajek")
wealthData <- read.csv("data/PadgettWealth.csv",header=TRUE)
```

You can then plot the network, or, for example, compute correlation between degree and wealth. Please note however, that in an environment where multiple network analysis packages are invoked, one may need to be explicit in calling a function like degree() since package precedence is unknown. In this particular case the function is provided by both sna and igraph libraries and failure to explcate which one is invoked may result in a failure:

```
#uncomment to plot
#plot(g)
cor(igraph::degree(g), wealthData$wealth)
## [1] 0.5589956
```

Krackhardt's Network of High-Tech Managers

Compiled by David Krackhardt, the dataset shows the advisory relationships among 21 managers working at a high-technology machinery manufacturing company (Krackhardt 1987). The researcher examined how advice-giving relationships affect the adoption of a managerial program within the company. The original dataset is available in the following link: http://networkdata.ics. uci.edu/netdata/html/krackHighTech.html

This dataset also included in NetData, an R package; perhaps the easiest way to invoke it for your exercises. The example below shows its usage:

```
require(NetData) #https://cran.r-project.org/web/packages/
NetData/NetData.pdf
data(kracknets)
head(advice_data_frame,3)
##   ego alter advice_tie
```

```
## 1    1      1           0
## 2    1      2           1
## 3    1      3           0
```

The dataset is provided in a very basic sociomatrix form. So you will need to convert it to a graph object according to the package you are using for plotting or analysis. An example conversion is for igraph package. Uncomment the line starting with plot(...) to see the network visualization.

```
edgelist <- as.matrix(
    # turn data into edgelist suitable for your package of
choice: igraph is shown below
    advice_data_frame[advice_data_frame[3]==1,1:2])
    # A value 1 in the third column of data indicates a tie
being present
require(igraph)
g<-graph_from_edgelist(edgelist)
#uncomment the following line to plot
#plot.igraph(g, layout=layout_with_kk)
```

International Trade

This dataset shows the import/export relations between 24 prominent countries. It is one of the basic datsets used in Wasserman and Faust book (Wasserman and Faust 1994). The original data can be found at http://vlado.fmf.uni-lj.si/pub/networks/data/WaFa/default.htm. It is also available on the book website: http://appliedsna.mgencer.com/data/CountriesTrade.paj . The data format is suitable for network package but not igraph. Thus you can import the data as follows:

```
require(network)
require(sna)
n<-read.paj("data/CountriesTrade.net")
n1 <- n$networks$ws0
# uncomment following line to plot
#plot.network(n1,displaylabels=T)
```

After that you will need to make a format conversion to use it in igraph package. The intergraph package provides functions for such conversion:

```
require(intergraph)
require(igraph)
```

```
g<-asIgraph(n1)
#uncomment the following line to plot
#plot(g)
```

Zachary's Karate Club Dataset

The data comes from a research in the field of anthropology, collected by Wayne Zachary (Zachary 1977). The data includes several relations between 34 members of a karate club in a university. Zachary studied a social duality what he labels as conflict and *fission*. There were two factions in this social group. Zachary have observed the group over some time and have found that the ties within factions became more intense (fission) whereas whatever ties existed between member from different groups has vanished over time (conflict).

This dataset and some others are available from an R library called igraphdata, as igraph objects. It is an undirected and weighted dataset.

```
require(igraphdata)
data(karate)
require(igraph)
summary(karate)
## IGRAPH 4b458a1 UNW- 34 78 -- Zachary's karate club network
## + attr: name (g/c), Citation (g/c), Author (g/c), Faction
(v/n),
## | name (v/c), label (v/c), color (v/n), weight (e/n)
#help(karate) # Please read the explanations for the dataset
#plot(karate)
```

Coleman's Highschool Boys' Friendship Network (Longitudinal)

This a dataset collected by Coleman (Coleman a,1964) and it shows the friendship ties between high school boys as assessed by the question: "What fellows here in school do you go around with most often?". The measurement was repeated twice, in 1957 and 1958 and the data shows the change in friendship network between the two years. The dataset is provided in both ggraph and sna packages, but note that their data object classes are different but can be converted to igraph:

```
require(ggraph)
data(highschool)
class(highschool)
## [1] "data.frame"
library(igraph)
g1 <- graph_from_data_frame(highschool)
#plot(g1)
require(sna)
data(coleman)
class(coleman)
## [1] "array"
g1957<-graph_from_adjacency_matrix(coleman[1,,])
#graph for 1957 converted to igraph
#plot(g1957)
```

Victor Hugo's Les Miserables Characters

This is a dataset about the "scene co-appearance" network of the characters in Victor Hugo's famous novel "Les Miserables". The original data is retrieved from the Stanford network database (Knuth 1993). This network has 77 actors/nodes, that appear throughout this voluminous novel.

```
require(igraph)
g <- read.graph("data/lesmiserables.gml", format="gml")
gu<-simplify(as.undirected(g)) #preferably
#plot(gu)
```

US air Traffic Dataset

This is a relatively larger network example. The Air Traffic network data comes from the Koblenz Network. It contains the data about the airline connection between US airports, with 1227 airport in the data. See: http://konect.uni-koblenz.de/networks/maayan-faa

```
require(igraph)
g<-read.graph("data/maayan-faa/out.maayan-
faa",format="edgelist")
gu<-simplify(as.undirected(g)) #preferably
#plot(gu)
```

APPENDIX B. BASIC STATISTICAL AND GRAPH DEFINITIONS

Graphs

A graph is a combination of nodes and ties, denoted as: $G=(N,T)$. The set of nodes is $N=n_1,n_2,...,n_n$, and the set of ties is $T=t_1,t_2,...,t_m$. The number of nodes, $n = N \vee$, and that of relations, $m = T \vee$, are the sizes of these sets.

Density of a directed/asymmetric graph is defined as $d = \dfrac{m}{n \cdot (n-1)}$ there may be relations between each of the n actors and each of the remaining n-1. for an undirected/symmetric graph, density is defined as $d = \dfrac{m}{n \cdot (n-1)/2}$ because the two directions of a symmetric tie between two nodes are the same, meaning that we need to divide the denominator of the formula by 2 in order not to count a symmetric tie twice.

Each tie is shown with the two actors it connects: $t_k=(n_{k1},n_{k2})$. If the relation is weighted, the strenght of the tie is also added to the notation: $t_k=(n_{k1},n_{k2},s_k)$.

Centrality: Local Degree

Degree of a node is denoted as d_k and it is the number of ties connected to the node:

$$d_k = (n_{k1},n_{k2}) \in T \vee k1 = k or k2 = k \vee$$

If the graph is directed than in-degree and out-degree are defined separately as the number of incoming and outgoing ties, respectively:

$$d_k = (n_{k1},n_{k2}) \in T \vee k2 = k \vee$$

$$d_k^{out} = (n_{k1},n_{k2}) \in T \vee k1 = k \vee$$

Centrality: Non-Local

Let u_{ij} denote the geodesic distance: the length of the shortest path between two individuals in a network. **Closeness centrality** of an individual, b_i, is found by first calculating the sum of distances between the individual and all others: $U_{b_i} = \sum_{\forall b_j \neq b_i} u_{ij}$. Closeness is reverse of this distance. However, such a measure would not be scale-free. It depends on the number of actors in the social network. If there are n people in the network and one individual is directly connected with all others the sum of distances is n-1 and closeness centrality is $\dfrac{1}{n-1}$. This value is used for normalization, such that closeness centrality is defined as follows:

$$C(b_i) = \frac{n-1}{U_{b_i}} = \frac{n-1}{\sum_{\forall b_j \neq b_i} u_{ij}}$$

With normalization, its value is between 0 and 1.

Betweenness centrality measures the proportion of shortest paths on which an individuals sits on the shortest paths between any other pair of individuals. It is more difficult to calculate. There may be more than one shortest path connecting two actors in the network. Let the number of geodesics connecting two individuals, b_k and b_l, be denoted as j_{kl}. The number of geodesics on which the individual we are concerned with, b_i, is located is denoted as j_{kl}^i. To compute betweenness centrality we first need the *betweenness sum* below in order to calculate the betweenness centrality of the actor, namely b_i:

$$a(i) = \sum_{k \neq l} j_{kl}^i / j_{kl}$$

Normalization is necessary by dividing the betweenness sum by the number of pairs excluding the actor. In a social network with n actors, the number of all possible pairs excluding the focal actor is $(n-1)(n-2)/2$. Therefore, betweenness centrality can be calculated as:

$$A(i) = \frac{a(i)}{(n-1)(n-2)/2} = \frac{\sum_{k \neq l} j_{kl}^i / j_{kl}}{(n-1)(n-2)/2}$$

This measure is also between 1 and 0

Distributions

Normal Distribution

A normal or Gaussian distribution is seen in collection of measurements that are centered around a value. The distribution is formulated as follows:

$$f\left(x \vee \mu, \sigma^2\right) = \frac{1}{\sqrt{2\pi\sigma^2}} e^{-}$$

An example is shown in Figure 1 and produced as follows:

```
x=0:1000
m=500
s=150
y=1/sqrt(2*pi*s^2)*exp(-(x-m)^2/(2*s^2))
plot(y~x, type="l")
```

Power-Law Distribution

A power-law distribution formulated as: $P(X=x) \propto x^{-\alpha}$. In the discrete case where degrees of nodes are distributed in this manner, on needs a zeta-distribution which is essentially same. A power distribution example is shown in Figure 2 and produced as follows:

```
x=1:1000
a=0.3
y=x^(-a)
plot(y~x, type="l")
```

Pearson Correlation

Pearson correlation measures how two measurement series are correlated:

$$\rho_{X,Y} = \text{corr}(X,Y) = \frac{\text{cov}(X,Y)}{\sigma_X \sigma_Y} = \frac{E\left[(X-\mu_X)(Y-\mu_Y)\right]}{\sigma_X \sigma_Y}$$

Figure 1. A normal distribution

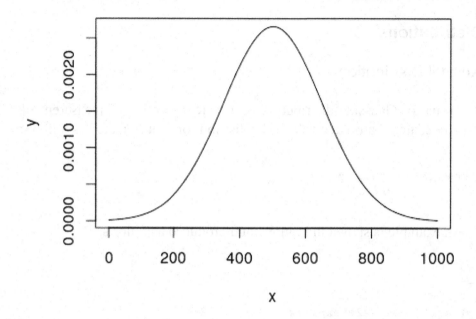

Figure 2. A power law distribution

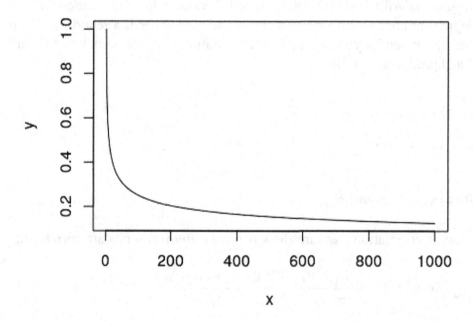

Here, the $E[\cdots]$ denotes a series average, X and Y denote the two data series, and μ_X and μ_Y denote their averages, and σ_X and σ_Y denote their standard deviations. These standard deviations are calculated as follows:

$$\sigma_X = \sqrt{E}$$

Linear Modeling

Linear modeling is a mathematical model involving a variable concerning each value in a sample (dependent variable) in terms of other variables (independent variables). This modeling method builds the dependent variable Y as the sum of independent variables $X_1, X_2, \ldots, X_n$ with certain weights and an additional error variable:

$$Y = \beta_1 X_1 + \beta_2 X_2 + \cdots + \beta_n X_n + \varepsilon$$

What we do in linear modeling is finding values for operation weights $\beta_1, \beta_2, \ldots, \beta_n$ that minimizes the error variable. It is easy to show this operation visually when there is only a single independent variable as in Figure 3. In this example, the coefficient that is optimal for connecting dependent variable values (vertical axis) with independent variable values (horizontal axis) is the one centers the values the best. This way, the distances of the real values from this centered line (as the name linear modeling suggests) will be minimized. To what extent the linear model is explanatory is measured with the datum. This value gives the correlation of the results provided by the model with the real measurements. Thus, values close to 1 signify a model with high explanatory power.

APPENDIX C. A QUICK INTRODUCTION TO R STATISTICS SYSTEM

Definition, Setup and Getting Started

R, a software tool for statistics (Venables and Smith 2002), is a software system developed continuously by many contributors from academia. Social network analysis is one of the analysis types applicable using R. Besides

Figure 3. Linear modeling with a single independent variable

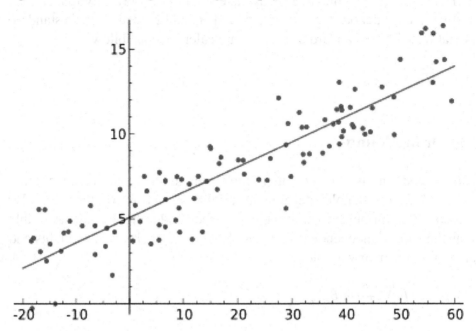

basic statistical methods such as general statistical methods, linear and other models, and hypothesis tests, R allows users to conduct various analyses including bioinformatic methods.

R is a core software package available for free download on http://www.R-project.org and can be run on different operating systems like Windows, Linux, and Mac. An introductory usage guide is provided for R on this website. Additionally, "Statistics. An Introduction using R" by Crawley is one of the most comprehensive reference sources (Crawley 2005).

After the setup, you will see an opening screen that is quite different from the attractive screens of software tools like Gephi (Bastian et al., 2009) and SPSS (another frequently used statistical software tool):

```
R version 3.5.2 (2018-12-20) -- "Eggshell Igloo"
Copyright (C) 2018 The R Foundation for Statistical Computing
Platform: x86_64-pc-linux-gnu (64-bit)
R is free software and comes with ABSOLUTELY NO WARRANTY.
You are welcome to redistribute it under certain conditions.
Type 'license()' or 'licence()' for distribution details.
  Natural language support but running in an English locale
R is a collaborative project with many contributors.
Type 'contributors()' for more information and
```

```
`citation()' on how to cite R or R packages in publications.
Type `demo()' for some demos, `help()' for on-line help, or
`help.start()' for an HTML browser interface to help.
Type `q()' to quit R.
>
```

This screen referred to as "command line" by Windows users waits for you to type commands to manage the program. This challenges the common habit of left/right clicking with the mouse and using the keyboard rarely. However, unlike the two buttons of a mouse, commands to be entered with a keyboard gives us an increased power of expression and control. I believe you will be satisfied with the experience if you try to surmount this emotional obstacle.

The prompt ">" on R's screen indicates that it is ready for our commands. When we type in a command, R will run it and show the results; then, this prompt will reappear, indicating that the program is ready for a new command. Each command consists of a name and parameters in parentheses. For instance, a command that reads as "quit()" allows quitting the program; we put the parentheses even though the operation requires no parameters. When you type in this command and press "ENTER", R will get the command and operate accordingly. To get help about any of the possible commands, the command "help" comes to our aid.

If you type in "help(solve)", R will show you a screen explaining what does the command "solve" do along with its parameters and examples. You can press "q" to quit the help screen.

To illustrate, let us solve the equation:

```
> solve(5,2)
[1] 0.4
>
```

The command "solve" gave us the solution for x consisting of one number ([1] shows the number of solutions): The result is 0.4, and now the program is ready for a new command as the marker suggests.

Besides commands, we can also type in numbers or arithmetic expressions:

```
> 2**3/7
[1] 1.142857
```

Instead of seeing the result of such an operation on the screen, it might be necessary to store it in a symbolic variable:

```
> x <- 2**3/7
>
```

This time, instead of directly showing the result, R stores it in a variable named "x". In the following operations, x will take this value. For example:

```
> x
[1] 1.142857
> x*10
[1] 11.42857
>
```

Instead of singular numbers, we may use the command "c(…)" to generate number sequences:

```
> c(7,3,2,4)
[1] 7 3 2 4
> c(7,3,2,4.3)
[1] 7.0 3.0 2.0 4.3
```

Please note that you can see if there is a real number in the list, R considers integer values as real numbers and generates a list accordingly. You can also embed the result of the command into a variable. Now, let us use multiple commands at once and solve a system of two equations with two unknowns. Keep in mind that you can use the command "help(…)" if you come across commands you are not familiar with:

```
> a <- matrix(c(1,2,3,4),nrow=2)
> a
     [,1] [,2]
[1,]    1    3
[2,]    2    4
> b <- c(5,6)
> solve(a,b)
[1] -1  2
>
```

The equation system we solved in this example is expressed in mathematical terms as follows:

$$\begin{bmatrix} 1 & 3 \\ 2 & 4 \end{bmatrix} \cdot X = \begin{bmatrix} 5 \\ 6 \end{bmatrix}$$

R shows us the result as

$$X = \begin{bmatrix} -1 \\ 2 \end{bmatrix}$$

Datasets

Conventional datasets we use consist of multiple data columns. In other words, they are formed with multiple lists such as the lists of values like those above coming together. In terms of R, such a dataset is called a "data frame". We can create such a dataset manually:

```
d <- data.frame(age=c(17,21,24,18,20))
```

Here, we created a dataset the sample of which consists of nothing but the ages of five individuals. We can add new data columns to the dataset if we want to:

```
> d$sex <- c("f","m","m","f","m")
> d
age sex
1  17       f
2  21       m
3  24       m
4  18       f
5  20       m
> d$age
[1] 17 21 24 18 20
>
```

We now have a dataset with two data columns (age and sex). As you can see, we can use and change different data columns in the dataset with the term "d$age". For instance, let us find the age average:

```
> mean(d$age) [1] 20
>
The command "summary()" will provide you with a summary of any
dataset you want:
> summary(d)
age sex
Min.  :17  Length:5
```

```
1st Qu.:18    Class:character   Median :20 Mode :character Mean
20
3rd Qu.:21 Max.  :24
>
```

We can show these data in a graphic or a histogram:

```
> plot(d$age)
> hist(d$age)
```

Such drawing commands show the graphic in a window on the screen. If you want to save the graphic as a separate file:

```
> jpeg("/tmp/agegraphic.jpg")
> hist(d$age)
> dev.off()
X11cairo
2
>
```

You may want to split and analyze the dataset based on categorical variables (e.g. sex):

```
> split <- split(d,d$sex)
> split$m
age sex
2   21       m
3   24       m
5   20       m
> split$f
> age       sex
1   17       f
4   18       f
>
```

Saving and Loading Datasets

Creating datasets manually every single time is not practical. Besides, we cannot use large datasets this way. To import such data to R or to export the data we generated, the best file format is the CSV (comma separated values) format. In this format, a data table is created like in spreadsheet tools (e.g. Microsoft Excel), but columns are separated with commas. The following example applies this to Krackhardt's case study on managerial relations (Krackhardt, 1997):

```
"",    "vertex", "age",   "tenure","centrality"
"1",   "v1",     33,      9.333,  13
"2",   "v2",     42,      19.583, 18
"3",   "v3",     40,      12.75,  5
"4",   "v4",     33,      7.5,    8
"5",   "v5",     32,      3.333,  5
"6",   "v6",     59,      28,     10
"7",   "v7",     55,      30,     13
"8",   "v8",     34,      11.333, 10
"9",   "v9",     62,      5.417,  4
"10",  "v10",    37,      9.25,   9
"11",  "v11",    46,      27,     11
"12",  "v12",    34,      8.917,  7
"13",  "v13",    48,      0.25,   4
"14",  "v14",    43,      10.417, 10
"15",  "v15",    40,      8.417,  4
"16",  "v16",    27,      4.667,  8
"17",  "v17",    30,      12.417, 9
"18",  "v18",    33,      9.083,  15
"19",  "v19",    32,      4.833,  4
"20",  "v20",    38,      11.667, 8
"21",  "v21",    36,      12.5,   15
```

Spreadsheet tools like Microsoft Excel or OpenOffice can export tables in CSV format. You can then import the file to R as a dataset and run it as follows:

```
> d <- read.csv("example.csv")
> d.summary()
...
> cor(d$age, d$centrality) ...
```

Or you can export the datasets after making alterations:

```
> write.csv(d, "ornek2.csv")
```

Setting up Additional Packages for R

In addition to the core software, there are some specialized packages making certain analysis methods available for use. You can discover them by looking at this website: http://cran.r-project.org/

After finding a package suitable for your task, you will set it up on R. For example, follow these steps to set up the statnet package used for social network analysis:

```
> install.packages("statnet")
```

This command will allow you to choose one of the international sites to download the packages and then will set up the package. Now you can use the following command to load the new package each time you need to use it in R:

```
> library(statnet)
```

An alternative way of loading packages is safer as it omits loading an already loaded package, instead just checking its status to satisfy that the required package is there:

```
> require(statnet)
```

Advanced Operations: Modeling and Hypothesis Tests

In Krackhardt's case study on managerial relations, we examined the relationship between the advice-giving role of managers and their ages and seniorities. The correlation provides clues in this respect. However, we need to formulate a hypothesis and test it with the numerical model if we want a more reliable study. For instance, let us take the hypothesis stating that the centrality in advice-giving is inversely correlated with both age and seniority. Our claim here corresponds to a linear model. We can, therefore, use the linear model command "lm()" on R:

```
> d <- read.csv("example.csv")
> mymodel <- lm(d$centrality ~ d$age + d$seniority)
> summary(mymodel) Call:
lm(formula = d$centrality ~ d$age + d$seniority)
```

```
Residuals:
Min 1Q  Median  3Q  Max
-4.3740 -1.9687 -0.5788 1.1362  6.4138
Coefficients:
Estimate Std. Error    t value Pr(>|t|)
(Intercept)  11.45894  3.16239  3.624  0.00194 **
d$age        -0.17130  0.08786 -1.950  0.06696 .
d$seniority   0.37389  0.10443  3.580  0.00214 **
---
Signif. codes:  0 '***' 0.001 '**' 0.01 '*' 0.05 '.' 0.1 ' ' 1
Residual standard error: 3.274 on 18 degrees of freedom
Multiple R-squared: 0.4169, Adjusted R-squared: 0.3521
F-statistic: 6.435 on 2 and 18 DF,  p-value: 0.007793
>
```

The summary R gives us regarding the model provides us with comprehensive knowledge rather than correlation. The effect of seniority on centrality is visible from the positive (0.37389) coefficient. Furthermore, the hypothesis concerning this effect is confirmed with a strong significance level ("significance code" 0.01). On the other hand, the impact of age is negative and weaker, and this impact is confirmed only with a significance level of 0.10. As a result, contradicting the correlation, seniority has a positive impact while we cannot confirm that of age statistically. Yet the explanatory power of the model is somewhat weak (R-squared value of 0.35). This suggests that we need to keep looking for other factors affecting centrality.

APPENDIX D. CORE NETWORK ANALYSIS PACKAGES IN R

In this appendix we will examine the libraries that are helpful in applying social network analysis methods. For many readers coming from a social sciences background these methods might be complicated to use.

For this reason, I believe a head start with Gephi, a software tool with an attractive visual interface, is quite appealing for many beginners when compared with other alternatives. Among the network software tools discussed in the book, Gephi, in particular, offers the "first-time experience" that is the closest to our daily computer usage habits. For instance, in Pajek, another software tool with a visual interface, you are expected to know exactly what you want while you browse through menus with equivalent appearances; therefore, it targets experts despite its visual interface. Gephi, on the other hand, has an intuitive user interface for novice social network analysts. Its interface consists of buttons for visualization, data organization, and analysis while being easy to navigate for beginner-level users.

However, this is where the problem starts. Analysis required by a scientific study do not fit in a simplified interface aiming to appeal to a general audience. After improving themselves in the application of these methods, the practitioner sees the limitations of this software tool.

Due to these reasons, throughout this book we concentrate on another software tool that might seem to be way too complex at first glance but is quite powerful and controllable once you get familiarized with it: R statistics system. Those who have never used R should read Appendix C thoroughly and acquire basic skills. They can then proceed with this chapter.

This appendix only provides an introduction to the use of R for analyzing social networks. The methods are theoretically discussed in the previous chapters. This appendix aims to overcome practical obstacles by reviewing the libraries altogether in a single place.

R consists of a basic software core and many additional compatible packages developed by different people enabling certain unique statistical analysis methods. Multiple R packages have emerged throughout years within the framework of social network analysis.

Graph Representation, Drawing and Basic Analyses with the "Igraph" Package

"igraph" is the most basic package on R used for social network analysis (Csardi and Nepusz, 2006; http://igraph.org). This package allows us to represent and visualize graphs along with other fundamental operations. Even though it was not designed specifically for "social network analysis", it is suitable for our basic operations. The chapter concerning the use of this package for social network analysis of the following book can be used as a comprehensive guide http://www.rdatamining.com/docs/r-and-data-mining-examples-and-case-studies.

You need to generate or load a graph on the igraph package and create nodes and ties. This operation is made manually in the example below, with results shown in Figure 4:

```
# The small network in this example was generated using R
commands
# In a real data analysis we would upload the network from the
```

```
data file
library(igraph) #gerekli ağ kitaplığını yükler
# the following function generates the network
g <- graph.formula(
   "Me"-"Adam",    # each pair in these rows
   "Me"-"Jane",    #   signifies a relationship
   "Me"-"John",
   "Me"-"Mary",
   "Adam"-"Jane",
   "Jane"-"John",
   "John"-"Mary",
   "Adam"-"Mary"
   )
V(g)$size <- 45
plot(g)
```

You can get the variable representing the nodes in the graph using the function V() and change the parameters interpreted by igraph (e.g. size). Similarly, you can use the function E() to obtain ties. In the following example, we change the graph features and draw it again. Here, using the weight parameter, we make the graph weighted, as in Figure 5:

```
V(g)$size <- 45 # change vertex size in plot
E(g)$weight <- 1/c(8,4,6,10,9,3,6,5) # weights of ties (Edges)
                                     # by taking the reverse
we make sure
                                     # the strong ties are
drawn shorter
E(g)$label <- c(8,4,6,10,9,3,6,5)    # labels of edges
```

Figure 4. Ego-network (artificial)

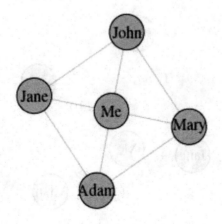

```
plot(g, # visualize the graph
     edge.curved=0.2) # make the ties drawn curved
```

Instead of creating a graph using commands as it is shown above, you can upload it from an external data file. For example, assume that you put the graph below given in the Pajek format (Batagelj and Mrvar, 1998) in a file named "example1.net" (you can access this file from the webpage of the book as http://appliedsna.mgencer.com/data/example1.net):

```
*Vertices 4
1 "Me"
2 "Mary"
3 "Adam"
4 "John"
5 "Jane"
*Edges
1 2 10
1 3 8
1 4 6
1 5 4
2 3 5
2 4 6
3 5 9
4 5 3
```

There are three figures in each row corresponding to the ties in the example because this is a weighted network and third figures show the weight or strength

Figure 5. Ego network re-drawn

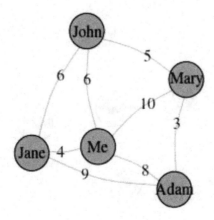

of the tie. Now we can run such a file using the command below; you are advised to change the file path to a local path of the file on your computer:

```
library(igraph)
g <- read.graph("http://appliedsna.mgencer.com/data/example1.
net",format="pajek")
#plot(g)
```

Unfortunately, sometimes igraph might not be able to read the node names correctly. You can come across such shortcomings while working with software tools developed dynamically.

You can get some basic network metrics with the igraph package. For more details, you should read the reference guide of the package and consult relevant sections of the book.

```
g <- read.graph("data/example1.net",format="pajek")
igraph::degree(g) #Find degrees
##    Me Mary Adam John Jane
##     4    3    3    3    3
V(g)$degree <- igraph::degree(g) # or better store them in
vertices
E(g)$weight  #see edge weights
## [1] 10  8  6  4  5  6  9  3
#plot(g, vertex.size = 10 * V(g)$degree, edge.label =
E(g)$weight)
```

You may, of course, want to export this drawing to a file:

```
jpeg("example1.jpg")
plot(g)
dev.off()
## png
##   2
```

Another dataset, the example dataset of Florentine families (Padgett, 2010), is provided for you to familiarize yourself with this package and use the example commands. it is accessed as a file or can be found in the network package:

```
library(network)
data(flo) #use dataset from package
library(igraph)
#convert to igraph
fg <- graph.adjacency(as.matrix(flo), mode="undirected", add.
```

```
rownames=TRUE)
#or read from file
g <- read.graph("data/PadgettMarital.net", format="pajek")
gs<-simplify(g)
plot(gs)
```

STATNET, SNA and Network Packages

As the igraph package is only aimed at graph representation and not social network analysis, we will need additional packages. Here, we will introduce statnet, sna and network packages.

First, we need to discuss the "statnet" package (Handcock et al. 2008b. It makes use of previously-written packages of "sna" and "network" while conducting certain methods that are frequently used in network analysis on them. On the other hand, developers of the package focused more on "random networks" mostly used by physicists and mathematicians and the aim of simulating them with stochastic models. Meanwhile, another social network analysis package called "RSiena" provides us with tools examining the changes in networks throughout the course of time (Ripley, Snijders, and Preciado 2015). These packages come into forefront among many others whose developments are either halted or in progress.

I prefer limiting the practical applications in this chapter with the statnet package because it seems to be the most popular package providing analyses and metrics. Detailed usage guides and helpful articles on statnet (and its sub-

Figure 6. Florentine families marriage network

packages) can be found in the Issue 24 of the Journal of Statistical Software: http://www.jstatsoft.org/v24

Statnet and other R social network packages use the data formats of a few other software tools used for network analysis that have their own strengths in different areas. Most of the time, they also define their unique formats. I opted, wherever possible, to use the Pajek format because it comes to the forefront as the best option to code the most common social network data in the most effective way,and it is compatible with many other software. We have seen the dataset files using this format in the previous chapters.

Before starting network analysis with statnet on R, you need to set up and install the package using the command install.packages("statnet") as shown in the package management examples at the end of the section making an introduction to R, in Appendix C. Then you invoke the package as:

```
require(statnet)
```

You may need two kinds of datasets while analyzing a social network. The first is the conventional type of data concerning measurements about actors forming the network (probably individuals), such as age, gender, etc.. The other kind is relational data.

We will use the dataset about the relationships among company managers compiled by Krackhardt as an example (Krackhardt, 1987). First, we will upload the relationship data. These data are, as before, in the Pajek format. Let us upload this dataset and save it in a variable named n. While using the commands below, you should change the file path in accordance with the file name and location on your computer:

```
require(statnet)
n <- read.paj("data/HighTech-advice.net")
```

If you look closely, you can see that this dataset is different from the usual "data frame", list or matrix format on R. Furthermore, the summary of the dataset will also be different (for instance, it also shows network density):

```
class(n)
## [1] "network"
summary(n,print.adj=FALSE)
## Network attributes:
##    vertices = 21
##    directed = TRUE
##    hyper = FALSE
```

```
##    loops = FALSE
##    multiple = FALSE
##    bipartite = FALSE
##    title = Krackhardt's High-tech managers
##  total edges = 190
##    missing edges = 0
##    non-missing edges = 190
##  density = 0.452381
##
## Vertex attributes:
##   vertex.names:
##     character valued attribute
##     21 valid vertex names
##
##  x:
##     numeric valued attribute
##     attribute summary:
##    Min. 1st Qu.  Median   Mean 3rd Qu.    Max.
##  0.1145  0.5325  0.6117  0.5949  0.7041  0.8855
##
##  y:
##     numeric valued attribute
##     attribute summary:
##    Min. 1st Qu.  Median   Mean 3rd Qu.    Max.
##  0.0784  0.3892  0.4775  0.4671  0.5533  0.9216
##
## Edge attributes:
##
##   Krackhardt's High-tech managers:
##     numeric valued attribute
##     attribute summary:
##    Min. 1st Qu.  Median   Mean 3rd Qu.    Max.
##       1       1       1       1       1       1
```

Now, we will upload the actor datasets. The best way of saving actor data and importing them to R is to use the CSV file format (see Appendix C). Programs we use for creating spreadsheets like Microsoft Excel can be used to export these data in the CSV format. Let us import our data file to R and then analyze the dataset type as well as its summary:

```
d <- read.csv("data/HighTech-variables.csv")
class(d)
## [1] "data.frame"
summary(d)
##      vertex          age             tenure
##   v1    : 1    Min.   :27.00   Min.   : 0.250
##   v10   : 1    1st Qu.:33.00   1st Qu.: 7.500
```

```
##   v11    : 1    Median:37.00    Median: 9.333
##   v12    : 1    Mean  :39.71    Mean  :11.746
##   v13    : 1    3rd Qu.:43.00    3rd Qu.:12.500
##   v14    : 1    Max.  :62.00    Max.  :30.000
##   (Other):15
```

This dataset is a "data frame", the R equivalent of datasets used in conventional statistical methods. Thus, its summary shows basic statistics like the average of each variable column and minimal/maximal values. These two datasets are compatible with one another. This means that the node data in the second data set are in the same order as in the first one: If an individual is shown in the fourth place in the first dataset, the same applies to the second dataset as well. This will help us make an alignment.

Network Visualization

Network visualization is provided by multiple packages including the "network" package. As the statnet package is an "umbrella" package, it comes with other packages including "network". Therefore, we do not need a separate setup.

To visualize the network we uploaded above and saved in the variable named n we run the following code chunk, whose result is shown in Figure 7:

```
require(statnet)
n <- read.paj("data/HighTech-advice.net")
plot.network(n, displaylabels=TRUE, interactive=FALSE)
```

If you change the "interactive" parameter in the command as TRUE, you will be able to select and move the actors of the drawing with your mouse, manipulating the drawing in accordance to your design.

If you would like to save this drawing in a file instead of seeing it on the screen, you should indicate a redirection of the output of the R and complete the redirection once the operation is done before typing the drawing command:

```
jpeg("plot.jpg")
plot.network(n, displaylabels=TRUE)
dev.off()
## png
##   2
```

Figure 7. Florentine families marriage network: node size indicates family wealth

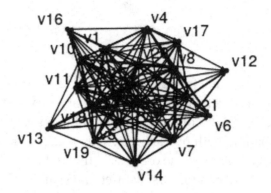

Measuring Density and Centrality

We already see the general density of the network in the dataset summary. In addition, we can use the command "density" in the network package to get it separately. If we assume that the variables n and d in the example above are defined the code is as follows:

```
require(statnet)
n <- read.paj("data/HighTech-advice.net")
network.density(n)
## [1] 0.452381
```

igraph also provides its own density function:

```
library(igraph)
g <- read.graph("data/HighTech-advice.net", format="pajek")
graph.density(g)
## [1] 0.452381
```

If we wish to separate the ego-networks of individuals and measure their densities, we need to follow several steps. here we will use the ego.extract() command from the sna package. The sapply() standard R function applies the given function to a vector of objects:

```
require(statnet)
n <- read.paj("data/HighTech-advice.net")
egonetdensities <- sapply(ego.extract(n), function (x)
{network.density(as.network(x))})
```

```
head(egonetdensities,n=3)
##        v1        v2        v3
## 0.5147059 0.4763158 0.4934641
```

Here, the command "ego.extract" separates the ego-networks in the network while the command "sapply" applies a function calculating their individual densities (while doing so, it also makes a data type conversion with the command as.network as commands come from different R packages). If you want, you can add the output of this command, individual ego-network densities, to the individual dataset instead of seeing them on the screen. Therefore, it will be easier to calculate, for example, the correlation of age and ego- network density:

```
require(statnet)
n <- read.paj("data/HighTech-advice.net")
d <- read.csv("data/HighTech-variables.csv")
d$density <- sapply(ego.extract(n), function (x) {network.
density(as.network(x))})
cor(d$age,d$density)
## [1] -0.3094646
```

We can infer from the analysis that the social network of an individual weakens as age increases.

We can measure centrality using the command "degree". This command supports (un)directed networks or different centrality measurements. For that reason, we need some parameters prompting the command. Let us both see the centrality measurements and add them into the individual dataset:

```
require(statnet)
n <- read.paj("data/HighTech-advice.net")
d <- read.csv("data/HighTech-variables.csv")
d$degree <- degree(n, cmode='outdegree', gmode='graph')
```

Same can be done using the igraph package. In this specific case one needs to take care about overlapping name spaces of the two libraries, in particular the degree() function:

```
require(igraph)
g <- read.graph("data/HighTech-advice.net",format="pajek")
d <- read.csv("data/HighTech-variables.csv")
d$degree <- igraph::degree(g, mode='out')
```

Analyzing how these measurements made based on individuals vary might prove to be quite useful. Using some basic commands on R would be sufficient to do that. Results are shown in Figures 8 and 9.

```
plot(d)
hist(d$degree,breaks=10)
```

The first command shows the change of all data columns when compared with one another in a single chart. The second one generates a histogram of the centrality measurements. The charts created with these commands are shown in the figures.

No parallelism is visible apart from the relationship between age and seniority in the multi-chart. The histogram of centrality measurements, on the other hand, is interesting. We instantly see a few clusters. There is a group with very low centrality. Then there are two clusters with centrality values of 8 and 14 and an individual with very high centrality on the far right. These clusters probably correspond to different groups of employees working in a firm. The individual on the far right with the highest centrality must be

Figure 8. Krackhardt database plot

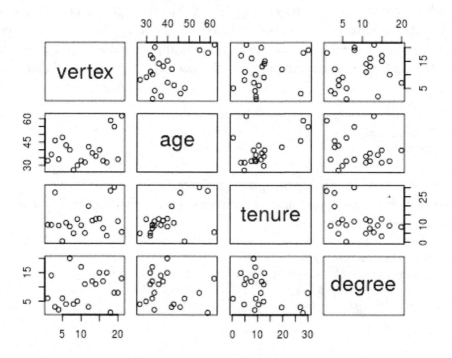

Figure 9. Krackhardt data: degree distribution

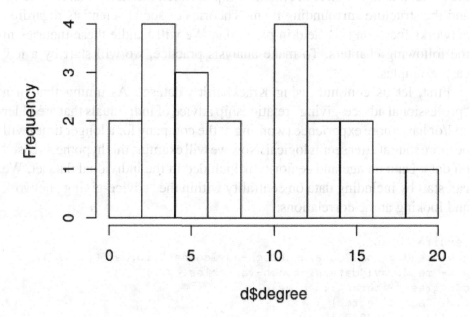

Histogram of d$degree

the company manager while the clusters in the middle are mid-to-high level managers. The group with high numbers and low centrality on the far left seems to be the lowest-ranking employees in the firm. Without additional data, we cannot confirm this interpretation. However, findings regarding clustering might help us in this respect.

Looking at the distribution of the structural features of the network, as we have done here, usually gives us interesting information about the general structure of the network. The clusters we saw in the centrality distribution indicate that individuals in the network are allocated to several different "roles". We were able to make a signification of this distribution in terms of our phenomenon (i.e. company managers) because clusters corresponding to different levels of company management were visible. As far as another phenomenon is concerned, this has the potential of revealing previously undetected roles.

Modeling Individual and Relational Data Together

Another field in which network analysis becomes significant in terms of the social phenomenon is the relationship between the state of an individual and the structure surrounding them. Theories of social scientists regarding networks focus on this field in particular. We will handle these theories in the following chapters. To make analysis practice, we will start by a few easy examples.

First, let us continue using Krackhardt's dataset. Assuming that in a "professional advice-giving" relationship advice of individuals that are older and/or have more experience (working at the company for a longer time) will be more sought after seems logical. Now we will examine this hypothesis based on data. Data on age and seniority is included in the individual dataset. We can start by including data on centrality within the "advice-giving" network and looking at the correlations:

```
require(igraph)
g <- read.graph("data/HighTech-advice.net",format="pajek")
d <- read.csv("data/HighTech-variables.csv")
d$degree <- igraph::degree(g)
cor(d$age,d$degree)
## [1] -0.1783847
cor(d$tenure,d$degree)
## [1] 0.003833262
```

There is a slightly negative correlation between age and centrality, meaning that unlike we assumed, older managers' advice does not seem to be more valuable. On the other hand, there is a positive correlation between tenure and centrality just like one would expect, but it is a weak correlation.

Naturally, our data are not the entire set of data determining one's value in terms of advice-giving. For instance, an individual's educational background, sex, and social skills will also play a role. However, we might question to what extent these data explain the value of giving advice. Looking at correlations is not sufficient on its own. A better and multivariate alternative is linear modeling or the method of linear regression. You can find the basic aspects of this method in other appendices of the book.

We want to model centrality on the basis of the data we have with using both age and centrality. We will use the standard command on R "lm()" (the initials for "linear model"):

```
m<-lm(d$degree ~ d$age + d$tenure)
summary(m)
##
## Call:
## lm(formula = d$degree ~ d$age + d$tenure)
##
## Residuals:
##    Min    1Q Median    3Q    Max
## -9.660 -4.501  1.319  2.576 13.185
##
## Coefficients:
##              Estimate Std. Error t value Pr(>|t|)
## (Intercept) 22.69093    5.65138   4.015 0.000812 ***
## d$age       -0.14073    0.15701  -0.896 0.381907
## d$tenure     0.08457    0.18662   0.453 0.655865
## ---
## Signif. codes:  0 '***' 0.001 '**' 0.01 '*' 0.05 '.' 0.1 ' '
1
##
## Residual standard error: 5.851 on 18 degrees of freedom
## Multiple R-squared:  0.04274,    Adjusted R-squared:
-0.06362
## F-statistic: 0.4018 on 2 and 18 DF,  p-value: 0.6749
```

This model confirms our inferences based on correlations to a great extent. However the R-squared information shows that the power of the model is very weak, indicating that one needs to look into structural aspects rather than age and tenure.

APPENDIX E. SOFTWARE FOR SOCIAL NETWORK ANALYSIS

Here, you will find some brief information and comparisons about some software tools frequently used for social network analysis. In many cases they are alternatives to R packages covered in the book. As there are many software tools out there, this list is not, by no means, an exhaustive one. However, my aim here, at the very least, was to compare software tools suitable for general use and being developed in an active manner.

Some of these software tools have an appealing user interface. Among these, I would recommend Gephi (Bastian et al., 2009), especially to beginners. The software tool can conduct, although not numerous, some general analyses and run different data formats.

Yet the user interface is not the only criterion. You need to choose a powerful tool for different analysis-related problems. For instance, Pajek might be more useful for those dealing with physics or mathematics. On the other hand, Pajek's methods concerning random networks may appeal to social researchers. However, the terminology employed more commonly by social researchers used in a software tool such as Gephi (in both the interface and documents) would be more familiar to them.

Furthermore, users may be comfortable with different styles of usage. For example, the R statistics system allows the user to work with command scripts. This makes it possible to repeat an entire analysis very quickly, bringing a significant advantage considering the frequent changes in the steps during the development of analysis. On the other hand, many users might prefer using a visual control panel instead of working with commands.

A certain analysis type may not be supported by every software tool. You might, therefore, need to use multiple tools at the same to complete a set of analysis you desire. For that reason, it is better to opt for tools supporting standard social network dataset formats (e.g. Pajek's .net format, a commonly used one).

One of the factors to be considered while choosing the best software tool is, apart from the software itself, the inclusion of an adequate user manual and the access to examples and documentation.

UCINET and NetDraw

One of the oldest social network analysis software around. UCINET (Borgatti et al., 2014) is not a free program. It can be downloaded from http://www.analytictech.com/archive/ucinet.htm for a 60 day free trial. The program is released for Microsoft Windows platform only. It parallels the most material in social network standard texts.

While the program is not free, its drawing component, NetDraw (Bogartti 2002), is free to download and use at https://sites.google.com/site/netdrawsoftware/home. This component, too, is only available for the Windows platform.

Pajek

Pajek (Batagelj and Mrvar 1998) is one of the software tools for network visualization and analysis that has been in use for a while. The contributions to the software mostly come from the fields of mathematics and physics, therefore, the presentation of the software reflects this orientation. This is an efficient system, especially for very large networks. You can get the software for free and access to additional materials such as a user manual from the following link: http://pajek.imfm.si/doku.php.

Pajek does not have a large community as the R igraph package has. But its ecosystem includes some books that provide a comprehensive introduction to its use.

Gephi

Gephi is one of the popular contemporary software tools available for social network visualization and analysis. As it is coded with Java language, it can be run on many systems (Windows, Linux, Mac). It has a relatively intuitive user interface and adopts popular network terminology, so that it is considerably easy to start with. You can use this tool for the initial stages of social network research. In comparison, however, R statistics system and related libraries allow increased control for serious analyses.

This software can be downloaded for free from http://gephi.org/ along with other basic user manuals. Gephi has a growing user community which is supportive. You can find examples and documentation in its website at https://gephi.org/users/. As common in open source software there is abundance of resources but no central quality control authority. For example, I have noticed a Facebook network analysis tutorial on Gephi website which is outdated. The analysis is not possible after Facebook has changed their usage policy several years ago. Thus users who came across this interesting tutorial will soon find themselves in a dead-end effort. Such encounters are common in open source ecosystems. But they accompany a rich variety of material so one should stay calm in the face of quality risks as such, but the pursuit is usually well worthed.

Siena and RSiena

Siena (Ripley, Snijders, and Preciado 2011) specializes in longitudinal modeling of network change. It implements sophisticated stochastic models for this purpose. It is freely available at https://www.stats.ox.ac.uk/~snijders/siena/, along with its sister package, Stocnet (Huisman and van Dujin, 2003).

RSiena makes the Siena software avaialable from within R. An obvious advantage is integration with the rest of analysis tools available in R. This also enables one to script the analysis as R code.

VOSviewer and Bibliometrix

Both of these software tools are for bibliometric analysis of collaboration, most often in academic fields. In particular, they can be used to process data in the standard format extracted from databases regarding scientific publications such as Scopus or Web-of-Science.

VOSviewer (Van Eck and Waltman 2007) conducts analyses specifically based on keywords in articles or relationships formed based on authors. It can be downloaded freeley from https://www.vosviewer.com/. One of its nice features is network-based clustering of keywords. A visual generated from an ongoing research study is given in Figure 10.

Bibliometrix is an R package used for similar analysis. It can be accessed at http://www.bibliometrix.org/. Its advantage when compared with VOSviewer is that it is programmable. This allows us to construct many different relational

Figure 10. A visual generated with VOSviewer: the network of keyword co-appearance in articles in scientific literature on workplace bullying

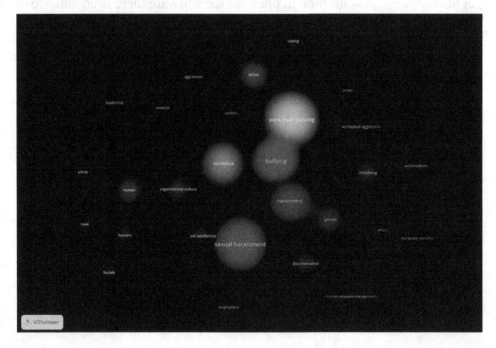

data, intergrate it with other analysis in R, or make youe analysis repeatable as a program.

NodeXL

NodeXL (Smith et al., 2009) is not a standalone software but an add-on for the popular spreadsheet program Excep, by Microsoft. Its free (but not open source) version can be downloaded from https://www.smrfoundation.org/ nodexl/ . NodeXL allows one to visualize graphs that are stored as edge lists in an Excel spreadsheet. Although the program lacks sophistication of other tools in our list, it can be useful for fast track workshops targeted at beginner level social network analysts.

NetworkX

NetworkX (Hagberg et al., 2013) is not a standalone tool but a software library for the popular programming language Python. Thus, it offers the advantage of extensibility: you can code your own analysis algorithms and metrics. In addition it offers access to Python's infamous variety of software libraries. For this reason it is advantageous in interdisciplinary research and applications. However, one must beware of the fact that a full quantitative research pipeline is what you want, you would need to take your data in and out of Python to manipulate it with more general statistical research tools such as R.

NetworkX is an open source and can be obtained from its website: https:// networkx.github.io/. The website also proves an extensive reference and tutorial documentation. You can also find pointers to a rich community of users that use and develop NetworkX, and help to answer each other's questions.

REFERENCES

Bastian, M., Heymann, S., & Jacomy, M. (2009). "Gephi: An Open Source Software for Exploring and Manipulating Networks." In *International Aaai Conference on Weblogs and Social Media*. http://www.aaai.org/ocs/index. php/ICWSM/09/paper/view/154

Batagelj, V., & Mrvar, A. (1998). Pajek-Program for Large Network Analysis. *Connections*, 21(2), 47–57.

Batagelj, V., & Mrvar, A. (2001). A subquadratic triad census algorithm for large sparse networks with small maximum degree. *Social Networks*, *23*(3), 237–243. doi:10.1016/S0378-8733(01)00035-1

Bogartti, S. P. (2002). *NetDraw Software for Network Visualization*. Lexington, USA: Analytic Technologies.

Borgatti, S. P., Everett, M. G., & Freeman, L. C. (2014). Ucinet. Encyclopedia of social network analysis and mining, 2261-2267.

Coleman, J. S. (1964). Introduction to Mathematical Sociology.NewYork, GlencoeCox, T. F, & Cox, M.A. (2000). Multidimensional Scaling. Chapman Hall/CRC.

Crawley, M. J. (2005). *Statistics: An Introduction using R*. Wiley.

Csardi, G., & Nepusz, T. (2006). The igraph software package for complex network research. *InterJournal. Complex Systems*, *1695*(5), 1–9.

Hagberg, A., Schult, D., Swart, P., Conway, D., Séguin-Charbonneau, L., Ellison, C., . . . Torrents, J. (2013). Networkx. High productivity software for complex networks. *Webová strá nka* https://networkx. lanl. gov/wiki

Handcock, M. S., Hunter, D. R., Butts, C. T., Goodreau, S. M., & Morris, M. (2008). statnet: Software tools for the representation, visualization, analysis and simulation of network data. *Journal of Statistical Software*, *24*(1), 1548.

http://www.stats.ox.ac.uk/{~}snijders/siena/RSiena{_}Manual.pdf.

Huisman, M., & Van Duijn, M. A. (2003). StOCNET: Software for the statistical analysis of social networks. *Connections*, *25*(1), 7–26.

Knuth, D E. (1993). Les miserables: coappearance network of characters in the novel les miserables. The Stanford GraphBase: A Platform for Combinatorial Computing.

Krackhardt, D. (1987). Cognitive social structures. *Social Networks*, *9*(2), 109–134. doi:10.1016/0378-8733(87)90009-8

Padgett, J. F. (2010). Open Elite? Social Mobility, Marriage, and Family in Florence, 1282–1494. *Renaissance Quarterly*, *63*(2), 357–411. doi:10.1086/655230

Ripley, R. M., Snijders, T. A., Boda, Z., Vörös, A., & Preciado, P. (2011). Manual for RSIENA. University of Oxford, Department of Statistics, Nuffield College, 1. http://www.stats.ox.ac.uk/{~}snijders/siena/RSiena{_}Manual.pdf

Smith, M. A., Shneiderman, B., Milic-Frayling, N., Mendes Rodrigues, E., Barash, V., Dunne, C., ... Gleave, E. (2009, June). Analyzing (social media) networks with NodeXL. In *Proceedings of the fourth international conference on Communities and technologies* (pp. 255-264). ACM.

Van Eck, N. J., & Waltman, L. (2007). VOS: A new method for visualizing similarities between objects. In *Advances in data analysis* (pp. 299–306). Berlin, Heidelberg: Springer.

Venables, W. N., Smith, D. M., & R Development Core Team. (2009). An introduction to R.

Wasserman, S., & Faust, K. (1994). *Social network analysis: Methods and applications* (Vol. 8). Cambridge university press.

Zachary, W. W. (1977). An Information Flow Model for Conflict and Fission in Small Groups. *Journal of Anthropological Research*, *33*(4), 452–473.

Related Readings

To continue IGI Global's long-standing tradition of advancing innovation through emerging research, please find below a compiled list of recommended IGI Global book chapters and journal articles in the areas of genetic algorithms, data clustering, and metaheuristic computing. These related readings will provide additional information and guidance to further enrich your knowledge and assist you with your own research.

Aggarwal, S., & Azad, V. (2017). A Hybrid System Based on FMM and MLP to Diagnose Heart Disease. In S. Bhattacharyya, S. De, I. Pan, & P. Dutta (Eds.), *Intelligent Multidimensional Data Clustering and Analysis* (pp. 293–325). Hershey, PA: IGI Global. doi:10.4018/978-1-5225-1776-4.ch011

Aherwar, A., Singh, A., Patnaik, A., & Unune, D. (2018). Selection of Molybdenum-Filled Hip Implant Material Using Grey Relational Analysis Method. In P. Vasant, S. Alparslan-Gok, & G. Weber (Eds.), *Handbook of Research on Emergent Applications of Optimization Algorithms* (pp. 675–692). Hershey, PA: IGI Global. doi:10.4018/978-1-5225-2990-3.ch029

Akkarapatty, N., Muralidharan, A., Raj, N. S., & P., V. (2017). Dimensionality Reduction Techniques for Text Mining. In V. Bhatnagar (Ed.), *Collaborative Filtering Using Data Mining and Analysis* (pp. 49-72). Hershey, PA: IGI Global. doi:10.4018/978-1-5225-0489-4.ch003

Alparslan-Gök, S. Z., Palancı, O., & Yücesan, Z. (2018). Peer Group Situations and Games With Grey Uncertainty. In P. Vasant, S. Alparslan-Gok, & G. Weber (Eds.), *Handbook of Research on Emergent Applications of Optimization Algorithms* (pp. 265–278). Hershey, PA: IGI Global. doi:10.4018/978-1-5225-2990-3.ch011

Amine, K. (2018). Insights Into Simulated Annealing. In S. Dash, B. Tripathy, & A. Rahman (Eds.), *Handbook of Research on Modeling, Analysis, and Application of Nature-Inspired Metaheuristic Algorithms* (pp. 121–139). Hershey, PA: IGI Global. doi:10.4018/978-1-5225-2857-9.ch007

Anish, C. M., Majhi, B., & Majhi, R. (2018). A Novel Hybrid Model Using RBF and PSO for Net Asset Value Prediction. In S. Dash, B. Tripathy, & A. Rahman (Eds.), *Handbook of Research on Modeling, Analysis, and Application of Nature-Inspired Metaheuristic Algorithms* (pp. 54–72). Hershey, PA: IGI Global. doi:10.4018/978-1-5225-2857-9.ch003

Antônio de Sousa, M., Carlson, C. M., & Vieira, F. H. (2015). Optimum Allocation of Transmission Technologies for Solving the BTS Interconnection Problem in Cellular Systems. In P. Vasant (Ed.), *Handbook of Research on Artificial Intelligence Techniques and Algorithms* (pp. 152–182). Hershey, PA: IGI Global. doi:10.4018/978-1-4666-7258-1.ch005

Banerjee, B., Saha, S., & Mohan Buddhiraju, K. (2017). Graph Theoretic Approaches for Image Analysis. In S. Bhattacharyya, S. De, I. Pan, & P. Dutta (Eds.), *Intelligent Multidimensional Data Clustering and Analysis* (pp. 193–224). Hershey, PA: IGI Global. doi:10.4018/978-1-5225-1776-4.ch008

Başaran, B., & Güneş, F. (2017). Data Clustering. In S. Bhattacharyya, S. De, I. Pan, & P. Dutta (Eds.), *Intelligent Multidimensional Data Clustering and Analysis* (pp. 28–72). Hershey, PA: IGI Global. doi:10.4018/978-1-5225-1776-4.ch002

Basu, A., & Talukdar, S. (2017). On the Implementation of a Digital Image Watermarking Framework Using Saliency and Phase Congruency. In S. Bhattacharyya, S. De, I. Pan, & P. Dutta (Eds.), *Intelligent Multidimensional Data Clustering and Analysis* (pp. 253–292). Hershey, PA: IGI Global. doi:10.4018/978-1-5225-1776-4.ch010

Behnamian, J. (2015). Combined Electromagnetism-Like Algorithm with Tabu Search to Scheduling. In P. Vasant (Ed.), *Handbook of Research on Artificial Intelligence Techniques and Algorithms* (pp. 478–508). Hershey, PA: IGI Global. doi:10.4018/978-1-4666-7258-1.ch015

Besbes, K., Allaoui, H., Goncalves, G., & Loukil, T. (2015). A Stochastic Approach to Product-Driven Supply Chain Design. In P. Vasant (Ed.), *Handbook of Research on Artificial Intelligence Techniques and Algorithms* (pp. 82–121). Hershey, PA: IGI Global. doi:10.4018/978-1-4666-7258-1.ch003

Bhargavi, P., Jyothi, S., & Mamatha, D. M. (2017). A Study on Hybridization of Intelligent Techniques in Bioinformatics. In S. Bhattacharyya, S. De, I. Pan, & P. Dutta (Eds.), *Intelligent Multidimensional Data Clustering and Analysis* (pp. 358–379). Hershey, PA: IGI Global. doi:10.4018/978-1-5225-1776-4.ch014

Bhatnagar, V., Majhi, R., & Devi, S. L. (2018). Development of an Efficient Prediction Model Based on a Nature-Inspired Technique for New Products: A Case of Industries From the Manufacturing Sector. In S. Dash, B. Tripathy, & A. Rahman (Eds.), *Handbook of Research on Modeling, Analysis, and Application of Nature-Inspired Metaheuristic Algorithms* (pp. 160–182). Hershey, PA: IGI Global. doi:10.4018/978-1-5225-2857-9.ch009

Biba, M., Vajjhala, N. R., & Nishani, L. (2017). Visual Data Mining for Collaborative Filtering: A State-of-the-Art Survey. In V. Bhatnagar (Ed.), *Collaborative Filtering Using Data Mining and Analysis* (pp. 217–235). Hershey, PA: IGI Global. doi:10.4018/978-1-5225-0489-4.ch012

Bouarara, H. A., Hamou, R. M., Rahmani, A., & Amine, A. (2015). Boosting Algorithm and Meta-Heuristic Based on Genetic Algorithms for Textual Plagiarism Detection. *International Journal of Cognitive Informatics and Natural Intelligence*, 9(4), 65–87. doi:10.4018/IJCINI.2015100105

Boudouaoui, Y., Habbi, H., & Harfouchi, F. (2018). Swarm Bee Colony Optimization for Heat Exchanger Distributed Dynamics Approximation With Application to Leak Detection. In P. Vasant, S. Alparslan-Gok, & G. Weber (Eds.), *Handbook of Research on Emergent Applications of Optimization Algorithms* (pp. 557–578). Hershey, PA: IGI Global. doi:10.4018/978-1-5225-2990-3.ch024

Bousson, K., & Velosa, C. (2015). Robust Control and Synchronization of Chaotic Systems with Actuator Constraints. In P. Vasant (Ed.), *Handbook of Research on Artificial Intelligence Techniques and Algorithms* (pp. 1–43). Hershey, PA: IGI Global. doi:10.4018/978-1-4666-7258-1.ch001

Cai, T. (2015). Application of Artificial Intelligence Techniques to Handle the Uncertainty in the Chemical Process for Environmental Protection. In P. Vasant (Ed.), *Handbook of Research on Artificial Intelligence Techniques and Algorithms* (pp. 446–477). Hershey, PA: IGI Global. doi:10.4018/978-1-4666-7258-1.ch014

Cai, T. (2015). Application of Soft Computing Techniques for Renewable Energy Network Design and Optimization. In P. Vasant (Ed.), *Handbook of Research on Artificial Intelligence Techniques and Algorithms* (pp. 204–225). Hershey, PA: IGI Global. doi:10.4018/978-1-4666-7258-1.ch007

Calzada-Orihuela, G., Urquiza-Beltrán, G., Ascencio, J. A., & Reyes-Salgado, G. (2017). Implementing Genetic Algorithms to Assist Oil and Gas Pipeline Integrity Assessment and Intelligent Risk Optimization. *International Journal of Organizational and Collective Intelligence*, 7(4), 63–82. doi:10.4018/IJOCI.2017100104

Cavallin, A., Frutos, M., Vigier, H. P., & Rossit, D. G. (2018). An Integrated Model of Data Envelopment Analysis and Artificial Neural Networks for Improving Efficiency in the Municipal Solid Waste Management. In P. Vasant, S. Alparslan-Gok, & G. Weber (Eds.), *Handbook of Research on Emergent Applications of Optimization Algorithms* (pp. 206–231). Hershey, PA: IGI Global. doi:10.4018/978-1-5225-2990-3.ch009

Chakraborty, S., Chatterjee, S., Ashour, A. S., Mali, K., & Dey, N. (2018). Intelligent Computing in Medical Imaging: A Study. In N. Dey (Ed.), *Advancements in Applied Metaheuristic Computing* (pp. 143–163). Hershey, PA: IGI Global. doi:10.4018/978-1-5225-4151-6.ch006

Chantrapornchai, C., Kaegjing, A., Srakaew, S., Piyanuntcharatsr, W., & Krakhaeng, S. (2017). Utilizing Architecture Aspects for in Data Mining for Computer System Design. In S. Bhattacharyya, S. De, I. Pan, & P. Dutta (Eds.), *Intelligent Multidimensional Data Clustering and Analysis* (pp. 225–252). Hershey, PA: IGI Global. doi:10.4018/978-1-5225-1776-4.ch009

Chatterjee, A., & Barik, N. (2018). A New Data Hiding Scheme Combining Genetic Algorithm and Artificial Neural Network. In S. Dash, B. Tripathy, & A. Rahman (Eds.), *Handbook of Research on Modeling, Analysis, and Application of Nature-Inspired Metaheuristic Algorithms* (pp. 94–103). Hershey, PA: IGI Global. doi:10.4018/978-1-5225-2857-9.ch005

Chatterjee, S., Sarkar, S., Dey, N., Ashour, A. S., & Sen, S. (2018). Hybrid Non-Dominated Sorting Genetic Algorithm: II-Neural Network Approach. In N. Dey (Ed.), *Advancements in Applied Metaheuristic Computing* (pp. 264–286). Hershey, PA: IGI Global. doi:10.4018/978-1-5225-4151-6.ch011

Chintalapudi, S. R., & Krishna Prasad, M. H. M. (2018). A Survey on Overlapping Communities in Large-Scale Social Networks. In H. Seetha, M. Murty, & B. Tripathy (Eds.), *Modern Technologies for Big Data Classification and Clustering* (pp. 198-215). Hershey, PA: IGI Global. doi:10.4018/978-1-5225-2805-0.ch008

Choudhury, D. K., & Dash, S. (2018). Defect Detection of Fabrics by Grey-Level Co-Occurrence Matrix and Artificial Neural Network. In S. Dash, B. Tripathy, & A. Rahman (Eds.), *Handbook of Research on Modeling, Analysis, and Application of Nature-Inspired Metaheuristic Algorithms* (pp. 285–297). Hershey, PA: IGI Global. doi:10.4018/978-1-5225-2857-9.ch014

Daneshfar, F., Fathy, W., & Alaqeband, B. (2015). A Metaheuristic Algorithm for OCR Baseline Detection of Arabic Languages. In P. Vasant (Ed.), *Handbook of Research on Artificial Intelligence Techniques and Algorithms* (pp. 708–735). Hershey, PA: IGI Global. doi:10.4018/978-1-4666-7258-1.ch023

Das, A. (2018). Automatic Mask Alignment for Optical Lithography Using GA- and PSO-Based Image Registration Technique. In P. Vasant, S. Alparslan-Gok, & G. Weber (Eds.), *Handbook of Research on Emergent Applications of Optimization Algorithms* (pp. 637–655). Hershey, PA: IGI Global. doi:10.4018/978-1-5225-2990-3.ch027

Dash, C. S., Behera, A. K., & Nayak, S. C. (2018). DE-Based RBFNs for Classification With Special Attention to Noise Removal and Irrelevant Features. In S. Dash, B. Tripathy, & A. Rahman (Eds.), *Handbook of Research on Modeling, Analysis, and Application of Nature-Inspired Metaheuristic Algorithms* (pp. 218–243). Hershey, PA: IGI Global. doi:10.4018/978-1-5225-2857-9.ch011

Dash, N., Debta, S., & Kumar, K. (2018). Application of ANN and PSO Swarm Optimization for Optimization in Advanced Manufacturing: A Case With CNC Lathe. In P. Vasant, S. Alparslan-Gok, & G. Weber (Eds.), *Handbook of Research on Emergent Applications of Optimization Algorithms* (pp. 386–406). Hershey, PA: IGI Global. doi:10.4018/978-1-5225-2990-3.ch017

Dash, S. (2018). Metaheuristic-Based Hybrid Feature Selection Models. In S. Dash, B. Tripathy, & A. Rahman (Eds.), *Handbook of Research on Modeling, Analysis, and Application of Nature-Inspired Metaheuristic Algorithms* (pp. 1–22). Hershey, PA: IGI Global. doi:10.4018/978-1-5225-2857-9.ch001

Dey, N., & Ashour, A. S. (2018). Meta-Heuristic Algorithms in Medical Image Segmentation: A Review. In N. Dey (Ed.), *Advancements in Applied Metaheuristic Computing* (pp. 185–203). Hershey, PA: IGI Global. doi:10.4018/978-1-5225-4151-6.ch008

Dhal, K. G., & Das, S. (2018). Chaotic Differential-Evolution-Based Fuzzy Contrast Stretching Method. In N. Dey (Ed.), *Advancements in Applied Metaheuristic Computing* (pp. 71–94). Hershey, PA: IGI Global. doi:10.4018/978-1-5225-4151-6.ch003

Dongre, S. S., & Malik, L. G. (2017). Data Stream Mining Using Ensemble Classifier: A Collaborative Approach of Classifiers. In V. Bhatnagar (Ed.), *Collaborative Filtering Using Data Mining and Analysis* (pp. 236–249). Hershey, PA: IGI Global. doi:10.4018/978-1-5225-0489-4.ch013

El Hassani, H., Benkachcha, S., & Benhra, J. (2018). Optimized Crossover JumpX in Genetic Algorithm for General Routing Problems: A Crossover Survey and Enhancement. In N. Dey (Ed.), *Advancements in Applied Metaheuristic Computing* (pp. 205–230). Hershey, PA: IGI Global. doi:10.4018/978-1-5225-4151-6.ch009

Ganesan, T., Aris, M. S., & I., E. (2018). Multiobjective Strategy for an Industrial Gas Turbine: Absorption Chiller System. In P. Vasant, S. Alparslan-Gok, & G. Weber (Eds.), *Handbook of Research on Emergent Applications of Optimization Algorithms* (pp. 531-556). Hershey, PA: IGI Global. doi:10.4018/978-1-5225-2990-3.ch023

Garg, H. (2015). A Hybrid GA-GSA Algorithm for Optimizing the Performance of an Industrial System by Utilizing Uncertain Data. In P. Vasant (Ed.), *Handbook of Research on Artificial Intelligence Techniques and Algorithms* (pp. 620–654). Hershey, PA: IGI Global. doi:10.4018/978-1-4666-7258-1.ch020

Ghosal, S. K., & Mandal, J. K. (2016). Genetic-Algorithm-Based Optimization of Fragile Watermarking in Discrete Hartley Transform Domain. In J. Mandal, S. Mukhopadhyay, & T. Pal (Eds.), *Handbook of Research on Natural Computing for Optimization Problems* (pp. 103–127). Hershey, PA: IGI Global. doi:10.4018/978-1-5225-0058-2.ch005

Goncalves, M., & Mendoza, J. N. (2017). A Physical Design Strategy for Datasets with Multiple Dimensions. In S. Bhattacharyya, S. De, I. Pan, & P. Dutta (Eds.), *Intelligent Multidimensional Data Clustering and Analysis* (pp. 1–27). Hershey, PA: IGI Global. doi:10.4018/978-1-5225-1776-4.ch001

Gopal, N., & Krishnan, V. (2017). Proficient Clustering algorithm for Wireless Sensor Networks. In S. Bhattacharyya, S. De, I. Pan, & P. Dutta (Eds.), *Intelligent Multidimensional Data Clustering and Analysis* (pp. 345–357). Hershey, PA: IGI Global. doi:10.4018/978-1-5225-1776-4.ch013

Goudos, S. K. (2018). Optimization of Antenna Design Problems Using Binary Differential Evolution. In P. Vasant, S. Alparslan-Gok, & G. Weber (Eds.), *Handbook of Research on Emergent Applications of Optimization Algorithms* (pp. 614–636). Hershey, PA: IGI Global. doi:10.4018/978-1-5225-2990-3.ch026

Gowri, R., & Rathipriya, R. (2018). Protein Motif Comparator Using Bio-Inspired Two-Way K-Means. In N. Dey (Ed.), *Advancements in Applied Metaheuristic Computing* (pp. 95–117). Hershey, PA: IGI Global. doi:10.4018/978-1-5225-4151-6.ch004

Goyal, M., & Bhatnagar, V. (2017). A Classification Framework on Opinion Mining for Effective Recommendation Systems. In V. Bhatnagar (Ed.), *Collaborative Filtering Using Data Mining and Analysis* (pp. 180–194). Hershey, PA: IGI Global. doi:10.4018/978-1-5225-0489-4.ch010

Gürsel, G. (2015). Fuzzy Logic in Healthcare. In P. Vasant (Ed.), *Handbook of Research on Artificial Intelligence Techniques and Algorithms* (pp. 679–707). Hershey, PA: IGI Global. doi:10.4018/978-1-4666-7258-1.ch022

Gürsel, G. (2017). For Better Healthcare Mining Health Data. In S. Bhattacharyya, S. De, I. Pan, & P. Dutta (Eds.), *Intelligent Multidimensional Data Clustering and Analysis* (pp. 135–158). Hershey, PA: IGI Global. doi:10.4018/978-1-5225-1776-4.ch006

Gurumoorthy, S., & Tripathy, B. K. (2018). Intelligent Technique to Identify Epilepsy Using Fuzzy Firefly System for Brain Signal Processing. In S. Dash, B. Tripathy, & A. Rahman (Eds.), *Handbook of Research on Modeling, Analysis, and Application of Nature-Inspired Metaheuristic Algorithms* (pp. 400–412). Hershey, PA: IGI Global. doi:10.4018/978-1-5225-2857-9.ch020

Hamdan, M., & Abderrazzaq, M. H. (2016). Optimization of Small Wind Turbines using Genetic Algorithms. *International Journal of Applied Metaheuristic Computing*, 7(4), 50–65. doi:10.4018/IJAMC.2016100104

He, Y., Liu, J. N., Hu, Y., & Wang, X. (2015). Fuzzy Integral-Based Kernel Regression Ensemble and Its Application. In P. Vasant (Ed.), *Handbook of Research on Artificial Intelligence Techniques and Algorithms* (pp. 378–410). Hershey, PA: IGI Global. doi:10.4018/978-1-4666-7258-1.ch012

Heidari, A. A., & Abbaspour, R. A. (2018). Enhanced Chaotic Grey Wolf Optimizer for Real-World Optimization Problems: A Comparative Study. In P. Vasant, S. Alparslan-Gok, & G. Weber (Eds.), *Handbook of Research on Emergent Applications of Optimization Algorithms* (pp. 693–727). Hershey, PA: IGI Global. doi:10.4018/978-1-5225-2990-3.ch030

Hudedagaddi, D. P., & Tripathy, B. K. (2017). Adaptive Clustering Techniques and Their Applications. In S. Bhattacharyya, S. De, I. Pan, & P. Dutta (Eds.), *Intelligent Multidimensional Data Clustering and Analysis* (pp. 380–397). Hershey, PA: IGI Global. doi:10.4018/978-1-5225-1776-4.ch015

Hudedagaddi, D. P., & Tripathy, B. K. (2018). Fuzziness in Ant Colony Optimization and Their Applications. In S. Dash, B. Tripathy, & A. Rahman (Eds.), *Handbook of Research on Modeling, Analysis, and Application of Nature-Inspired Metaheuristic Algorithms* (pp. 363–376). Hershey, PA: IGI Global. doi:10.4018/978-1-5225-2857-9.ch018

Hussain, S. A., Mondal, S. P., & Mandal, U. K. (2018). A Holistic-Based Multi-Criterion Decision-Making Approach for Solving Engineering Sciences Problem Under Imprecise Environment. In S. Dash, B. Tripathy, & A. Rahman (Eds.), *Handbook of Research on Modeling, Analysis, and Application of Nature-Inspired Metaheuristic Algorithms* (pp. 298–330). Hershey, PA: IGI Global. doi:10.4018/978-1-5225-2857-9.ch015

Islam, S. M., Banerjee, M., & Bhattacharyya, S. (2017). Dealing with Higher Dimensionality and Outliers in Content-Based Image Retrieval. In S. Bhattacharyya, S. De, I. Pan, & P. Dutta (Eds.), *Intelligent Multidimensional Data Clustering and Analysis* (pp. 109–134). Hershey, PA: IGI Global. doi:10.4018/978-1-5225-1776-4.ch005

J, A. K., S, A., & Trueman, T. E. (2018). Sentiment Mining Approaches for Big Data Classification and Clustering. In H. Seetha, M. Murty, & B. Tripathy (Eds.), *Modern Technologies for Big Data Classification and Clustering* (pp. 34-63). Hershey, PA: IGI Global. doi:10.4018/978-1-5225-2805-0.ch002

Jagatheesan, K., Anand, B., Dey, N., & Ashour, A. S. (2018). Effect of SMES Unit in AGC of an Interconnected Multi-Area Thermal Power System With ACO-Tuned PID Controller. In N. Dey (Ed.), *Advancements in Applied Metaheuristic Computing* (pp. 164–184). Hershey, PA: IGI Global. doi:10.4018/978-1-5225-4151-6.ch007

Jain, A., Bhatnagar, V., & Sharma, P. (2017). Collaborative and Clustering Based Strategy in Big Data. In V. Bhatnagar (Ed.), *Collaborative Filtering Using Data Mining and Analysis* (pp. 140–158). Hershey, PA: IGI Global. doi:10.4018/978-1-5225-0489-4.ch008

Janssens, G. K., Soonpracha, K., Manisri, T., & Mungwattana, A. (2015). Robust Vehicle Routing Solutions to Manage Time Windows in the Case of Uncertain Travel Times. In P. Vasant (Ed.), *Handbook of Research on Artificial Intelligence Techniques and Algorithms* (pp. 655–678). Hershey, PA: IGI Global. doi:10.4018/978-1-4666-7258-1.ch021

Jenicka, S. (2018). Sugeno Fuzzy-Inference-System-Based Land Cover Classification of Remotely Sensed Images. In P. Vasant, S. Alparslan-Gok, & G. Weber (Eds.), *Handbook of Research on Emergent Applications of Optimization Algorithms* (pp. 326–363). Hershey, PA: IGI Global. doi:10.4018/978-1-5225-2990-3.ch015

Kaffash, S., & Torshizi, M. (2018). Data Envelopment Analysis Development in Banking Sector. In P. Vasant, S. Alparslan-Gok, & G. Weber (Eds.), *Handbook of Research on Emergent Applications of Optimization Algorithms* (pp. 462–484). Hershey, PA: IGI Global. doi:10.4018/978-1-5225-2990-3.ch020

Ke, S., & Lee, W. (2017). Combining User Co-Ratings and Social Trust for Collaborative Recommendation: A Data Analytics Approach. In V. Bhatnagar (Ed.), *Collaborative Filtering Using Data Mining and Analysis* (pp. 195–216). Hershey, PA: IGI Global. doi:10.4018/978-1-5225-0489-4.ch011

Kenwright, B. (2018). Smart Animation Tools. In P. Vasant, S. Alparslan-Gok, & G. Weber (Eds.), *Handbook of Research on Emergent Applications of Optimization Algorithms* (pp. 52–66). Hershey, PA: IGI Global. doi:10.4018/978-1-5225-2990-3.ch003

Khan, L., Badar, R., Ali, S., & Farid, U. (2015). Comparison of Uncertainties in Membership Function of Adaptive Lyapunov NeuroFuzzy-2 for Damping Power Oscillations. In P. Vasant (Ed.), *Handbook of Research on Artificial Intelligence Techniques and Algorithms* (pp. 260–321). Hershey, PA: IGI Global. doi:10.4018/978-1-4666-7258-1.ch009

Khare, N., Rajput, D. S., & D, P. (2017). Association Rules-Based Analysis in Multidimensional Clusters. In S. Bhattacharyya, S. De, I. Pan, & P. Dutta (Eds.), *Intelligent Multidimensional Data Clustering and Analysis* (pp. 73-89). Hershey, PA: IGI Global. doi:10.4018/978-1-5225-1776-4.ch003

Kim, E., Jha, M. K., & Kang, M. (2015). A Sensitivity Analysis of Critical Genetic Algorithm Parameters: Highway Alignment Optimization Case Study. *International Journal of Operations Research and Information Systems*, *6*(1), 30–48. doi:10.4018/ijoris.2015010103

Klepac, G., Kopal, R., & Mrsic, L. (2015). Early Warning System Framework Proposal Based on Structured Analytical Techniques, SNA, and Fuzzy Expert System for Different Industries. In P. Vasant (Ed.), *Handbook of Research on Artificial Intelligence Techniques and Algorithms* (pp. 763–796). Hershey, PA: IGI Global. doi:10.4018/978-1-4666-7258-1.ch025

Krawiec, K., Simons, C., Swan, J., & Woodward, J. (2018). Metaheuristic Design Patterns: New Perspectives for Larger-Scale Search Architectures. In P. Vasant, S. Alparslan-Gok, & G. Weber (Eds.), *Handbook of Research on Emergent Applications of Optimization Algorithms* (pp. 1–36). Hershey, PA: IGI Global. doi:10.4018/978-1-5225-2990-3.ch001

Kumar, G. V., Rao, B. V., Chowdary, D. D., & Sobhan, P. V. (2018). Multi-Objective Optimal Power Flow Using Metaheuristic Optimization Algorithms With Unified Power Flow Controller to Enhance the Power System Performance. In N. Dey (Ed.), *Advancements in Applied Metaheuristic Computing* (pp. 1–33). Hershey, PA: IGI Global. doi:10.4018/978-1-5225-4151-6.ch001

Kumar, H. (2018). Computational Intelligence Approach for Flow Shop Scheduling Problem. In P. Vasant, S. Alparslan-Gok, & G. Weber (Eds.), *Handbook of Research on Emergent Applications of Optimization Algorithms* (pp. 298–313). Hershey, PA: IGI Global. doi:10.4018/978-1-5225-2990-3. ch013

Kumar, M., Nallagownden, P., Elamvazuthi, I., & Vasant, P. (2018). Optimal Placement and Sizing of Distributed Generation in Distribution System Using Modified Particle Swarm Optimization Algorithm: Swarm-Intelligence-Based Distributed Generation. In P. Vasant, S. Alparslan-Gok, & G. Weber (Eds.), *Handbook of Research on Emergent Applications of Optimization Algorithms* (pp. 485–507). Hershey, PA: IGI Global. doi:10.4018/978-1-5225-2990-3. ch021

Kumar, R. R., Viswanath, P., & Bindu, C. S. (2018). Data Compaction Techniques. In H. Seetha, M. Murty, & B. Tripathy (Eds.), *Modern Technologies for Big Data Classification and Clustering* (pp. 64–98). Hershey, PA: IGI Global. doi:10.4018/978-1-5225-2805-0.ch003

Leung, C. K., Jiang, F., Dela Cruz, E. M., & Elango, V. S. (2017). Association Rule Mining in Collaborative Filtering. In V. Bhatnagar (Ed.), *Collaborative Filtering Using Data Mining and Analysis* (pp. 159–179). Hershey, PA: IGI Global. doi:10.4018/978-1-5225-0489-4.ch009

Li, C., Liu, J., Lin, C., & Lo, W. (2015). On the Accelerated Convergence of Genetic Algorithm Using GPU Parallel Operations. *International Journal of Software Innovation*, 3(4), 1–17. doi:10.4018/IJSI.2015100101

Li, S., & Zheng, Y. (2015). A Memetic Algorithm for the Multi-Depot Vehicle Routing Problem with Limited Stocks. In P. Vasant (Ed.), *Handbook of Research on Artificial Intelligence Techniques and Algorithms* (pp. 411–445). Hershey, PA: IGI Global. doi:10.4018/978-1-4666-7258-1.ch013

Lienland, B., & Zeng, L. (2015). A Review and Comparison of Genetic Algorithms for the 0-1 Multidimensional Knapsack Problem. *International Journal of Operations Research and Information Systems*, 6(2), 21–31. doi:10.4018/ijoris.2015040102

Liñán-García, E., De la Barrera-Gómez, H. I., Vázquez-Esquivel, A. L., Aguirre-García, J., Cervantes-Payan, A. I., Escobedo-Hernández, E. O., & López-Alday, L. A. (2018). Solving Vehicle Routing Problem With Multi-Phases Simulated Annealing Algorithm. In P. Vasant, S. Alparslan-Gok, & G. Weber (Eds.), *Handbook of Research on Emergent Applications of Optimization Algorithms* (pp. 508–530). Hershey, PA: IGI Global. doi:10.4018/978-1-5225-2990-3.ch022

M., V., & K., T. (2017). History and Overview of the Recommender Systems. In V. Bhatnagar (Ed.), *Collaborative Filtering Using Data Mining and Analysis* (pp. 74-99). Hershey, PA: IGI Global. doi:10.4018/978-1-5225-0489-4.ch004

Mahajan, R. (2017). Review of Data Mining Techniques and Parameters for Recommendation of Effective Adaptive E-Learning System. In V. Bhatnagar (Ed.), *Collaborative Filtering Using Data Mining and Analysis* (pp. 1–23). Hershey, PA: IGI Global. doi:10.4018/978-1-5225-0489-4.ch001

Maitra, I. K., & Bandhyopadhyaay, S. K. (2017). Adaptive Edge Detection Method towards Features Extraction from Diverse Medical Imaging Technologies. In S. Bhattacharyya, S. De, I. Pan, & P. Dutta (Eds.), *Intelligent Multidimensional Data Clustering and Analysis* (pp. 159–192). Hershey, PA: IGI Global. doi:10.4018/978-1-5225-1776-4.ch007

Majumder, A., & Majumder, A. (2015). Application of Standard Deviation Method Integrated PSO Approach in Optimization of Manufacturing Process Parameters. In P. Vasant (Ed.), *Handbook of Research on Artificial Intelligence Techniques and Algorithms* (pp. 536–563). Hershey, PA: IGI Global. doi:10.4018/978-1-4666-7258-1.ch017

Mankad, K. B. (2015). An Intelligent Process Development Using Fusion of Genetic Algorithm with Fuzzy Logic. In P. Vasant (Ed.), *Handbook of Research on Artificial Intelligence Techniques and Algorithms* (pp. 44–81). Hershey, PA: IGI Global. doi:10.4018/978-1-4666-7258-1.ch002

Márquez, A. E., & Expósito-Izquierdo, C. (2018). An Overview of the Last Advances and Applications of Greedy Randomized Adaptive Search Procedure. In S. Dash, B. Tripathy, & A. Rahman (Eds.), *Handbook of Research on Modeling, Analysis, and Application of Nature-Inspired Metaheuristic Algorithms* (pp. 264–284). Hershey, PA: IGI Global. doi:10.4018/978-1-5225-2857-9.ch013

Mehrotra, S., & Kohli, S. (2017). Data Clustering and Various Clustering Approaches. In S. Bhattacharyya, S. De, I. Pan, & P. Dutta (Eds.), *Intelligent Multidimensional Data Clustering and Analysis* (pp. 90–108). Hershey, PA: IGI Global. doi:10.4018/978-1-5225-1776-4.ch004

Mellal, M. A., & Williams, E. J. (2018). A Survey on Ant Colony Optimization, Particle Swarm Optimization, and Cuckoo Algorithms. In P. Vasant, S. Alparslan-Gok, & G. Weber (Eds.), *Handbook of Research on Emergent Applications of Optimization Algorithms* (pp. 37–51). Hershey, PA: IGI Global. doi:10.4018/978-1-5225-2990-3.ch002

Mezzoudj, S., & Melkemi, K. E. (2018). A Hybrid Approach for Shape Retrieval Using Genetic Algorithms and Approximate Distance. *International Journal of Computer Vision and Image Processing*, 8(1), 75–91. doi:10.4018/IJCVIP.2018010105

Miriyala, S. S., & Mitra, K. (2018). A Proposal for Parameter-Free Surrogate Building Algorithm Using Artificial Neural Networks. In P. Vasant, S. Alparslan-Gok, & G. Weber (Eds.), *Handbook of Research on Emergent Applications of Optimization Algorithms* (pp. 232–264). Hershey, PA: IGI Global. doi:10.4018/978-1-5225-2990-3.ch010

Mishra, B. S., Mishra, S., & Singh, S. S. (2016). Parallel Multi-Criterion Genetic Algorithms: Review and Comprehensive Study. *International Journal of Applied Evolutionary Computation*, 7(1), 50–62. doi:10.4018/IJAEC.2016010104

Mishra, S., Mishra, B. K., Tripathy, H. K., Mishra, M., & Panda, B. (2018). Use of Social Network Analysis in Telecommunication Domain. In H. Seetha, M. Murty, & B. Tripathy (Eds.), *Modern Technologies for Big Data Classification and Clustering* (pp. 152–178). Hershey, PA: IGI Global. doi:10.4018/978-1-5225-2805-0.ch006

Mittal, M., Sharma, R. K., Singh, V., & Mohan Goyal, L. (2017). Modified Single Pass Clustering Algorithm Based on Median as a Threshold Similarity Value. In V. Bhatnagar (Ed.), *Collaborative Filtering Using Data Mining and Analysis* (pp. 24–48). Hershey, PA: IGI Global. doi:10.4018/978-1-5225-0489-4.ch002

Mittal, P., & Mitra, K. (2018). Decomposition-Based Multi-Objective Optimization of Energy Noise Trade-Off in a Wind Farm: A Hybrid Approach. In P. Vasant, S. Alparslan-Gok, & G. Weber (Eds.), *Handbook of Research on Emergent Applications of Optimization Algorithms* (pp. 177–205). Hershey, PA: IGI Global. doi:10.4018/978-1-5225-2990-3.ch008

Mohammadian, M. (2017). Modelling, Control and Prediction using Hierarchical Fuzzy Logic Systems: Design and Development. *International Journal of Fuzzy System Applications*, 6(3), 105–123. doi:10.4018/IJFSA.2017070105

Mokadem, D., Amine, A., Elberrichi, Z., & Helbert, D. (2018). Detection of Urban Areas using Genetic Algorithms and Kohonen Maps on Multispectral images. *International Journal of Organizational and Collective Intelligence*, 8(1), 46–62. doi:10.4018/IJOCI.2018010104

Mukhopadhyay, A. (2016). MRI Brain Image Segmentation Using Interactive Multiobjective Evolutionary Approach. In J. Mandal, S. Mukhopadhyay, & T. Pal (Eds.), *Handbook of Research on Natural Computing for Optimization Problems* (pp. 10–29). Hershey, PA: IGI Global. doi:10.4018/978-1-5225-0058-2.ch002

Mukhopadhyay, S., & Das, S. (2016). A System on Chip Development of Customizable GA Architecture for Real Parameter Optimization Problem. In J. Mandal, S. Mukhopadhyay, & T. Pal (Eds.), *Handbook of Research on Natural Computing for Optimization Problems* (pp. 66–102). Hershey, PA: IGI Global. doi:10.4018/978-1-5225-0058-2.ch004

Narayanan, S. J., Perumal, B., & Rohra, J. G. (2018). Swarm-Based Nature-Inspired Metaheuristics for Neural Network Optimization. In S. Dash, B. Tripathy, & A. Rahman (Eds.), *Handbook of Research on Modeling, Analysis, and Application of Nature-Inspired Metaheuristic Algorithms* (pp. 23–53). Hershey, PA: IGI Global. doi:10.4018/978-1-5225-2857-9.ch002

Nayak, S. C., Misra, B. B., & Behera, H. S. (2018). Escalation of Prediction Accuracy With Virtual Data: A Case Study on Financial Time Series. In S. Dash, B. Tripathy, & A. Rahman (Eds.), *Handbook of Research on Modeling, Analysis, and Application of Nature-Inspired Metaheuristic Algorithms* (pp. 433–461). Hershey, PA: IGI Global. doi:10.4018/978-1-5225-2857-9.ch022

Nayak, S. C., Misra, B. B., & Behera, H. S. (2018). On Developing and Performance Evaluation of Adaptive Second Order Neural Network With GA-Based Training (ASONN-GA) for Financial Time Series Prediction. In N. Dey (Ed.), *Advancements in Applied Metaheuristic Computing* (pp. 231–263). Hershey, PA: IGI Global. doi:10.4018/978-1-5225-4151-6.ch010

Nishani, L., & Biba, M. (2017). Statistical Relational Learning for Collaborative Filtering a State-of-the-Art Review. In V. Bhatnagar (Ed.), *Collaborative Filtering Using Data Mining and Analysis* (pp. 250–269). Hershey, PA: IGI Global. doi:10.4018/978-1-5225-0489-4.ch014

Ochoa-Zezzatti, A., Olivier, T., Camarena, R., Gutiérrez, G., Axpeitia, D., & Vázque, I. (2018). Intelligent Drones Improved With Algae Algorithm. In P. Vasant, S. Alparslan-Gok, & G. Weber (Eds.), *Handbook of Research on Emergent Applications of Optimization Algorithms* (pp. 279–297). Hershey, PA: IGI Global. doi:10.4018/978-1-5225-2990-3.ch012

P, K. A., & N, S. K. (2018). A Comprehensive Review of Nature-Inspired Algorithms for Feature Selection. In S. Dash, B. Tripathy, & A. Rahman (Eds.), *Handbook of Research on Modeling, Analysis, and Application of Nature-Inspired Metaheuristic Algorithms* (pp. 331-345). Hershey, PA: IGI Global. doi:10.4018/978-1-5225-2857-9.ch016

Pal, A., & Kumar, M. (2017). Collaborative Filtering Based Data Mining for Large Data. In V. Bhatnagar (Ed.), *Collaborative Filtering Using Data Mining and Analysis* (pp. 115–127). Hershey, PA: IGI Global. doi:10.4018/978-1-5225-0489-4.ch006

Pal, B. B., Roy, S., & Kumar, M. (2016). A Genetic Algorithm to Goal Programming Model for Crop Production with Interval Data Uncertainty. In J. Mandal, S. Mukhopadhyay, & T. Pal (Eds.), *Handbook of Research on Natural Computing for Optimization Problems* (pp. 30–65). Hershey, PA: IGI Global. doi:10.4018/978-1-5225-0058-2.ch003

Panda, M., & Dash, S. (2018). Automatic Test Data Generation Using Bio-Inspired Algorithms: A Travelogue. In S. Dash, B. Tripathy, & A. Rahman (Eds.), *Handbook of Research on Modeling, Analysis, and Application of Nature-Inspired Metaheuristic Algorithms* (pp. 140–159). Hershey, PA: IGI Global. doi:10.4018/978-1-5225-2857-9.ch008

Pantula, P. D., Miriyala, S. S., & Mitra, K. (2018). Efficient Optimization Formulation Through Variable Reduction for Clustering Algorithms. In P. Vasant, S. Alparslan-Gok, & G. Weber (Eds.), *Handbook of Research on Emergent Applications of Optimization Algorithms* (pp. 135–162). Hershey, PA: IGI Global. doi:10.4018/978-1-5225-2990-3.ch006

Pauline, O., & Zainuddin, Z. (2017). A Combinational Fuzzy Clustering Approach for Microarray Spot Segmentation. In S. Bhattacharyya, S. De, I. Pan, & P. Dutta (Eds.), *Intelligent Multidimensional Data Clustering and Analysis* (pp. 326–344). Hershey, PA: IGI Global. doi:10.4018/978-1-5225-1776-4.ch012

Pires, D. S., & Serra, G. L. (2015). Robust Fuzzy Digital PID Controller Design: A Contribution for Advanced Studies in Control and Automation. In P. Vasant (Ed.), *Handbook of Research on Artificial Intelligence Techniques and Algorithms* (pp. 226–259). Hershey, PA: IGI Global. doi:10.4018/978-1-4666-7258-1.ch008

Pombo, N., Garcia, N., Bousson, K., & Felizardo, V. (2015). Machine Learning Approaches to Automated Medical Decision Support Systems. In P. Vasant (Ed.), *Handbook of Research on Artificial Intelligence Techniques and Algorithms* (pp. 183–203). Hershey, PA: IGI Global. doi:10.4018/978-1-4666-7258-1.ch006

Pratihar, D. K. (2016). Realizing the Need for Intelligent Optimization Tool. In J. Mandal, S. Mukhopadhyay, & T. Pal (Eds.), *Handbook of Research on Natural Computing for Optimization Problems* (pp. 1–9). Hershey, PA: IGI Global. doi:10.4018/978-1-5225-0058-2.ch001

Pujari, P., & Majhi, B. (2018). Application of Natured-Inspired Technique to Odia Handwritten Numeral Recognition. In S. Dash, B. Tripathy, & A. Rahman (Eds.), *Handbook of Research on Modeling, Analysis, and Application of Nature-Inspired Metaheuristic Algorithms* (pp. 377–399). Hershey, PA: IGI Global. doi:10.4018/978-1-5225-2857-9.ch019

Punurai, W., & Pholdee, N. (2018). Optimal Structural Elements Sizing Using Neural Network and Adaptive Differential Algorithm. In P. Vasant, S. Alparslan-Gok, & G. Weber (Eds.), *Handbook of Research on Emergent Applications of Optimization Algorithms* (pp. 93–134). Hershey, PA: IGI Global. doi:10.4018/978-1-5225-2990-3.ch005

Rahman, A. U. (2018). Applications of Hybrid Intelligent Systems in Adaptive Communication. In S. Dash, B. Tripathy, & A. Rahman (Eds.), *Handbook of Research on Modeling, Analysis, and Application of Nature-Inspired Metaheuristic Algorithms* (pp. 183–217). Hershey, PA: IGI Global. doi:10.4018/978-1-5225-2857-9.ch010

Rathi, R., & Acharjya, D. P. (2018). A Rule Based Classification for Vegetable Production Using Rough Set and Genetic Algorithm. *International Journal of Fuzzy System Applications*, 7(1), 74–100. doi:10.4018/IJFSA.2018010106

Recioui, A. (2018). Application of Teaching Learning-Based Optimization to the Optimal Placement of Phasor Measurement Units. In P. Vasant, S. Alparslan-Gok, & G. Weber (Eds.), *Handbook of Research on Emergent Applications of Optimization Algorithms* (pp. 407–438). Hershey, PA: IGI Global. doi:10.4018/978-1-5225-2990-3.ch018

Recioui, A. (2018). Application of the Spiral Optimization Technique to Antenna Array Design. In P. Vasant, S. Alparslan-Gok, & G. Weber (Eds.), *Handbook of Research on Emergent Applications of Optimization Algorithms* (pp. 364–385). Hershey, PA: IGI Global. doi:10.4018/978-1-5225-2990-3.ch016

Recioui, A. (2018). Optimal Placement of Power Factor Correction Capacitors Using Taguchi Optimization Method. In P. Vasant, S. Alparslan-Gok, & G. Weber (Eds.), *Handbook of Research on Emergent Applications of Optimization Algorithms* (pp. 777–812). Hershey, PA: IGI Global. doi:10.4018/978-1-5225-2990-3.ch033

Rout, S. S., & Misra, B. B. (2018). Competency Mapping in Academic Environment: A Swarm Intelligence Approach. In S. Dash, B. Tripathy, & A. Rahman (Eds.), *Handbook of Research on Modeling, Analysis, and Application of Nature-Inspired Metaheuristic Algorithms* (pp. 244–263). Hershey, PA: IGI Global. doi:10.4018/978-1-5225-2857-9.ch012

S, C. (2018). Twitter Data Analysis. In H. Seetha, M. Murty, & B. Tripathy (Eds.), *Modern Technologies for Big Data Classification and Clustering* (pp. 124-151). Hershey, PA: IGI Global. doi:10.4018/978-1-5225-2805-0.ch005

S, J. (2018). Texture-Based Land Cover Classification Algorithm Using Hidden Markov Model for Multispectral Data. In P. Vasant, S. Alparslan-Gok, & G. Weber (Eds.), *Handbook of Research on Emergent Applications of Optimization Algorithms* (pp. 579-613). Hershey, PA: IGI Global. doi:10.4018/978-1-5225-2990-3.ch025

Sahin, M. A., & Tuzkaya, G. (2018). Operations Research Problems for Airline Industry: A Literature Survey for Maintenance Routing Problem. In P. Vasant, S. Alparslan-Gok, & G. Weber (Eds.), *Handbook of Research on Emergent Applications of Optimization Algorithms* (pp. 163–176). Hershey, PA: IGI Global. doi:10.4018/978-1-5225-2990-3.ch007

Sahoo, S., Mishra, S., Mishra, B. K., & Mishra, M. (2018). Analysis and Implementation of Artificial Bee Colony Optimization in Constrained Optimization Problems. In S. Dash, B. Tripathy, & A. Rahman (Eds.), *Handbook of Research on Modeling, Analysis, and Application of Nature-Inspired Metaheuristic Algorithms* (pp. 413–432). Hershey, PA: IGI Global. doi:10.4018/978-1-5225-2857-9.ch021

Saini, A. (2017). Big Data Mining Using Collaborative Filtering. In V. Bhatnagar (Ed.), *Collaborative Filtering Using Data Mining and Analysis* (pp. 128–138). Hershey, PA: IGI Global. doi:10.4018/978-1-5225-0489-4.ch007

Samui, P. R., V., J., J., & Kurup, P. U. (2018). Determination of Spatial Variability of Rock Depth of Chennai. In S. Dash, B. Tripathy, & A. Rahman (Eds.), Handbook of Research on Modeling, Analysis, and Application of Nature-Inspired Metaheuristic Algorithms (pp. 462-479). Hershey, PA: IGI Global. doi:10.4018/978-1-5225-2857-9.ch023

Samui, P., & Dalkilic, H. Y. (2015). GPR and RVM-Based Predictions of Surface and Hole Quality in Drilling of AISI D2 Cold Work Tool Steel. In P. Vasant (Ed.), *Handbook of Research on Artificial Intelligence Techniques and Algorithms* (pp. 736–762). Hershey, PA: IGI Global. doi:10.4018/978-1-4666-7258-1.ch024

Sangeetha, J., Nagaraj, K., Murthy, K. N., & Rustagi, R. P. (2018). Analyzing and Predicting the QoS of Traffic in WiMAX Network Using Gene Expression Programming. In N. Dey (Ed.), *Advancements in Applied Metaheuristic Computing* (pp. 34–70). Hershey, PA: IGI Global. doi:10.4018/978-1-5225-4151-6.ch002

Sangwan, N., & Dahiya, N. (2017). A Classification Framework Towards Application of Data Mining in Collaborative Filtering. In V. Bhatnagar (Ed.), *Collaborative Filtering Using Data Mining and Analysis* (pp. 100–114). Hershey, PA: IGI Global. doi:10.4018/978-1-5225-0489-4.ch005

Sarkar, A., & Maulik, U. (2015). Cancer Biomarker Assessment Using Evolutionary Rough Multi-Objective Optimization Algorithm. In P. Vasant (Ed.), *Handbook of Research on Artificial Intelligence Techniques and Algorithms* (pp. 509–535). Hershey, PA: IGI Global. doi:10.4018/978-1-4666-7258-1.ch016

Seethapathy, B. K., & R, P. (2018). A Review on Spatial Big Data Analytics and Visualization. In H. Seetha, M. Murty, & B. Tripathy (Eds.), *Modern Technologies for Big Data Classification and Clustering* (pp. 179-197). Hershey, PA: IGI Global. doi:10.4018/978-1-5225-2805-0.ch007

Sen, B., Mandal, U. K., & Mondal, S. P. (2018). A Statistical Scrutiny of Three Prominent Machine-Learning Techniques to Forecast Machining Performance Parameters of Inconel 690. In S. Dash, B. Tripathy, & A. Rahman (Eds.), *Handbook of Research on Modeling, Analysis, and Application of Nature-Inspired Metaheuristic Algorithms* (pp. 104–120). Hershey, PA: IGI Global. doi:10.4018/978-1-5225-2857-9.ch006

Sheibani, K. (2017). An Incorporation of the Fuzzy Greedy Search Heuristic With Evolutionary Approaches for Combinatorial Optimization in Operations Management. *International Journal of Applied Evolutionary Computation*, 8(2), 58–72. doi:10.4018/IJAEC.2017040104

Shiming, Q., Dehuri, S., & Wang, G. (2015). Interactive Genetic Algorithms for Optimal Assignment of Blocks into Workspaces of Shipbuilding Industry. *International Journal of Applied Evolutionary Computation*, 6(1), 30–48. doi:10.4018/IJAEC.2015010102

Simanjuntak, B. H., Prasetyo, S. Y., Hartomo, K. D., & Purnomo, H. D. (2015). Application of Fuzzy Logic for Mapping the Agro-Ecological Zones. In P. Vasant (Ed.), *Handbook of Research on Artificial Intelligence Techniques and Algorithms* (pp. 351–377). Hershey, PA: IGI Global. doi:10.4018/978-1-4666-7258-1.ch011

Singh, U. P., Jain, S., Jain, D. K., & Singh, R. K. (2018). An Improved RBFNN Controller for a Class of Nonlinear Discrete-Time Systems With Bounded Disturbance. In P. Vasant, S. Alparslan-Gok, & G. Weber (Eds.), *Handbook of Research on Emergent Applications of Optimization Algorithms* (pp. 656–674). Hershey, PA: IGI Global. doi:10.4018/978-1-5225-2990-3.ch028

Singh, U. P., Jain, S., Tiwari, A., & Singh, R. K. (2018). Nature-Inspired-Based Adaptive Neural Network Approximation for Uncertain System. In P. Vasant, S. Alparslan-Gok, & G. Weber (Eds.), *Handbook of Research on Emergent Applications of Optimization Algorithms* (pp. 439–461). Hershey, PA: IGI Global. doi:10.4018/978-1-5225-2990-3.ch019

Singha, A., & Namgay, P. (2018). Methodologies and Technologies to Retrieve Information From Text Sources. In H. Seetha, M. Murty, & B. Tripathy (Eds.), *Modern Technologies for Big Data Classification and Clustering* (pp. 99–123). Hershey, PA: IGI Global. doi:10.4018/978-1-5225-2805-0.ch004

Survey, A. H. Seetha, M. Murty, & B. Tripathy (Eds.), *Modern Technologies for Big Data Classification and Clustering* (pp. 244–259). Hershey, PA: IGI Global. doi:10.4018/978-1-5225-2805-0.ch010

Swayamsiddha, S., Singhal, C., & Roy, R. (2018). Nature-Inspired-Algorithms-Based Cellular Location Management: Scope and Applications. In S. Dash, B. Tripathy, & A. Rahman (Eds.), *Handbook of Research on Modeling, Analysis, and Application of Nature-Inspired Metaheuristic Algorithms* (pp. 346–362). Hershey, PA: IGI Global. doi:10.4018/978-1-5225-2857-9.ch017

Szkaliczki, T. (2018). Combinatorial Optimization Problems in Multimedia Delivery. In P. Vasant, S. Alparslan-Gok, & G. Weber (Eds.), *Handbook of Research on Emergent Applications of Optimization Algorithms* (pp. 67–92). Hershey, PA: IGI Global. doi:10.4018/978-1-5225-2990-3.ch004

Tallamaraju, R. B., & Kirti, M. (2018). A Brief Study of Approaches to Text Feature Selection. In H. Seetha, M. Murty, & B. Tripathy (Eds.), *Modern Technologies for Big Data Classification and Clustering* (pp. 216–243). Hershey, PA: IGI Global. doi:10.4018/978-1-5225-2805-0.ch009

Tavares, Y. M., Nedjah, N., & Mourelle, L. D. (2017). Tracking Patterns with Particle Swarm Optimization and Genetic Algorithms. *International Journal of Swarm Intelligence Research*, 8(2), 34–49. doi:10.4018/IJSIR.2017040103

Tripathy, B. K. T. R., S., & Mohanty, R. K. (2018). Memetic Algorithms and Their Applications in Computer Science. In S. Dash, B. Tripathy, & A. Rahman (Eds.), Handbook of Research on Modeling, Analysis, and Application of Nature-Inspired Metaheuristic Algorithms (pp. 73-93). Hershey, PA: IGI Global. doi:10.4018/978-1-5225-2857-9.ch004

Tripathy, B. K., Seetha, H., & Murty, M. N. (2018). Uncertainty-Based Clustering Algorithms for Large Data Sets. In H. Seetha, M. Murty, & B. Tripathy (Eds.), *Modern Technologies for Big Data Classification and Clustering* (pp. 1–33). Hershey, PA: IGI Global. doi:10.4018/978-1-5225-2805-0.ch001

Unune, D. R., & Aherwar, A. (2018). A Multiobjective Genetic-Algorithm-Based Optimization of Micro-Electrical Discharge Drilling: Enhanced Quality Micro-Hole Fabrication in Inconel 718. In P. Vasant, S. Alparslan-Gok, & G. Weber (Eds.), *Handbook of Research on Emergent Applications of Optimization Algorithms* (pp. 728–749). Hershey, PA: IGI Global. doi:10.4018/978-1-5225-2990-3.ch031

Usta, P., Ergun, S., & Alparslan-Gok, S. Z. (2018). A Cooperative Game Theory Approach to Post- Disaster Housing Problem. In P. Vasant, S. Alparslan-Gok, & G. Weber (Eds.), *Handbook of Research on Emergent Applications of Optimization Algorithms* (pp. 314–325). Hershey, PA: IGI Global. doi:10.4018/978-1-5225-2990-3.ch014

Virivinti, N., & Mitra, K. (2018). Handling Optimization Under Uncertainty Using Intuitionistic Fuzzy-Logic-Based Expected Value Model. In P. Vasant, S. Alparslan-Gok, & G. Weber (Eds.), *Handbook of Research on Emergent Applications of Optimization Algorithms* (pp. 750–776). Hershey, PA: IGI Global. doi:10.4018/978-1-5225-2990-3.ch032

Vora, M., & Mirnalinee, T. T. (2015). From Optimization to Clustering: A Swarm Intelligence Approach. In P. Vasant (Ed.), *Handbook of Research on Artificial Intelligence Techniques and Algorithms* (pp. 594–619). Hershey, PA: IGI Global. doi:10.4018/978-1-4666-7258-1.ch019

Yuce, B., Mastrocinque, E., Packianather, M. S., Lambiase, A., & Pham, D. T. (2015). The Bees Algorithm and Its Applications. In P. Vasant (Ed.), *Handbook of Research on Artificial Intelligence Techniques and Algorithms* (pp. 122–151). Hershey, PA: IGI Global. doi:10.4018/978-1-4666-7258-1.ch004

Zadshakoyan, M., & Pourmostaghimi, V. (2018). Metaheuristics in Manufacturing: Predictive Modeling of Tool Wear in Machining Using Genetic Programming. In N. Dey (Ed.), *Advancements in Applied Metaheuristic Computing* (pp. 118–142). Hershey, PA: IGI Global. doi:10.4018/978-1-5225-4151-6.ch005

Zeblah, A., Rami, A., & Châtelet, E. (2015). A Comparison for Optimal Allocation of a Reliability Algorithms Production System. In P. Vasant (Ed.), *Handbook of Research on Artificial Intelligence Techniques and Algorithms* (pp. 564–593). Hershey, PA: IGI Global. doi:10.4018/978-1-4666-7258-1.ch018

Zigh, E. (2015). New Neural Buildings Stereo Matching Method Applied to Very High Resolution Ikonos Images. In P. Vasant (Ed.), *Handbook of Research on Artificial Intelligence Techniques and Algorithms* (pp. 322–350). Hershey, PA: IGI Global. doi:10.4018/978-1-4666-7258-1.ch010

About the Author

Mehmet Gençer is currently a professor of Organization Studies at the Izmir University of Economics, Department of Business Administration. After a training in Electrical and Electronics Engineering (BSc, MSc, 1986-1994), Physics (1986-1989), and Developmental Economics (1995-1996), he has practiced software development and software project management at private companies in Turkey (1994-1999) and US (1994-2001). Soon after joining the Computer Science department at Istanbul Bilgi University in 2002 as a lecturer, he has started his PhD at the Social Sciences Institute's Organization Studies programme in 2004, which he has finished in 2009. Since then he has been teaching across undergraduate and graduate programs in business, informatics, and computing. His main research focus has been on the social and organizational aspects of innovation in general, and software industry cases in particular. Based on structural features of organizing and knowledge exchange, his studies are concerned with nature and efficiency of collaboration and social networks in innovation, knowledge creation and transfer across individuals and firms; with cases in software, technology, and manufacturing industries. Prof. Gençer has published several research articles in various journals including Technology Analysis and Strategic Management, and The Journal of Organizational Change Management, in addition to book chapters and proceedings. Mehmet Gençer's research approach reflect the inter-disciplinary character of his background: in computing and computational methods, and in organization studies. With this dual background, his research involves application of computational methods to empirical studies regarding collective production and innovation ecosystems, how do such systems sustain, and how people and organizations manage to collaborate and gain advantage in such systems, or why they fail. Subject of these work includes structural features of organizing and knowledge exchange, nature and efficiency of collaboration in knowledge creation and transfer across individuals and firms, and evolution of community features and dynamics over time. Analysis of social networks has a special place in his approach as it is a truly computational methodology for exploring the social structure of innovation.

Index

Printed in the United States
By Bookmasters